Communalism, Caste and Hindu Nationalism

D1086922

Belligerent Hindu nationalism, accompanied by recurring communal violence between Hindus and Muslims, has become a compelling force in Indian politics over the last two decades of the twentieth century. Ornit Shani's book, which examines the rise of communalism, asks why distinct groups of Hindus, deeply divided by caste, mobilised on the basis of unitary Hindu nationalism? And why was the Hindu national-ist rhetoric about the threat from the essentially impoverished Muslim minority so persuasive to the Hindu majority? Shani uses evidence from communal violence in Ahmedabad, the largest and most prosperous city in Gujarat, long considered the 'laboratory' of Hindu nationalism, as the basis for her investigations. She argues that the growth of communalism did not lie in Hindu–Muslim antagonisms alone. It was rather an expres-sion of intensifying tensions among Hindus, nurtured by changes in the caste regime and associated state policies. The causes for the resulting uncertainties among Hindus were frequently displaced onto Muslims, thus enabling caste tensions to develop and deepen communal rivalries. The book offers a significant and persuasive challenge to previous schol-arship on the rise of communalism, which will be welcomed by students and readers with a professional interest in the region.

Ornit Shani is Lecturer in Asian Studies at Haifa University.

Communalism, Caste and Hindu Nationalism

The Violence in Gujarat

Ornit Shani

CAMBRIDGE
UNIVERSITY PRESS

CAMBRIDGE UNIVERSITY PRESS
Cambridge, New York, Melbourne, Madrid, Cape Town, Singapore, São Paulo

Cambridge University Press
The Edinburgh Building, Cambridge CB2 8RU, UK

Published in the United States of America by Cambridge University Press, New York

www.cambridge.org
Information on this title: www.cambridge.org/9780521683692

© Ornit Shani 2007

First published 2007

Printed in the United Kingdom at the University Press, Cambridge

A catalogue record for this publication is available from the British Library

ISBN 978-0-521-86513-5 hardback
ISBN 978-0-521-68369-2 paperback

To my father and the memory of my mother

Contents

Acknowledgements

I will always be indebted to Raj Chandavarkar: a uniquely indefatigable, knowledgeable and extremely clever teacher. His relentless critiques on drafts of this study and his shrewd questions and comments in long conversations and arguments, always accompanied by his distinctive humour, first as my research supervisor, and then when I wrote this book, taught me how to rethink my own thoughts, against my own grain. Above all, he was a very real source of support and loyal friendship. Raj died very suddenly at the time these words were written. He will for ever be sorely missed. His seminal scholarship and academic guidance were of such an impact that parts of him certainly live on in this book.

The research on which this book is based and the ideas developed in it would have been impossible without the generosity with their time, knowledge and the will to share their experiences of numerous people in India. In addition to the many interviewees who made the times I stayed in Ahmedabad significantly memorable, I would like particularly to thank Varsha Ganguly, Manish Jani, Professor Makrand Mehta, Bhartiben Patel, Girish Patel, Valjibhai Patel, Ashok Shrimali, Monali Soni, Pravinaben Soni and Anand Yagnik. I am heartily grateful to Suchitra Seth for her provoking questions about my work, her interest and above all her genuine care and friendship. I am beholden to Achyut Yagnik who was an infallible guide to the city as well as a partner for lengthy, stirring discussions. His friendship, the knowledge he shared and the access he provided to a wide variety of sources helped throughout the time of my fieldwork.

For their generous financial support I am grateful to the master and fellows of St John's College, Cambridge, the Wingate Foundation, the Cambridge Overseas Trust and the Managers of the Smuts Memorial Fund. I am thankful for the indispensable assistance of librarians and staff of various institutions: in Ahmedabad, Setu library, mostly to Parulben and Udaysingh; the Ahmedabad Municipal Corporation and its Town Planning Department; the Gujarat University Library; the School of Planning; India Institute of Management; Sardar Patel Institute of

Economic and Social Research; Ahmedabad Mill Owners Association; Textile Labour Association; the Gujarat State Archives in Gandhinagar; Centre for Social Studies, Surat; the India Office Library and the British Library in London; the University Library in Cambridge; and the Centre for South Asian Studies in Cambridge, especially to Kevin Greenbank.

William Gould, Geoff Hawthorn, Ira Katznelson, Yoav Peled and David Shulman read earlier drafts of the manuscript at the various stages of its development and provided valuable comments and encouragement. Through the summers of Cambridge I have had the privilege of benefiting from stimulating discussions with Ira Katznelson. I am grateful for his support and insights into my work. Yoav Peled first drove me to pursue doctoral studies and has since provided an unflagging friendship. I owe him a particular debt of gratitude. Since my return to Israel, David Shulman has given ceaseless encouragement and advice. Gordon Johnson and David Washbrook, who were my Ph.D. examiners, encouraged me to develop the dissertation further into a book. At Cambridge University Press, Marigold Acland, Isabelle Dambricourt and Joanna Breeze provided great help in getting this book ready for publication. Two anonymous Cambridge University Press reviewers gave valuable suggestions and criticism. Shahd Wa'ary generously produced the map.

Friends and colleagues have been supportive in numerous ways over the years and it is a pleasure to thank Gadi Algazi, Subho Basu, Bela Bhatia, Joya Chatterji, Jennifer Davis, Ana and Noa Galtung, Azar Gat, Suzanne Goldenberg, Riho Isaka, Jen Simms and Ashelly Tellis. I greatly value the warm and supportive friendship of Jackie Dugard who helped to sustain me during hard times.

I always drew strength and encouragement from my beloved sisters, Ifat and Shimrit, who persistently believed in me. I am doubly indebted to my father Hanan and treasure his unconditional love and invaluable support. My son Rom was born at the time I decided to embark on this research; growing up through the trajectory of Cambridge, Ahmedabad and Tel Aviv. His playfulness, humour and innocence were always an inspiration for me, reminding me of questions I long ago forgot one could ask.

Fredrik Galtung painstakingly read many drafts of this book and provided constant intellectual challenges. This book, and so much beyond it, would not have been possible, or as enjoyable, without his precious companionship, love and understanding.

Glossary

adivasis	(the 'original inhabitants') used to describe the scheduled tribes
akhada	gymnasium
avarna	a generic term for lower-caste Hindus
badli	temporary worker
banakhata	an agreement prior to the sale of land wherein some money is given to the owner but the property is not transferred
bandh	shutting down of businesses, shops and offices
caste panchayat	caste council – decides over matters that arise within the caste
chawl	a form of neighbourhood: a row of rooms with either no sanitary conveniences or with community facilities built around the textile mills for the labour; tenement
dada	used to describe a neighbourhood tough
dalit	(oppressed) former untouchables
galla	small shop
goonda	thug
hapta	bribery, an instalment
harijans	(children of God) term coined by Gandhi for the former untouchables
Hindu rashtra	Hindu nation
Hindutva	Hinduness, the quality of being a Hindu
kakada	lit rags
karsevaks	religious volunteers
kuccha housing	dwellings made of provisional building materials
lakh	100,000
lari	four-wheel cart
lathi	stick, truncheon
Lok Sabha	Indian Parliament
majdoor	labourer

moholla	neighbourhood; usually in reference to a Muslim neighbourhood
otla	platform in front of the main entrance to a house
paan	a type of snack served in a betel leaf
panchayati raj	official local self-government institutions
pol (pole)	traditional neighbourhoods in the walled city of Ahmedabad – narrow streets lined with buildings
pucca housing	cement housing
savarna	a generic term for upper-caste Hindus (also referred to as twice-born or Caste Hindus)
Sangh Parivar	the family (network) of Hindu organisations
taluka	administrative unit taluka below level of the district
varna order	caste hierarchy among Hindus

Abbreviations

ABVP	Akhil Bharatiya Vidyarthi Parishad (student wing of the BJP)
AGERAC	All-Gujarat Educational Reform Action Committee
AIBCF	All-India Backward Class Federation
AJGAR	Ahir (Yadav), Jat Gujar and Rajput alliance
AMC	Ahmedabad Municipal Corporation
AUDA	Ahmedabad Urban Development Authority
BIDA	Bombay Industrial Dispute Act
BJP	Bharatiya Janata Party
BKD	Bharatiya Kranti Dal Party
BSP	Bahujan Samaj Party
COI	*Commission of Inquiry*
CPI (ML)	Communist Party of India (Marxist-Leninist)
GHB	Gujarat Housing Board
GPCC	Gujarat Pradesh Congress Committee
GW	Government Worker
JD	Janata Dal
KHAM	Kshatriyas, Harijans, Adivasis, Muslims
KMLP	Kisan Mazdoor Lok Paksha Party
MLA	Member of Legislative Assembly
MP	Member of Parliament
NSA	National Security Act
OBCs	Other Backward Classes/Castes
PDS	Public Distribution System
PSI	Police Sub-Inspector
PW	Public Witness
RJP	Rashtriya Janata Party
RSS	Rashtriya Swayamsevak Sangh
SC	Scheduled Caste (Dalits, Harijans)
SEBC	Socially and Educationally Backward Classes/Castes
SETU	Centre for Social Knowledge and Action, Ahmedabad
SEWA	Self-Employed Women's Association

SRP	State Reserve Police
ST	Scheduled Tribe
TLA	Textile Labour Association (Majoor Mahajan)
TOI	*Times of India*
ULCRA	Urban Land (Ceiling and Regulation) Act, 1976
UP	Uttar Pradesh
VHP	Vishva Hindu Parishad

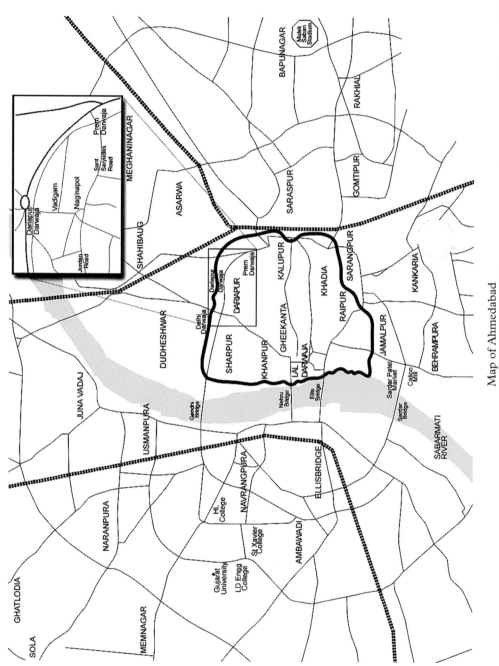

Map of Ahmedabad

Introduction

Communalism has been an important theme in Indian politics since the 1880s. During the first three decades after independence, even after the partition of the subcontinent into India and Pakistan in 1947, no political force gained substantial power in the name of Hinduism. From the mid-1980s there has been a resurgence of a belligerent and new kind of Hindu nationalism in India's public life and in its political institutions. In the main, the Hindu nationalist movement has defined itself in opposition to Islam and Muslims. Hindu revivalists have promoted a claim that the Muslim minority in India threatens Hindus and have sought to establish India as a primarily Hindu nation (*rashtra*), based on a notion of Hindu ethos, values and religion. The ideology and politics of *Hindutva* – the quality of being a Hindu – was accompanied by a rapid increase in large-scale communal (Hindu–Muslim) riots in the 1980s and 1990s.[1] Major communal violence spread throughout India in 1990 and following the destruction of the Babri Masjid mosque at Ayodhya in 1992.

Gujarat, one of India's most prosperous states, has been vital for the growth of communalism. Since the mid-1980s Gujarat became the site of recurring communal violence. The state turned into a nerve centre for the Hindu nationalist movement and has come to be seen as the Hindutva laboratory. The rising communalism in Gujarat culminated in a massacre of Muslims in many parts of the state in February 2002. The complicity of state officials in the killings raised doubts about the ability of the state to govern and to uphold the rule of law. It also demonstrated that such carnage in a country with one of the largest Muslim populations in the world had the potential for destabilising India's democracy and the secular consensus on which it was built.

Hindu nationalist politics rose with the growth of the popularity of a family of extremist Hindu organisations, known as the Sangh Parivar.

---

[1] Recurring communal violence since the 1980s took place, for example, in Ahmedabad, Aligarh, Bhagalpur, Bhiwandi, Coimbatore, Maliana, Meerut, Mumbai, Kanpur and Surat. The term Hindutva originates from V. D. Savarkar's book, *Hindutva, Who is a Hindu?*, Bombay: Veer Savarkar Prakashan, 1969.

The most prominent organisations have been the Rashtriya Swayamsevak Sangh (RSS), the Vishva Hindu Parishad (VHP) and the Bajrang Dal. These groups, with tens of thousands of members, had their origins, respectively, in the 1920s, 1960s and 1980s. The political face of the Hindutva movement, the Bharatiya Janata Party (BJP), was founded in 1980 as a reconstitution of the Jan Sangh Party. Both at the national level and in Gujarat the BJP became a leading political force and came to power in the 1990s. In 1996 the party was able to form a minority government at the centre, but it fell after two weeks. In both the 1998 and 1999 parliament (Lok Sabha) elections the BJP emerged as the largest party, winning 182 out of the 543 Lok Sabha seats, forming a government with its allies in the National Democratic Alliance. The BJP and its allies lost the 2004 elections, with BJP seats in parliament declining to 138, even though its share of the vote only decreased slightly.

The BJP's Performance in the Parliament (Lok Sabha) and Gujarat Assembly Elections[2]

| | Gujarat Assembly | | Parliament (Lok Sabha) | |
	% of vote	No. of seats	% of vote	No. of seats
1980	14.02	9		
1984			7.40	2
1985	14.96	11		
1989			11.36	85
1990	26.69	67		
1991			20.07	120
1995	42.51	121		
1996			20.29	161
1998	44.81	117	25.59	182
1999			23.75	182
2002	49.85	127		
2004			22.16	138

Communalism has conventionally been understood by scholars, colonial administrators and policy makers as a sectarian conflict between Hindus and Muslims. In recent years, a significant scholarship has questioned the sectarian nature of this conflict. This book is a contribution to this literature, and sets out to trace the nature of the revival of communalism since the 1980s from a different point of departure. Its central

---

[2] *Election Commission of India*, http://eci.gov.in/ElectionResults/ElectionResults_fs.htm, 3/1/05.

hypothesis is that the growth of communalism in the last two decades of the twentieth century did not lie in Hindu–Muslim antagonism alone. The growing appeal of Hindutva, and its inherent antagonism towards Muslims, was in fact an expression of deepening tensions among Hindus, nurtured by an instability in the relations between castes and by the ways in which changes in the caste regime were experienced by diverse groups of Hindus. These processes were conditioned by state policies and their political discourses.

The rise of Hindu nationalism since the 1980s was surprising. Hindu nationalism was able to attract widespread support despite several under-lying contradictions. The notion of a monolithic Hindu identity, no more than a homogenous Muslim identity, is inherently implausible. Hinduism has been the bearer of diverse theological interpretations. Hindus have been deeply divided as much by caste, as by ritual observance and sec-tarian differences.[3] It is therefore unclear why distinct groups of Hindus would mobilise on the basis of a unitary Hindu nationalism. Moreover, the idea that there are two homogenous communities of Hindus and Mus-lims in India that are hostile to each other is not borne out by historical evidence. The partition of India in 1947 was not a result of an endur-ing Hindu–Muslim strife at the national level of Indian politics.[4] Finally, Hindu revivalists have rallied around the claim that the Muslim minor-ity in India has been appeased by the state and are a threat to Hindus. Yet, Muslims have not organised themselves politically as a single com-munity since independence, nor is it clear that they ever did so before.[5] The general impoverishment of the Muslim minority in India also makes it difficult to explain why and how the rhetoric about their peril to the Hindu majority became so persuasive.

Scholars have broadly offered either a culturalist or a materialist expla-nation for the rise of communalism and the formation of a Hindu identity, or they have tried to find a golden mean between these two

---

[3] See Romila Thapar, 'Imagined Religious Communities? Ancient History and the Modern Search for a Hindu Identity', in Thapar (ed.), *Interpreting Early India*, Delhi: Oxford University Press, 1992, p. 67. Also see Gyanendra Pandey, 'Which of Us Are Hindus?', in G. Pandey (ed.), *Hindu and Others*, Delhi: Viking, 1993, pp. 238–72. In many ways, caste also exists among Muslims as a basis for social relations. See Mushirul Hasan, *Legacy of a Divided Nation: India's Muslims since Independence*, Delhi: Oxford University Press, 1997, pp. 7–8; Robert W. Stern, *Changing India*, Cambridge: Cambridge University Press, 1993, pp. 71–4.

[4] Ayesha Jalal, *The Sole Spokesman*, Cambridge: Cambridge University Press, 1985; Joya Chatterji, *Bengal Divided*, Delhi: Cambridge University Press, 1994; Mushirul Hasan, 'Indian Muslims since Independence: In Search of Integration and Identity', *Third World Quarterly*, vol. 10, no. 2, April 1988, p. 818; Hasan, *Legacy of a Divided Nation*, pp. 71–2, 198.

[5] Hasan, *Legacy of a Divided Nation*.

approaches.[6] In the culturalist view, communal identity is often characterised as existing prior to, and independently of, the conflict.[7] From a materialist standpoint, the appeal of communalism is attributed to economic and social factors or to manipulations of the masses by political elites, or even by the state.[8] In the golden mean approach scholars have attempted to negotiate a way through the shortcomings of these dichotomous explanations. They accommodate the notion of a Hindu mentality, but reject the concept that it is natural or given. They recognise the political or religious processes and cultural symbols and practices that produce it and emphasise the emergence of a Hindu identity in opposition to an external threatening Other, through which it is defined.[9]

Culturalist approaches assume a transcendental Hindu identity.[10] Communal conflict stems from the very reality, and permanence, of cultural differences between Hindus and Muslims. However, on closer examination, these cultural differences appear to be neither consistent nor fixed but often contingent on changing social circumstances. Moreover, divisions and differences among Hindus are sometimes even greater than those between some Hindus and some Muslims. If communal conflicts were the product of cultural differences, it would not be unreasonable to assume that such conflicts also developed among Hindus themselves.

Some works within the culturalist position deny the relevance of secularism for India. In their view, since secularism as a basis for the practices of the state is incompatible with the values derived from religious faith,

---

[6] Also see Ornit Shani, 'The Resurgence of *EthnoHinduism* – a Theoretical Perspective', in Shlomo Ben-Ami, Yoav Peled and Alberto Spektrovski (eds.), *Ethnic Challenges to the Modern Nation State*, London: Macmillan, 2000, pp. 268–76. For other mapping of the literature see, for example, Ashutosh Varshney, *Ethnic Conflict and Civic Life: Hindus and Muslims in India*, New Haven and London: Yale University Press, 2002, pp. 23–39.

[7] This view is based especially on Clifford Geertz, 'The Integrative Revolution: Primordial Sentiments and Civil Politics in the New States', *The Interpretation of Culture*, London: Fontana, 1995, pp. 255–310.

[8] This approach is also known as the constructivist approach in the study of ethnic conflicts.

[9] These writings can be attributed, at least partly, to the appearance of the postcolonial discourse and the cultural turn in the study of Indian society and ethnicity and nationalism in general. To some extent, this discourse is a part of the realisation of Foucault's perspicacious view of Western 'truth' as 'another rule of knowledge'. Edward Said in his study of Orientalism applied this view. See Edward W. Said, *Orientalism*, New York: Vintage Books, 1979. Other works that form the intellectual base for these writings are, for example, Homi K. Bhabha, *The Location of Culture*, London: Routledge, 1994; Robert J. C. Young, *Colonial Desire*, London: Routledge, 1995, pp. 1–28, 159–82; Slavoj Zizek, 'Eastern Europe's Republic of Gilead', in Chantal Mouffe (ed.), *Dimensions of Radical Democracy: Pluralism, Citizenship, Community*, London: Verso, 1993.

[10] See Louis Dumont, *Homo Hierarchicus*, Chicago: University of Chicago Press, 1980, Appendix D, pp. 314–34; Daniel Gold, 'Organised Hinduism: From Vedic Truth to Hindu Nation', in Martin Marty and R. Scott Appleby (eds.), *Fundamentalism Observed*, Chicago: University of Chicago Press, 1991, pp. 531–93; Stanley Wolpert, 'Resurgent Hindu Fundamentalism', *Contention*, vol. 2, no. 3, Spring 1995, pp. 9–18.

which are intrinsic to Indian culture, it cannot be an adequate guide for moral or political action. Some scholars suggest that 'the traditional ways of life have, over the centuries, developed internal principles of tolerance . . . [which] must have a play in contemporary politics'.[11] In this perspective, religious neutrality and policies derived from it seem irrelevant to Indian politics, precisely because these policies ignore what is claimed to be the authentic indigenous tradition of religious tolerance in Hinduism. In this emphasis on an innate tolerance in Hinduism, these arguments legitimise, sometimes unintentionally, the 'politics of religious identity', thus playing into the hands of Hindutva forces. Indeed, the proponents of Hindutva have not been slow to present arguments from similar culturalist positions. They look back, for instance, to the 'real' traditions of a Hindu Golden Age, which declined under Muslim rule and which they seek to revive. They have also imagined a persistent historical friction between the two communities, dating it to the period of the Mughal Aurangzeb, who began, in their view, the 'tradition' of destroying Hindu temples in the seventeenth century.[12]

In the culturalist analysis, religious Hindu identity has an ontological existence and therefore does not call for an explanation. The communal conflict will continue to beset India since the state underestimates the strength of these real religious and cultural identities. However, the assumption of a pre-existing Hindu identity is belied by the evidence that Hindu identity often appears to be contingent on different social circumstances, at times playing a prominent role, or at others, disappearing altogether. In the 1960s, for example, the main politically relevant identities in the subcontinent were largely shaped by linguistic divides rather than religious affiliation. Even recent ideologies of Hindutva have proven to be unstable. The Ayodhya Ram Mandir (temple) issue, for example, was not equally appealing in all regions of India. From 1993 it became less prominent and was only revived in 2002, a decade later. Moreover, if a Hindu identity is latent and natural, why was its appeal, for such a long period, largely limited to upper castes and to urban middle-class Hindus? Even from a culturalist approach, it would be plausible to suggest that

---

[11] Ashish Nandy, 'The Politics of Secularism and the Recovery of Religious Tolerance', in Veena Das (ed.), *Mirrors of Violence*, Delhi: Oxford University Press, 1990, p. 84. Also see T. N. Madan, 'Whither Indian Secularism?', *Modern Asian Studies*, vol. 27, no. 3, 1993, pp. 680–2; Partha Chatterjee, 'Secularism and Tolerance', *Economic and Political Weekly*, 9 July 1994, pp. 1768–77. For an analysis and critiques of these positions see, Achin Vanaik, *The Furies of Indian Communalism*, London: Verso, 1998, pp. 150–62, 187–205; Aijaz Ahmad, 'Fascism and National Culture: Reading Gramsci in Days of Hindutva', *Social Scientist*, vol. 21, no. 3–4, March–April 1993, pp. 32–68; Rajeev Bhargava (ed.), *Secularism and Its Critics*, New Delhi: Oxford University Press, 1998.

[12] See, for example, Tapan Basu *et al.*, *Khaki Shorts and Saffron Flags*, Delhi: Orient Longman, 1993, pp. 72–3; Amartya Sen, 'The Threats to Secular India', *New York Review of Books*, 8 April 1993.

Hindutva has no relevance to the multiple expressions of religious faith that have historically been intrinsic to Hinduism. Indeed, Hindutva ideology homogenises the plurality of traditions and cultures in a similar manner to that which its spokesmen accuse secularism of doing.

Materialist analyses focus on the social, economic and political aspects of communalism. In this approach communal identities are constructed. Some scholars identify Hindutva's social backbone in the urban, educated middle class, or the upper-caste component of the urban petty bourgeoisie. Both groups feel threatened by the political and economic mobilisation of the lower castes.[13] These analyses have explanatory value, but they do not provide a full account of the mechanisms by which social and economic processes lead to communalism, especially when economic factors cannot account fully, in themselves, for communal conflicts. Another explanation suggests that the predatory commercialisation and capitalism that developed in India, and their effects upon poor Muslims and Hindus, made them prone to communal violence. It contends that the insecurity of the poor, the overcrowded conditions of most cities and the competition for valuable urban space, which can be divided and re-divided for profit, create a fertile ground for 'major communal conflagration'.[14] Yet, the urban poor are not the fomenters of communal conflicts.

Materialist-instrumentalist explanations ascribe the formation of a Hindu identity to strategies adopted by politicians and political parties for their own particular purposes. Some writers focus on the Hindu turn of the Congress Party, from which the BJP profited, and view the rise of Hindu militancy as a result of the transformation of secular politics in India by a process of communal polarisation. They highlight the effects of the tactics of political elites who emphasise religious differences in order to gain popular support.[15] Although political stratagems certainly

---

[13] See, for example, Tapan Rayachaudhri, 'Shadows of the Swastika: Historical Reflection on the Politics of Hindu Communalism', *Contention*, vol. 4, no. 2, 1995, p. 154; Vinay Lal, 'Hindu "Fundamentalism" Revisited', *Contention*, vol. 4, no. 2, Winter 1995, pp. 169–70; Ashish Nandy *et al.*, *Creating a Nationality: The Ramjanmabhumi Movement and Fear of the Self*, Delhi: Oxford University Press, 1997, p. 101; Sujata Patel, 'Urbanization, Development and Communalisation of Society in Gujarat', in Takashi Shinoda (ed.), *The Other Gujarat*, Mumbai: Popular Prakashan, 2002, pp. 207–15; Achyut Yagnik and Suchitra Sheth, *The Shaping of Modern Gujarat: Plurality, Hindutva and Beyond*, New Delhi: Penguin Books, 2005, pp. 252–7.

[14] Amiya Bagchi, 'Predatory Commercialisation and Communalism in India', in Sarvepalli Gopal (ed.), *Anatomy of a Confrontation: Ayodhya and the Rise of Communal Politics in India*, London: Zed Books, 1991, pp. 210–11.

[15] See Paul Brass, 'Elite Groups Symbol Manipulation and Ethnic Identity among the Muslims of South Asia', in David Taylor and Malcolm Yapp (eds.), *Political Identity in South Asia*, London: Curzon Press, 1979, p. 41; Brass, 'Ethnic Groups and the State', in Brass (ed.), *Ethnic Groups and the State*, Totowa, NJ: Barnes & Noble Books, 1985, pp. 1–56; Robert Eric Frykenberg, 'Hindu Fundamentalism and the Structural Stability

play a role in the growth of communalism, this approach is limited by its instrumentalist logic. It takes for granted rather than explains how leaders convince significant numbers of people to do as they are told, and as a result presumes people to be inherently passive.[16] By focusing on high-level politics this approach neglects the different forces in the society and the wider social meaning and implications of political processes, and frequently depends on the claim, for example, that some groups are culturally prone to violence. In this way materialist explanations rely on categories and presumptions that underlie the culturalist view.

In their efforts to address the problem of communal conflicts and violence, some scholars within the materialist approach developed state-oriented explanations for their growth. These analyses view the state and the politically dominant as the agents of both communal conflicts and Hindu patterns of politicisation. For instance, they explain the growth of communalism as the consequence of the institutional decline of the state. But they often also attribute a centrality to social disorder in the process of the state's degeneration.[17] These arguments are tautological. Another variety of state-oriented explanations suggests that communal violence and its scale is the result of manipulations by political elites and the state. 'The persistence of riots helps local, state and national leaders of different persuasions in capturing or maintaining institutional and state power by providing convenient scapegoats, and alleged perpetrators of the events, and by providing as well dangers and tensions useful in justifying the exercise of state authority.'[18] This position claims that communal riots are

of India', in Martin Marty and R. Scott Appleby (eds.), *Fundamentalism and the State: Remaking Politics, Economies and Militance,* Chicago: University of Chicago Press, 1993, pp. 233–55; Rajni Kothari, *Politics and the People,* Vol. II, Delhi: Ajanta, 1990, pp. 440–79. Steven Wilkinson examines the relations between the occurrence of communal riots, as well as the state's efforts to stop them, and electoral incentives at the town and state level. See Steven I. Wilkinson, *Votes and Violence: Electoral Competition and Ethnic Riots in India,* Cambridge: Cambridge University Press, 2004, pp. 4–9, 137–71.

[16] Also see a discussion on this point in, James D. Fearon and David D. Laitin, 'Violence and the Social Construction of Ethnic Identity', *International Organization,* vol. 54, no. 4, 2000, p. 846; Amrita Basu, 'Mass Movement or Elite Conspiracy? The Puzzle of Hindu Nationalism', in David Ludden (ed.), *Making India Hindu: Religion, Community and the Politics of Democracy in India,* Delhi: Oxford University Press, 1996, p. 56.

[17] See Atul Kohli, *Democracy and Discontent,* Cambridge: Cambridge University Press, 1990; Sumantra Bose suggests 'an organic crisis' of the Indian state in facilitating the rise of Hindu nationalism. Sumantra Bose, '"Hindu Nationalism" and the Crisis of the Indian State: A Theoretical Perspective', in Sugata Bose and Ayesha Jalal (eds.), *Nationalism, Democracy and Development,* Oxford: Oxford University Press, 1997, pp. 104–64. For a critique of arguments about the weakness of state institutions as a cause for failing to prevent communal riots see Wilkinson, *Votes and Violence,* pp. 85–96.

[18] Paul Brass, *Theft of an Idol,* Princeton, NJ: Princeton University Press, 1997, pp. 6–7. Brass defines 'an institutionalized riot system', which works 'to keep a town or city in a permanent state of awareness of Hindu–Muslim relationship', *ibid.,* p. 284. Brass

manoeuvred by elites and persons and groups that specialise in producing riots, while at the same time insisting that communal violence became 'endemic in India'.[19] Furthermore, while assuming that disorder and violent conflicts are intrinsic to India, this explanation nevertheless suggests that these conflicts can be managed and controlled. State and political elites do play a role in energising communal conflicts. But state-oriented explanations are limited by their narrow focus on electoral politics and political strategies for coalition building. They explain and understand social events from above, looking at them through the state, or the political elites, and subsequently deprive social groups of agency. In the cases when these explanations do attribute agency to society, they are often constrained by the presumptions that they hold about the state and the society, such as its proneness to violence.

Conversely, an approach that focuses on social networks and civic associations links the occurrences of communal riots to the existence or absence of associations and networks of civic engagement between the communities in strife. 'Where such networks of engagement exist, tensions and conflicts were regulated and managed; where they are missing, communal identities led to endemic and ghastly violence.'[20] In this society-centred approach communal riots are understood in isolation from the state, even though the state's basic role is to maintain law and order. Consequently, in this analysis the onus for maintaining communal peace is laid on the society, specifically on prominent members of social groups and civic organisations. Neither state-oriented nor society-centred approaches account for the complex patterns of reciprocal relations between the various state institutions and the society.

Some scholars understand the communal predicament as the effect of the homogenising pressures of the modern state.[21] In one view, colonial policies and their assumptions about the nature of the society in

---

further develops this analysis in a seminal study of Hindu–Muslim violence, conducted over more than four decades of field study in Aligarh, in Uttar Pradesh. See Paul R. Brass, *The Production of Hindu–Muslim Violence in Contemporary India*, London: University of Washington Press, 2003, pp. 32–3, 258. Wilkinson argues that electoral incentives determine whether state governments will prevent communal violence, suggesting that in a state with a high degree of party fractionalisation, wherein the government relies on minority votes, it will prevent riots. Wilkinson, *Votes and Violence*, pp. 137–40.

[19] Brass, *Theft of an Idol*, p. 6; *The Production of Hindu–Muslim Violence*, p. 9.

[20] Varshney, *Ethnic Conflict and Civic Life*, p. 9. Also see p. 265.

[21] Sudipta Kaviraj, for instance, looks at the logic of modernity's reconstitution of identities in order to understand the relations between religion and political processes in India. Sudipta Kaviraj, 'Religion, Politics and Modernity', in U. Baxi and B. Parekh (eds.), *Crisis and Change in Contemporary India*, Delhi: Sage Publications, 1995, pp. 295–316.

purely communal or religious terms created, constructed and promoted an imperative of animosity between Hindus and Muslims.[22]

In the golden mean approach, scholars tried to reconcile both culturalist and materialist analyses, by identifying mechanisms by which the 'naturalness' of religious identities is produced by political processes.[23] From one viewpoint, the formation of a Hindu identity and the rise of Hindu nationalism are explained through a hybrid approach that combines three 'strategies', which prospered in the 1980s as the result of propitious conditions. First, Hindu identity is formed as a result of a process of stigmatisation and emulation that is based on the 'threatening Other', on stereotypes of the Muslim and on Hindu feelings of inferiority and vulnerability.[24] Hindus imitated and assimilated those cultural traits from which the Muslim–Other were believed to have derived their strength, in order to resist the Other, to rediscover those traits in their own culture, and to regain the self-esteem they had lost with the passing of the Golden Age.[25] The aspiration of Hindu nationalists, for instance, to build immense temples that would function as common meeting places, as mosques are thought to do, is an example of this process of imitation and assimilation. Second, Hindu nationalism has also been an instrument in the hands of elites who manipulate Hindu symbols. Third, its growth has been the result of party-building and organisation of the Hindu forces.

Explaining Hindu militancy, even partly, by the character of a collective Hindu psyche and its complex of vulnerability in relation to other defined collectives is problematic.[26] It assumes that such an organic collective exists in the first place. Yet, it is scarcely credible to speak of a homogenous community psyche that is cut off from its sociogenesis, or to assume, rather than explain, the 'Freudian short cut' that some of

[22] See Gyanendra Pandey, 'The Colonial Construction of "Communalism"', in Veena Das (ed.), *Mirrors of Violence*, Delhi: Oxford University Press, 1990, pp. 94–132; Aditya Mukherjee, 'Colonialism and Communalism', in Sarvepalli Gopal (ed.), *Anatomy of a Confrontation: Ayodhya and the Rise of Communal Politics in India*, London: Zed Books, 1991, pp. 164–78. Part of the analysis in this book also examines the role of state policies and their discourses to understand the growth of communalism in the 1980s.

[23] Peter van der Veer, *Religious Nationalism*, London: University of California Press, 1994, p. 7; Christophe Jaffrelot, *The Hindu Nationalist Movement, and Indian Politics 1925–1990s*, Delhi: Viking, 1996, p. 5.

[24] See Jaffrelot, *The Hindu Nationalist Movement*, pp. 1–10, 359, 400, 410.

[25] *Ibid.* Also see a similar line of argument in Ashish Nandy's discussion on the meeting between east and west in the context of British colonialism. Ashish Nandy, *The Intimate Enemy Loss and Recovery of Self under Colonialism*, Delhi: Oxford University Press, 1993; Sudhir Kakar, *The Colors of Violence: Cultural Identities, Religion, Conflict*, Chicago: Chicago University Press, 1996, pp. 154–5, 157, 166.

[26] See the analysis by Sudhir Kakar, 'Some Unconscious Aspects of Ethnic Violence in India', in Veena Das (ed.), *Mirrors of Violence*, Delhi: Oxford University Press, 1990, pp. 135–45; Kakar, *The Colors of Violence*.

these scholars take from the individual to the society. Moreover, although this approach recognises the material aspects of the question, it takes the cultural traits of large social collectives for granted, and in this respect becomes indistinguishable from culturalist arguments and tends to be ahistorical. Finally, the proposition that Hindu militancy can be the outcome of a matter of consciousness, a state of mind, implies that it stands outside social interaction. In this way consciousness attains an essentialist status.

Culturalist and golden mean approaches to the rise of communal conflicts and the formation of a Hindu identity since the 1980s employ different emphases, but they share essentialist assumptions about the society, particularly that there is a cultural essence. Even materialist explanations that emphasise the processes of the construction of communalism rather than its ontological nature ultimately dwell on essentialist assumptions. The various approaches remain within a purview of an almost fundamental divide, and often inherent antagonism, between Hindus and Muslims. The explanations that acknowledge the construction and instability of communal identities fail to attend to the processes that explain how communal identities change, without relying on assumptions about the cultural essence of groups or without depriving agency from people. In their final account, therefore, the various approaches inevitably arrive at a predicament of endemic violence that derives from groups' cultural traits. These analyses do not account for caste as a factor in the growth of communalism.

While Hindu nationalism gained power and communal violence between Hindus and Muslims intensified, there was also a considerable increase in caste conflicts around redistributive policies for the lower and backward caste Hindus, particularly over the reservations of places in educational institutions and government jobs.[27] Moreover, conflicts between the forward and backward castes sometimes appeared to be closely linked with communal tensions. Either they occurred at the same time, or, at a more complex level, caste conflicts turned into communal violence. This happened in Gujarat in 1985 and at an all-India level in 1990. This book explores the relationships between caste conflicts, particularly over redistributive policies and the rise of communalism.

The coincidence of the rise of communal violence with the growth of caste conflicts seems paradoxical. While militant Hinduism assumes and

---

[27] Agitations and social protests against the reservation of quotas for the lower- and backward-caste Hindus in government jobs and educational institutions took place from the end of the 1970s and particularly in the 1980s and early 1990s in Bihar, Andhra Pradesh, Delhi, Gujarat, Madhya Pradesh and Uttar Pradesh.

tries to promote the principle of a unitary Hindu identity, caste conflicts demonstrate deep divisions among Hindus.[28] Furthermore, the Hindu caste groups that propelled Hindu nationalism were also the primary generative forces behind caste agitations. Indeed, the rhetoric of Hindutva about the appeasement of Muslims by the state, and the attempt to portray them as a threat to Hindus, has appealed primarily to upper-caste and urban middle-class Hindus, who are particularly anxious about compensatory reservation policies for lower- and backward-caste Hindus.[29] Muslims were lumped together with these minorities, even though religion was excluded as a category qualifying a candidate for positive discrimination. It is therefore important to investigate the dynamic processes by which caste reservation conflicts, which were exclusive to Hindus, translated into tensions between Hindus and Muslims. The many commentaries on communalism have either neglected the relations between caste conflicts and communalism; have viewed caste conflicts as a barrier to the further growth of Hindu nationalism; or have perceived caste and communalism as competing identities, particularly in the context of electoral politics.[30] In the cases where a link between communalism and caste conflict is made, the dynamics by which caste conflicts relate or turn to communal antagonism between Hindus and Muslims is not

---

[28] It is important to note that a contradiction between caste conflicts and communalism arises precisely because of the presupposition about the existence of coherent Hindu and Muslim communities. Otherwise, as phenomena in themselves, caste conflicts and Hindu–Muslim conflicts are not necessarily contradictory. By simple reasoning a group (or an individual) can be in a conflict with another group, but on another occasion unite against a third group.

[29] Some scholars within the materialist approach suggest that both the urban middle class and upper castes, who form Hindutva's social basis, feel threatened by political and economic mobilisation of the lower castes and by policies of positive discrimination. Hamza Alavi, 'Politics of Ethnicity in India and Pakistan', in H. Alvi and H. John (eds.), Sociology of Developing Societies, London: Macmillan, 1989, pp. 232–4; Rayachaudhri, 'Shadows of the Swastika', p. 154; Lal, 'Hindu "Fundamentalism" Revisited', p. 170. Peter van der Veer indicates the possibility of a link between positive discrimination and communalism. Peter van der Veer, 'The Foreign Hand: Orientalist Discourse in Sociology and Communalism', in Carol A. Breckenridge and Peter van der Veer (eds.), Orientalism and the Post-Colonial Predicament, Philadelphia: University of Pennsylvania Press, 1993, p. 38; Peter van der Veer, 'Writing Violence', in Ludden (ed.), Making India Hindu, p. 261. Also see Basu, 'Mass Movement or Elite Conspiracy?', p. 58; Thomas Blom Hansen, The Saffron Wave: Democracy and Hindu Nationalism in Modern India, Princeton, NJ: Princeton University Press, 1999, pp. 142–5. Ghanshyam Shah suggested that '[i]nter-caste conflicts get softened by communal clashes between the Hindus and Muslims'. Ghanshyam Shah, 'Polarised Communities', Seminar, 470, October 1998, p. 34.

[30] See, for example, Varshney, Ethnic Conflict and Civic Life, pp. 85, 161. For a view of caste and communalism as competing identities, see for example Basu, 'Mass Movement or Elite Conspiracy?', pp. 58, 74–6.

explained.[31] This book argues that both caste and communal conflicts, despite the potential contradiction between them, stem from similar social processes, and that caste is inextricably linked to the rise of communalism since the 1980s. It was precisely these caste conflicts that fostered communalism in the 1980s and 1990s.

Preferential policies for backward castes in the 1980s, like reservations, had served to complicate and antagonise caste relations, especially as they appeared to offer lower and backward castes greater opportunities for social mobility. As some segments of the lower and backward castes appeared to improve their economic situation, forward-caste Hindus feared that their own opportunities were being restricted and their dominance challenged. They were now suddenly forced to compete with the lower castes, of lesser status, on terms that they perceived to be disadvantageous. The intensification of communal antagonism since the 1980s reflected the resulting and growing uncertainties within the Hindu moral order.

The growth of Hindu militancy and the formation of a 'Hindu identity' were informed by the changes in the caste order and the complex interrelationship between caste and class. The dynamic of these interrelations, as well as the ascent of communal antagonism, was largely energised and reproduced by the state's policies and political discourse. The intervention of the state, especially in its reservations policy, appeared to bestow favours on minorities, which were seen as including Muslims. State policies addressed issues of equality as if they were synonymous with the rights of religious minorities, thereby enabling caste conflicts to develop and deepen communal rivalries. The disposition of all-Hindus against Muslims was formed as some segments of forward-caste Hindus found the cause of their own 'limited' mobility in these governments' preferential treatment of minorities.

Communalism grew, then, in the interstices between the interrelations of caste and class. The threat that Hindu nationalists claimed to be posed by Muslims actually expressed a fear about the peril of violating the Hindu social and moral order from within. The rise of communalism and the formation of a 'Hindu identity' since the 1980s are therefore described in this book as ethnoHinduism: they were driven by tensions between members of minority groups among Hindus. The analysis examines how communalism is related to caste and to the state's reservation policies and their discourse. It also draws inferences from the relations between communalism and caste for the understanding of caste. This analysis of

---

[31] For example, Alavi, 'Politics of Ethnicity in India and Pakistan'; van der Veer, 'The Foreign Hand'; Shah, 'Polarised Communities'.

the interconnections between caste, class, communalism and the state is developed gradually in the book, and is explicated as a discourse and practice of the politics of social differentiation. In order to take into account the changeable character of communal, caste and social identities in general, the approach developed in this book views the construction of these identities as a relational process. In this formation process, distinct categories of social differentiation, like caste and class, interact with each other and with the state. These dynamics of interactions are most clearly revealed in the context of struggles over various state resources. In the effect of the interrelations among and between distinct categories of social differentiation and the state, and their inadvertent outcomes, ethnic relations are constituted. Understanding ethnoHindu identity formation as a relational process avoids a predetermination or essentialisation of communal identities.

The explanation of the rise of communalism, as well as the conceptual framework for understanding its rise, is developed through a case study of the large-scale riots that occurred in Ahmedabad in 1985, as well as an inquiry into the pogrom against Muslims in the city in 2002 and reflections on the Ahmedabad riots of 1969. In the 1985 riots, conflicts around the reservation of places in educational and government institutions for backward-caste Hindus transmogrified into communal violence even though there was no prior religious tension between Hindus and Muslims, and local Muslims had no part in the reservation dispute between forward- and backward-caste Hindus. These riots marked the beginnings of the shift from several decades of Congress dominance to the triumph of the Hindu nationalist BJP in Gujarat as well as in Indian national politics.[32]

Ahmedabad is one of India's most important metropolitan centres. Between 1991 and 1997 it attracted the highest levels of industrial investment in India. With a population of over 3 million in the early 1990s it is the largest city in Gujarat, one of India's fastest growing states,

---

[32] For other analyses of the Ahmedabad riots of 1985 see Howard Spodek, 'From Gandhi to Violence: Ahmedabad's 1985 Riots in Historical Perspective', *Modern Asian Studies*, vol. 23, no. 4, 1989, pp. 765–95; Sujata Patel, 'The Ahmedabad Riots, 1985: An Analysis', *Reports-Papers*, Surat: Centre for Social Studies, 1985; Upendra Baxi, 'Reflections on the Reservations Crisis in Gujarat', in Veena Das (ed.), *Mirrors of Violence*, 1990, New Delhi: Oxford University Press, pp. 215–39; Kohli, *Democracy and Discontent*, pp. 257–65; Ghanshyam Shah, 'Middle Class Politics: A Case of Anti-Reservation Agitation in Gujarat', *Economic and Political Weekly*, Annual Number, May 1987, pp. 155–72; Subrata Mitra, 'The Perils of Promoting Equality: The Latent Significance of the Anti-Reservation Movement in India', *Journal of Commonwealth and Comparative Politics*, vol. 25, no. 3, 1987, pp. 292–312; John R. Wood, 'Reservation in Doubt: The Backlash against Affirmative Action in Gujarat', in Ramashray Roy and Richard Sisson (eds.), *Diversity and Dominance in Indian Politics*, Vol. II, London: Sage, 1990, pp. 146–69.

and the seventh largest city in India.[33] The milestones in the politics of Gujarat and Ahmedabad have frequently been critical historical moments in India's national politics. Ahmedabad gained importance in India's national politics especially after the late 1910s, when Mahatma Gandhi became deeply involved in the city's political and social activities. The city was the centre of the struggle of the Maha Gujarat Janata Parishad movement for the formation of Gujarat as a linguistically defined state between 1956 and 1960.[34]

In 1984 the Hindu nationalist party won one of its two seats in the Lok Sabha from Gujarat. In 1987 the party won the Ahmedabad Municipal Corporation elections. From the mid-1980s, the BJP's share of the vote in the state grew steadily, and in contrast to other states, from the late 1990s the party has ruled on its own in Gujarat without reliance on political allies. From the mid-1980s, frequent communal violence arose in Ahmedabad.[35] In 2002 this violence climaxed in the pogrom against Muslims in the city and in large parts of Gujarat. Communal riots since the 1980s have largely been an urban phenomenon.[36] In a recent study Ahmedabad was defined as one of the most 'riot prone' cities in India.[37]

The propagators of Hindu nationalism have perceived Gujarat as strategically important to the success of their agenda. Senior members of the Sangh Parivar have seen the state as the Hindutva laboratory. After the BJP's victory in the 2002 Gujarat assembly elections the VHP leader, Pravin Togadia, asserted that 'the experiment of Hindutva "lab" would be repeated . . . The Gujarat elections will change the ideology, colour and composition of all political parties.'[38] The VHP's president at the time, Ashok Singhal, declared that 'Gujarat was an experiment which was to be replicated in other parts of the country, and one assumes, eventually

---

[33] In 1981 the Ahmedabad population was 2,059,725 and in 1991 it was 2,876,710. *Statistical Outline of Ahmedabad City 1994–95*, Ahmedabad: Planning and Statistics Department Ahmedabad Municipal Corporation, 1996, Table 3.2, p. 9. Also see *Socio-Economic Review: Gujarat State 1999–2000*, Gandhinagar: Directorate of Economics and Statistics, Government of Gujarat, February 2000.

[34] Indulal Yagnik's, *Aatmakathaa* [Autobiography], Vol. VI, Dhanwant Oza (ed.), Ahmedabad: Maha Gujarat Seva Trust, 1973 (unpublished translation into English by Devaurat Pathak, Howard Spodek and John Wood).

[35] Major communal conflagrations occurred in Ahmedabad in 1985, 1986, 1990 and 1992. During the 1990s sporadic communal riots transpired in the city and in other parts of Gujarat.

[36] Nandy *et al.*, *Creating a Nationality*, pp. 9–10.

[37] Varshney, *Ethnic Conflict and Civic Life*, pp. 6–7.

[38] http://www.newsindia-times.com/2002/12/27/tow-vhp20.html; 'Experiment of "Hindutva lab" to be repeated in Delhi: Togadia', *The Hindustan Times*, http://www.hindustan times. com/news/5905_120559,0008.htm, 4/1/05.

throughout the country. The State had been carefully chosen as the laboratory for putting into practice the Hindutva ideology of the RSS.'[39] This perception was also widely held beyond the membership of Hindu nationalists. An editor of a Muslim newspaper explained that Gujarat was the laboratory for the Hindutva agenda especially because 'the VHP has built a vast network throughout the state. They have offices in small villages and talukas in remote parts and their members there can spring into action at a short notice.'[40] Similarly, a Human Rights Watch Report suggested that 'since first assuming power in 1995, the state has stacked its inner ranks with VHP and RSS members and others that shared and would actively promote Sangh Parivar's policies and programs.'[41] For some scholars, Gujarat appeared even to 'set the pace' in the decline of the Congress and the growth of Hindu nationalism.[42] It 'has been a harbinger of change in India and often the battleground on which issues are first tested'.[43] The elites of Gujarat always boasted that 'what Gujarat is today India is tomorrow'.[44]

Gujarat and Ahmedabad in particular, then, have been identified as an extreme case of the rise of communalism and communal violence. Although the first major post-independence communal riots in India took place in Ahmedabad in 1969, the 1970s and 1980s saw relatively little Hindu–Muslim tension in the city. The ethnic conflicts of the 1980s were primarily about reservations and the status of the backward castes, and communalism began gaining political prominence in the city and in the state only from the middle of that decade. The emergence of communalism in Ahmedabad at this time can be traced to tensions among Hindus rather than to a deepening conflict between Hindus and Muslims. Indeed, the riots of 1985, which marked the rise of communalism in Gujarat, developed initially over preferential policies for the benefit of the backward castes. The case of Ahmedabad undermines the conventional view

---

[39] *The Hindu*, 8/12/02.

[40] 'This Was a BJP Lab Experiment', *Outlookindia.com*, 18 March 2002. Also see Asghar Ali Engineer, 'Gujarat: Laboratory of Hindutva', http://www.dawoodi-bohras.com/ spotlight/riots.htm, March 2002, 4/1/05; John Dayal (ed.), *Gujarat 2002: Untold and Retold Stories of the Hindutva Lab*, Delhi: Media House, 2002.

[41] Human Rights Watch Report, '*We Have No Order to Save You' State Participation and Complicity in Communal Violence in Gujarat*, vol. 14, no. 3(C), April 2002, p. 41.

[42] David Ludden, 'Introduction', in David Ludden (ed.), *Making India Hindu*, Delhi: Oxford University Press, 1996, p. 19.

[43] John R. Wood, 'On the Periphery but in the Thick of it: Some Current Indian Political Crises Viewed from Gujarat', paper presented at the International Seminar on Gujarat Society: Development and Deprivation, 6–9 December 1994, Surat, Centre for Social Studies.

[44] Girish Patel, 'Narendra Modi's One-Day Cricket', *Economic and Political Weekly*, 30 November 2002, p. 4827.

of the origins of communalism as lying in Hindu–Muslim antagonism. It also calls into question the rise and nature of communalism in states where the BJP has gained less prominence and communal violence has recurred less frequently. The case of Ahmedabad, therefore, has a strategic importance in relation to understanding the rise and intensification of communal conflicts since the 1980s.[45]

The pattern of events in the Ahmedabad riots of 1985 reveals the dynamics of the relations between caste and class, which have underlain the growth of Hindu nationalism and a communal Hindu identity since the 1980s. The 1985 riots erupted over social and economic reservation benefits for the backward castes, but transformed into communal violence between Hindus and Muslims. In August 1990, large-scale anti-reservation riots erupted throughout India over the V. P. Singh government's decision to implement the Mandal Commission recommendations on reservation for the Other Backward Classes (OBCs) at the national level. By September 1990, the BJP, which at that time backed Singh's National Front coalition, withdrew its support from the government and announced the demolition of the Babri Masjid mosque in Ayodhya as its major priority. The party initiated a Rath Yatra religious procession to Ayodhya, which sparked communal violence throughout the subcontinent. The destruction of the mosque in Ayodhya in December 1992 also coincided with a dispute over reservations. In the weeks that preceded the events the Supreme Court upheld the Report of the Mandal Commission for reservations for the backward castes at the national level. Although the same dynamics, wherein a caste reservation conflict preceded communal violence, could be discerned in the Ahmedabad riots of 1985, the religious issues that gained prominence in the late 1980s were still absent. The long period of sustained violence that Ahmedabad experienced in 1985 should therefore be seen in the context of what, in the coming decade, would become a feature of the rise of ethnoHinduism.

The riots of 1985 took place before the Sangh Parivar entrenched itself in India and developed a wide appeal. By examining these riots, this study seeks to throw light on the deeper causes of its rise and on the origins of the communalisation of the state and society. Moreover, through a detailed investigation of communal violence, it examines the underlying processes in the urban context that contributed to the growth of communalism, as well as the role that violence played in its development.[46] It offers a lens for observing the intensification of communalism in everyday life.

---

[45] See Bent Flyvbjerg's discussion on what constitutes a critical case in Bent Flyvbjerg, *Making Social Science Matter*, Cambridge: Cambridge University Press, 2001, p. 77–8.

[46] For ethnographic studies and detailed case studies of communal violence, see for example Veena Das, 'The Spatialization of Violence: Case Study of a "Communal Riot"', in

This book explores how shifts in the caste order were related to the rising antagonism against Muslims and how the Indian government, as well as state governments and various state agencies, had bearing on these processes. The book focuses on the dynamics of interactions, their intended and unintended consequences, between social groups and the state. It centres on the points and processes where the exchanges between state and society converge. The making of state redistribution policies, for example, as well as their discourse and implementation, is always subject to power struggles by various groups within the society and various components within the state. In the effect of these struggles state and society impinge on each other in many, and often intricate, ways. At the conjunction of these interactions the boundaries between state and society become blurred. The analysis in this study is guided by the view that the elusiveness of the boundary between state and society 'should not be overcome by sharper definitions but explored as a clue to the state's nature'.[47] In this analysis both the state and the society are viewed as disaggregated rather than monolithic entities, and as 'mutually transforming'.[48] This approach suggests investigating the state in a way that recognises the 'unified dimension of the state – its wholeness – expressed in its image, and one that dismantles this wholeness in favor of examining the reinforcing and contradictory practices and alliances of its disparate parts'.[49] The state is studied in its social context, with attention given to the processes whereby it affects as well as is affected by various social forces.

The first part of the book, Chapters 1 and 2, establishes the background in which the relations between various social groups evolved in Ahmedabad by the 1980s. It also analyses the effects of various state

---

Kaushik Basu and Sanjay Subrahmanyam (eds.), *Unravelling the Nation*, India: Penguin, 1996, pp. 157–203; Stanley Tambiah, *Levelling Crowds: Ethnonationalist Conflicts and Collective Violence in South Asia*, Berkeley: University of California Press, 1996; Brass, *Theft of an Idol*; Thomas B. Hansen, *Wages of Violence*, Princeton and Oxford: Princeton University Press, 2001; Brass, *The Production of Hindu–Muslim Violence*.

[47] Timothy Mitchell, 'The Limits of the State: Beyond Statist Approaches and Their Critics', *American Political Science Review*, vol. 85, no. 1 March 1991, p. 77. Also see Akhil Gupta, 'Blurred Boundaries: The Discourse on Corruption, the Culture of Politics, and the Imagined State', *American Ethnologist*, vol. 22, no. 2, 1995, pp. 375–402.

[48] Joel S. Migdal, 'The State in Society: An Approach to Struggles for Domination', in Migdal, Atul Kohli and Vivienne Shue (eds.), *State Power and Social Forces: Domination and Transformation in the Third World*, Cambridge: Cambridge University Press, 1994, p. 3; Migdal, 'Studying the State', in Mark Irving Lichbach and Alan S. Zuckerman (eds.), *Comparative Politics: Rationality, Culture and Structure*, Cambridge: Cambridge University Press, 1997, pp. 208–35; Migdal, *State in Society: Studying How States and Societies Transform and Constitute One Another*, Cambridge: Cambridge University Press, 2001.

[49] Migdal, *State in Society*, p. 22.

policies on the changes in the interrelations between and among castes. The first chapter describes the demographic, social and economic processes in the urban context. In particular, it examines the city's growth, housing developments and policies and processes of de-industrialisation. The way the city had developed played a role in the shaping of group identities and relations. The impact of these processes of urban development on the interrelations between caste and class led to increasing identity concerns among some Hindu groups, which resulted in growing social tensions, particularly from the 1980s. Some of these dynamic processes, as well as their effects, were driven by state policies and the struggles by various groups to exploit these political agendas. The chapter, therefore, indicates the processes by which state power is exercised, and how it is appropriated and re-appropriated in relation to groups in the society.

Chapter 2 focuses on the reservations policy, which became a major source of caste conflicts in the 1980s. It explicates how in the designation and discourse of reservations, policy makers and the judiciary intricately created a link between redistributive policies on the basis of caste and class, and communalism. The chapter also discusses the political context in which caste conflicts grew in the 1980s, driven by changes in the Hindu caste regime. The chapter analyses the processes by which castes were constructed through the dynamic interplay between the state and groups in the society over reservations. Thus, the analysis offers a non-essentialising view of caste. It demonstrates the shifting expressions of caste as an effect of its interrelations with other social categories of difference, like class and religion. It illustrates what specific kinds of state affirmative action meant for these changing dimensions of caste as well as for the shaping and acceleration of group tensions.

The second part of the book explores how the links between caste reservations and communalism were expressed in people's day-to-day interactions through a detailed investigation of the Ahmedabad riots of 1985. It unfolds two of the main themes of the book: first, the origins of the rise of communalism in the 1980s and the formation of a communal Hindu identity; and second, the growth of communal violence and the apparent inability of the state to contain this violence. Following a summary of the course of events, the book establishes two narrative views of the riots. One presents the state's Commission of Inquiry assessment of the events and the other examines these events from a grass-roots perspective. The first account, presented in Chapter 3, recaptures the official views of the riots as they were seen by the various agencies of the state and represented in their documents. This account is drawn from the formal documentation of the Dave Commission of Inquiry into the incidents.[50] The Commission based its explanation of the events on affidavits it collected from various state and public representatives and survivors.[51]

As an amalgamation of different public and state apparatus interests, the Commission reflects the prevailing official opinion. In the official views, these events were to be explained either by a culture of violence or by manipulations of communal politicians. This view corresponds to the conventional narrative explanations of communal violence. However, this explanation does not adequately explain the shift in the riots from caste reservation agitation to communal violence between Hindus and Muslims. Why did a conflict that was ostensibly about reservations and would thus seem naturally to intensify the divisions among Hindus turn into a battle between Hindus and Muslims and consequently lead to a consolidation of a unitary Hindu identity? The analysis in this chapter probes the relations among and between the state apparatuses and different groups within the society. It demonstrates that although the state is composed of fragmented parts that are sometimes in competition with each other, these agencies held relatively similar and consistent presumptions about society and the particular characteristics of social groups. The official account also discloses the active role of state apparatuses in exacerbating the violence. Finally, the analysis sheds light on the functioning of state institutions in everyday life.

Chapter 4 offers a second account of the event, using other sources, in order to broaden the perspective on the communal turn in the riots. It is based on oral testimonies of survivors and witnesses, documents collected by various groups and other reports and materials from the time of the riots. Because this is an account of the events as they were recalled by those who experienced and participated in them it forms the 'living text' of the riots. The chapter provides a chronicle of the riots in three areas of Ahmedabad, in the localities where some of the most significant events took place and which were most affected during the riots: the Dariapur area in the old city of Ahmedabad, where the anti-reservation agitation first transformed into communal riots; the Bapunagar area in the eastern industrial belt of the city, where large-scale destruction occurred and

---

[50] Judge V. S. Dave, *Report of the Commission of Inquiry: Into the Incidents of Violence and Disturbances which Took Place at Various Places in the State of Gujarat since February, 1985 to 18th July, 1985* (henceforth *COI*), Ahmedabad: Government of Gujarat, April 1990.

[51] The Commission collected affidavits of government workers, policemen and senior police officers, representatives of Muslims, Dalits and political parties, intellectuals, social activists and religious organisations. The Commission also collected hospital and police reports.

thousands of people were rendered homeless; and finally, a few areas in western Ahmedabad, where the dispute over the reservations policy erupted.

The oral testimonies are based on repeated in-depth interviews with extended families, individuals and public officials from these areas.[52] I located people who used to live or were still living in the localities, which the study focuses on, during the time of the riots. In this endeavour I found some people that were mentioned by the Dave Report and in other documents and publications, as well as by social activists in the city. The initial introduction to interviewees, particularly to Dalits and Muslims in the Dariapur and Bapunagar areas, was done with the help of a few social activists, especially through the staff of SETU (the Centre for Social Knowledge and Action).[53] After the first connections were made and as the fieldwork developed and I established my relations with people in the various localities, I made further contacts independently or through my interviewees. I also met some of the witnesses and survivors from the riots of 1985 through my daily interactions and experiences as a resident of a local Ahmedabad neighbourhood during the time of my fieldwork. I located some people that my interviewees mentioned in their narratives. I was conscious of interviewing both women and men who experienced the riots as adults and as youths.

Many families and their members were interviewed on different occasions, during long hours spent with them throughout their daily routine. The interviews focused on three dimensions of the residents' lives. First, the background of the locality was studied: its history; the caste and class character of its residents; their places of origin; the character of their houses; the status of the land and its ownership; the nature of the local social interactions before the riots; and the residents' political views. The second set of questions centred on the period of the riots, examining how the violence started and what happened during the seven months of riots. The questions covered life during the riots from the most mundane details to the violent incidents themselves: what people talked about; what they ate; which social activities took place; how many times they had to leave their homes; whether they were injured; how they engaged in the violence or defended themselves; who helped them; how they obtained the weapons; what was the nature of violence and of life under the curfew.

---

[52] The interviews were conducted and the material collected by the author during a year of fieldwork in 1997–8. A short field trip was also conducted in 2002. Pseudonyms are used in all citations.

[53] I am particularly grateful to Achyut Yagnik and Ashok Shrimali.

The third set of questions focused on the changes that took place in the wake of the riots.

The examination of the events from the viewpoint of people who lived through them, on the basis of their memories and from their different localities, reveals that a range of conflicts surfaced in the riots. These tensions were often unrelated to the anti-reservation agitations or to the communal antagonism. Thus, the chapter delineates the many riots within the riot. By focusing on 'little questions' and on the details of regular daily practices, the second account discloses the way in which everyday life is regulated.[54] On the one hand, it indicates how various groups in the society that are often considered to be simply tools in the hands of elites manoeuvred to gain a firm hold on the state. On the other hand, it unveils the informal regulating mechanisms that prevailed within the society beyond the purview of the state. Moreover, the second account of the riots further unravels the active role of state apparatuses in the violence.

The second account of the riots of 1985 reveals what gained significance in the memory of ordinary people twelve years after the events. Personal memory is a selective mechanism. It relates to the past through the present historical circumstances of the actors, and generates knowledge that may not always represent accurate facts. Yet, the way people recollected the events, what they remembered as much as what they forgot, provides a more nuanced understanding of the growing communalism, as well as of the discourse on communal violence. The disparities between the official views of the riots and the views of the riots as they were elicited from memories of witnesses and survivors sharpen the underlying questions, practical and theoretical, for the analysis of the revival of communalism since the 1980s in the following chapters.

The third and final part of the book develops a framework for understanding the making of ethnoHinduism since the mid-1980s. It also analyses the role of violence in relation to the formation process of ethnic identities. Chapter 5 develops an approach for thinking of ethnic identity formation. It then analyses the relations between communalism and caste, and their interplay with the state as a discourse and practice of ethnic politics, by examining the implications of the case of Ahmedabad for these interrelations. The analysis of the making of ethnoHinduism takes place by examining three arenas of social operation and the ways in which these arenas interrelate. The three domains of operation are: high politics; social and economic dynamics; and the experiences of everyday

---

[54] Flyvbjerg, *Making Social Science Matter*, pp. 132–3.

life at the local level. Chapter 6 explores why, despite the changeability of caste and communal identities, violence recurred from the mid-1980s along what appeared to be communal boundaries. It examines the rise of communalism in relation to Ahmedabad's history of violence since independence. This analysis of the role and effects of large-scale violence in ethnic politics reveals the dynamics by which the state's communalised practices, as well as the communalisation of the society, developed and consolidated, culminating in the massacre of Muslims in Gujarat in 2002.

Part I

The background

1   Setting the scene

Until the beginning of the twentieth century most of Ahmedabad's population resided within the Fort Walls on the eastern bank of the Sabarmati river.[1] The opening of the first Ahmedabad textile mill in 1861 and of the railway line between Ahmedabad and Bombay three years later was a harbinger of the city's rapid expansion. The developing textile industry generated waves of migration into the city and extensive growth of its population and territory. In 1872 Ahmedabad's population was 119,672; it had increased to 185,889 by the turn of the century; by 1961, immediately after the formation of Gujarat, it had risen to 1,149,918, and by 1985 had more than doubled to 2,387,938.[2] Over a century the city's area grew seventeen-fold: from 5.72 sq. km in 1872 to 98.15 sq. km in 1981.

The growth of the city and the demographic developments wrought profound social and economic changes among its social groups. Processes of urbanisation also restructured the city's layout. These transformations affected the dynamics of interrelations between caste and class and resulted in growing tensions among Hindus. The way the city developed was a factor in the shaping of these patterns of intra-Hindu group relations. The emerging social conflicts were inscribed on Ahmedabad's urban landscape. In particular, the social and economic transformation, the changing spatial organisation of the city and the developing pattern of settlements reflected processes of growing class segregation and fissures among castes. These changes unsettled the location of various groups within the 'Hindu order'. The resulting tensions among Hindus intensified in the 1980s, when the textile industry began to disintegrate. This chapter outlines the dynamics of these processes through an examination of Ahmedabad's urban profile, its de-industrialisation and land and housing policies. It focuses on the one hand on economic pressures on

---

[1] The old city of Ahmedabad is also referred to as the walled city and the Fort Walls.
[2] *Statistical Outline of Ahmedabad City 1984–85*, Ahmedabad: Ahmedabad Municipal Corporation, 1986, Table 3.6.

the city's social groups, and on the other hand on changes in the social context and identity.

The chapter is divided into four parts. The first section introduces the city's population to set the background for the subsequent understanding of the group relations and tensions that emerged in Ahmedabad by the mid-1980s. The second unfolds the restructuring of the city's layout, which shaped people's social dispositions and resulted in changes in the interrelations between caste and class. The third part focuses on the effects of de-industrialisation in the 1980s on various social groups. It examines why at a moment that seemed likely to generate a class conflict, caste and communal tensions developed instead. The fourth part discusses government land redistribution and housing policies and their adverse effects, which exacerbated the social tensions that arose with the city's growth and processes of de-industrialisation.

The urban profile

In 1971 Hindus constituted 78 per cent of Ahmedabad's population, and Muslims 15 per cent.[3] Both groups are deeply stratified and divided into distinct groups. Brahmins, Vanias (Banias) and Rajputs comprise the traditional upper-caste layer in Gujarat. According to a projection based on the 1931 census, the last that used caste categories, they formed 4 per cent, 3 per cent and 5 per cent of the population, respectively.[4] In the urban setting of Ahmedabad, Brahmins, traditionally priests, often held white-collar jobs. Vanias (Banias) were traditionally merchants and economically wealthier than Brahmins. The Rajputs (Kshatriyas) were descendants of ruling families who had enjoyed political power in the past. During the 1940s, the Kshatriya caste in Gujarat 'grew' when the Kshatriya Sabha (association) accepted the backward-caste Kolis into its fold. This decision, which was taken in the context of the expansion of their electoral base, aimed to increase the number of Kshatriyas and thereby advance the group politically.[5] The Kolis are the largest caste group in

---

[3] *Statistical Outline of Ahmedabad City*, Ahmedabad: Ahmedabad Municipal Corporation, 1976, table 11 (the figures are based on the 1971 census). Muslims form 8 per cent of Gujarat's total population. See *Statistical Outline of Ahmedabad City 1984–85*, Table 3.24.

[4] These figures, as well as other figures for castes in Gujarat, are based on the 1931 census. The discussion above presents a broad outline of the local caste social structure. The various castes are divided into many sub-groups. The Brahmins in Ahmedabad district, for example, are divided into eighty-four castes. *Ahmedabad District Gazetteer*, Ahmedabad: Gazetteer of India, Gujarat State, 1984, p. 190.

[5] See Ghanshyam Shah, 'Strategies of Social Engineering: Reservation and Mobility of Backward Communities of Gujarat', in Ramashray Roy and Richard Sisson (eds.), *Diversity and Dominance in Indian Politics*, Vol. II, New Delhi: Sage Publications, 1990,

Gujarat, constituting around 24 per cent of the population.[6] The British categorised the Kolis as a criminal class and in some official publications of Gujarat state into the 1980s they were still described as 'formerly engaged in roadside robberies and dacoities'.[7] From the end of the nineteenth century, the Kolis attempted to attain Kshatriya status through the census and by imitating Rajput customs.[8] The second largest and particularly influential caste group in Gujarat is the Patidars (contemporarily known as Patels), who constitute 12 per cent of the population.[9] According to Hindu Law they are Shudras, the fourth in the caste hierarchy. Until the nineteenth century they were also considered to be a low caste, but subsequently the Patidars gradually strengthened their social and economic position and attained higher caste status. Mainly as a result of land policies during British rule they were transformed from agricultural cultivators (Kanbis) into a powerful land-owning group and also became dominant among the professional classes.[10] The *Ahmedabad District Gazetteer* described the group as an enterprising community which 'earned their status, wealth and power by ability and tactful behaviour'.[11] The Patels became politically dominant in Ahmedabad and well entrenched in the Congress Party under the leadership of Vallabhbhai Patel.[12] The Patels

pp. 122–31; Shah, 'Caste Sentiments, Class Formation and Dominance in Gujarat', in Francine R. Frankel and M. S. A. Rao (eds.), *Dominance and State Power in Modern India*, Vol. II, Delhi: Oxford University Press, 1990, p. 64; Shah, 'Polarised Communities', *Seminar*, 470, October 1998, p. 31.

[6] Kolis are estimated to form between 20 and 24 per cent of the population, depending on the amalgamation of different social groups into a caste group and the inclusion of the relevant territories. The census of 1931, upon which these caste figures are based, was conducted before the formation of Gujarat.

[7] *Ahmedabad District Gazetteer*, 1984, p. 197. Also see, Lancy Lobo, 'Social Stratification and Mobility among the Kolis of North Gujarat', *International Seminar on 'Gujarat Society'*, Surat: Centre for Social Studies, 17–20 December 1986.

[8] See Shah, 'Strategies of Social Engineering', pp. 122–31; Shah, *Caste Association and Political Process in Gujarat: A Study of Gujarat Kshatriya Sabha*, Bombay: Popular Prakashan, 1975.

[9] Patidars are estimated to compose 12–14 per cent of the population. The term Patels will mostly be used in the book. Originally, Patidars were those among the Kanbi peasants who were jointly responsible for paying the land revenue to the Mughal ruler. David Hardiman, *Peasant Nationalists of Gujarat: Kheda District 1917–1934*, Delhi: Oxford University Press, 1981, pp. 36–7; Kenneth L. Gillion, *Ahmedabad: A Study in Indian Urban History*, Berkeley and Los Angeles, University of California Press, 1968, p. 161.

[10] In the 1931 Census the caste name was changed from Kanbi to Patidar. See Hardiman, *Peasant Nationalists of Gujarat*, pp. 42–5; David Pocock, *Kanbi and Patidar: A Study of the Patidar Community of Gujarat*, Oxford: Clarendon, 1972; Ashish Nandy et al., *Creating a Nationality: The Ramjanmabhumi Movement and Fear of the Self*, Delhi: Oxford University Press, 1997, p. 101.

[11] *Ahmedabad District Gazetteer*, 1984, p. 196.

[12] Hardiman, *Peasant Nationalists of Gujarat*.

are divided into two main groups, Leva Patel and Kadva Patel, the former being considered higher in the status hierarchy.[13]

The scheduled castes/Dalits (former untouchables) constitute 13 per cent of Ahmedabad's population.[14] The distinct inter-caste divisions among the Dalits form a status hierarchy among them. The main groups of Dalits in Ahmedabad are the Vankars, traditionally weavers; the Chamars, leather workers; Bhangis, sweepers; and Garodas – the priests.[15] Members of the various groups do not generally intermarry. Among the Dalits in Ahmedabad, the Vankars and the Chamars are the socially and politically prominent groups, having integrated early on in the burgeoning city's textile industry. The Vankars, who are considered to be higher in status, came to the city at the turn of the twentieth century in search of jobs and established themselves before other Dalits within the textile mills and the textile labour union. In the early 1930s the Vankar population in the city doubled the Chamars and outnumbered the other Dalit groups.[16] The Mulgami Dalits are considered to be indigenously Ahmedabadi. Members of this group have advanced through education and government jobs.

Social stratification among Muslims in Ahmedabad is similar in many ways to the caste divisions among Hindus, with occupational, sectarian and regional groupings. Muslim groupings include Sayads, Shaikhas, Pathans, Mughals, Memons, Bohras and Khojas. Among the Muslims, there are those who claim to be of foreign origin and those who are of Hindu descent. The large majority of Muslims in India were originally converted to Islam from the intermediate and lower Hindu castes. Often, Islamisation served to reinforce rather than weaken or eliminate caste distinctions among them.[17] The Bohras, Khojas and the Memons

---

[13] The economically established Leva Patels originate from central Gujarat; the newly enterprising Kadva Patels are from north Gujarat and Saurashtra. See Atul Kohli, *Democracy and Discontent*, Cambridge: Cambridge University Press, 1990, p. 254; Nandy *et al.*, *Creating a Nationality*, pp. 101–2.

[14] The scheduled castes form 7 per cent of the Gujarat state's population. *Statistical Outline of Ahmedabad City 1994–95*, Planning and Statistics Department, Ahmedabad: Ahmedabad Municipal Corporation, 1996, Table 3.20.

[15] Achyut Yagnik and Anil Bhatt, 'The Anti-Dalit Agitation in Gujarat', *South Asia Bulletin*, vol. 4, no. 1, Spring 1984, p. 48.

[16] Makrand Mehta, 'The Dalit Temple Entry Movement in Maharashtra and Gujarat, 1930–1948', in Takashi Shinoda (ed.), *The Other Gujarat*, Mumbai: Popular Prakashan, 2002, p. 11. The data are based on a census conducted by Ahmedabad Municipality in 1931–32.

[17] Imtiaz Ahmed, 'Introduction', in Imtiaz Ahmed (ed.), *Caste and Social Stratification among the Muslims*, Delhi: Manohar, 1973, pp. xxix, xxx. Also see, *Ahmedabad District Gazetteer*, 1984, pp. 210–16; *Gazetteer of the Bombay Presidency*, 1879, p. 40; Mushirul Hasan, *Legacy of a Divided Nation: India's Muslims since Independence*, Delhi: Oxford University Press, 1997, pp. 7–8; Satish C. Mishra, *Muslim Communities in Gujarat*, London: Asia Publishing House, 1964.

are traditionally the main traders and business groups among Muslims. These groups are considered to be descendants of Hindu upper castes and are generally better off economically. They tend not to intermarry with other Muslim communities.[18] Overall, Muslim business groups in Ahmedabad were not significant in numbers.[19] The majority of the Muslims in Ahmedabad are economically deprived. Many are petty traders and industrial workers. Large numbers of Muslims, mainly weavers, migrated to the city with the rise of the textile mills in the 1860s and became an important segment of the labour force. There were no Muslim mill-owners in Ahmedabad when the industry developed.[20] The economic decline of Muslims in the city began during the Maratha rule, when the Muslim administrative and military elite lost their positions. The decline continued under the British.[21] The proportion of Muslims in the city decreased significantly from the 1930s, from about 27 per cent in 1931 to 15 per cent in 1961 and 1976.[22] During partition there was very little emigration of Muslims to Pakistan.[23] A few leading Muslim families and professionals migrated to Pakistan, leaving behind a socially fragmented community.[24]

Social and political relations between various groups in Ahmedabad were informed by the distinct history of land-ownership and land reforms in the different regions of Gujarat. The state of Gujarat was formed in May 1960 as a result of the split of the Bombay presidency and the unification between British Gujarat and the region of the former princely states of Saurashtra. The two regions differed significantly in their social-hierarchical structure and relations. In British Gujarat the Patels began gaining dominance when the Maratha rule appointed many of them as revenue collectors. Later, the British gave them lands in what were then backward areas. Many Patels bought more lands from Kolis at throwaway

[18] Asghar Ali Engineer, *The Muslim Communities of Gujarat*, Delhi: Ajanta Publications, 1989, p. 22. Also see J. C. Masselos, 'The Khojas of Bombay: The Defining of Formal Membership Criteria during the Nineteenth Century', in Ahmed (ed.), *Caste and Social Stratification*, pp. 2–6.

[19] Ashutosh Varshney, *Ethnic Conflict and Civic Life: Hindus and Muslims in India*, New Haven and London: Yale University Press, 2002, pp. 229–30.

[20] Hasan, *Legacy of a Divided Nation*, p. 288; Gillion, *Ahmedabad*, p. 89.

[21] Reports of the Collector of Ahmedabad, 1854, suggest that Muslims had generally experienced economic decline since the imposition of British rule. Quoted in Siddhartha Raychaudhuri, 'Indian Elites, Urban Space and the Restructuring of Ahmedabad City 1890–1947', Ph.D. thesis, Cambridge University, 1997, p. 48. Also see Gillion, *Ahmedabad*, pp. 54, 71, 89–90.

[22] See B. K. Roy Burman, 'Social Profile', *Seminar*, 125, 1969, pp. 33–8.

[23] Achyut Yagnik and Suchitra Sheth, *The Shaping of Modern Gujarat: Plurality, Hindutva and Beyond*, New Delhi: Penguin Books, 2005, p. 225.

[24] *Interview* with Shiraz B. Tirmizi, president of *Gujarat Today* (a Muslim newspaper), 11/3/98, Ahmedabad.

prices under distress sales during the 1899 famine. Land reforms in the area after independence in the late 1940s and early 1950s, which aimed to transfer ownership rights to the tenants, were not effectively implemented. The Patels, who dominated the Congress Party at that time, utilised their links with the government in order to bypass the reform acts and to keep their lands. A large number of tenants belonging to the upper and intermediate castes were able to acquire land from absentee caste-fellow landowners who had moved to urban areas. Lower-caste tenants rarely gained land on the basis of high-caste absentees from their lands.[25] Thus, hostile relations prevailed between the Patels and the Kolis in British Gujarat. The land reforms in the area after independence failed and reinforced social inequalities and animosities between the groups.

Different social relations predominated in Saurashtra. Rajputs were the main land-owning class, oppressing the economically backward Patels and Kolis. The government rigorously implemented the land reforms in this area in order to transfer the rights over the land from the former princely states. With the formation of the Union of Saurashtra in 1950, the Indian government enacted the Girasdari Abolition Act for the uprooting of absentee landlords and granted occupancy rights to the tenants. The main beneficiaries of the reforms in Saurashtra were the Patel cultivators. Consequently, land reforms in this area yielded a change in the local power structure. The Rajput landowners lost lands to the generally poorer Patels. The latter suddenly attained ownership over land and gradually became economically and politically influential. Land reform policies in Gujarat, therefore, resulted in the empowerment of Patels in both regions of the state. The social and political hostilities, which emanated from the histories of landownership and reforms in the different regions of Gujarat, migrated with the various communities as they came to Ahmedabad with the developing textile industry.

In 1870, a decade after the first textile mill opened, the first road linking Ahmedabad's Fort Walls with the western side of the Sabarmati river was established with the opening of Ellis Bridge. In the same year the Ahmedabad Municipality attained the status of a city municipality. At the turn of the twentieth century there were twenty-seven textile mills in the city, and their number increased to fifty-one by 1920. With the growth of the industry, communities of weavers gradually migrated to the city. Most of them were Dalits or Muslims. Initially, they came from Ahmedabad district and the neighbouring Mehsana and Kheda districts.

[25] Shah, 'Caste Sentiments, Class Formation and Dominance in Gujarat', pp. 81–2.

They settled around the mills, near other Dalit and Muslim communities. Between 1872 and 1930 the industrial and residential growth was principally confined to the eastern side of the river. Only in 1911 did the city also extend to the Ellisbridge area on the western side of the river. Over that sixty-year period the city area grew four-fold and its population more than trebled to over 380,000 inhabitants.[26]

The textile industry was at its height in the years 1931–60. More groups of Muslims, Dalits and Patels migrated to Ahmedabad in quest of work. By 1939 there were seventy-seven mills in the city and eighty-three by 1941.[27] As more mills were established, surrounding villages east of the walled city, such as Asarwa, Saraspur and Gomtipur, progressively transformed into industrial townships, and the industrial activities expanded further to the eastern side. In 1939 the city also developed significantly on the western bank of the Sabarmati. The residential expansion in this area occurred with the opening of the Sardar and Gandhi bridges between the two riverbanks in 1939 and 1940, respectively. In 1939 the city limits were extended by 22 sq. km, an increase of about 73 per cent.[28] In 1950 Ahmedabad Municipal Corporation (AMC) came into existence. Non-textile industries began to develop in the eastern area of Ahmedabad at that time. Another remarkable spurt of expansion occurred in 1958, when the city was extended by a further 21 sq. km – an increase of 39 per cent.[29] The industrial area of Bapunagar next to the national highway was formed at that time with the city's eastward expansion. Even the 'green belt', which the AMC designated in its first development plan in 1959, failed to contain this dynamic growth.[30] The residential growth on the western side of the river gradually increased after the establishment of Gujarat University in 1952 in the Navrangpura area. In spite of the growth in outlying areas, the increase in population and congestion within the old city continued unabated, 'with more and more central activities

---

[26] The data are compiled from *Growth of the City Ahmedabad*, Estate Department, Ahmedabad Municipal Corporation, 1991; *Statistical Outline of Ahmedabad City 1994–95* and *1984–85*; *Ahmedabad Municipal Corporation Revised Development Plan 1975–1985*, Vols. I and II, Town Development Department, Ahmedabad Municipal Corporation, 1975, and *Growth of the City (1857–1986)* [map], Ahmedabad Estate Department, Ahmedabad Municipal Corporation.

[27] 'Ahmedabad Municipal Corporation at a Glance' (Table VII) in *Is Ahmedabad Dying?*, Seminar and Publication coordinated by Jayendra N. Bhatt, CEPT Ahmedabad and Gujarat Institute of Civil Engineering and Architects, Ahmedabad, 1987, p. 4; *Ahmedabad Municipal Corporation Revised Development Plan 1975–1985*, Vol. I, p. 45.

[28] *Growth of the City Ahmedabad*, pp. 26–7.

[29] *Ibid.*, pp. 30–1. Between 1951 and 1961 Ahmedabad's area grew by 77.22 per cent. See *Statistical Outline of Ahmedabad City 1994–95*, Table 3.1, p. 8.

[30] *Ahmedabad Municipal Corporation Revised Development Plan 1975–1985*, Vol. I, p. 35.

than its infra-structure could cater for'.[31] The population of the whole city over the three decades between 1931 and 1960 trebled.[32]

In the decade that followed the formation of the state of Gujarat, between 1961 and 1971, the city's territory did not expand, but its population grew by almost 38 per cent.[33] During that time, residential neighbourhoods continued developing on the western side of the city, and commercial businesses were established along Ashram Road, on the western riverbank. The opening of Nehru Bridge in the early 1960s accelerated these processes.[34] Until the 1970s the continuing migration to the city was mainly from other districts of Gujarat.[35] Between 1971 and 1981 the administrative area of the city grew insignificantly, by only 5.5 per cent, but the city's population grew by 30 per cent.[36] Although migration to Ahmedabad began at the turn of the century, only during the 1970s did the population of the old city start to decrease.[37]

Along with the migration to Ahmedabad, there were also population shifts within the city. As the city and its economy grew, upwardly mobile groups among the upper castes moved beyond the walled city to the western side of the river. Workers concentrated around the burgeoning textile mills and other industries on the eastern side of the river, further beyond the old city. These trends were accompanied by the establishment of new patterns of residential settlements outside the walled city on both its eastern and western sides. The developing neighbourhoods had distinct characteristics, which reflected newly forming social segregations. These processes resulted in the re-structuring of Ahmedabad's spatial layout and appearance. Socially, economically and in its structural and spatial design, the city had gradually been divided into three parts. From the end of the 1960s Ahmedabad became the story of three cities.[38] The division

---

[31] Ibid.; *Statistical Outline of Ahmedabad City 1994–95*, Table 3.3, p. 9.

[32] During this period the city experienced its highest population growth rates. In 1932 Ahmedabad's population was 382,768; in 1941, 591,267; in 1951, 837,163; and in 1961, 1,149,918: *Statistical Outline of Ahmedabad City 1994–95*, Table 3.2, p. 9.

[33] *Ibid.*, Table 3.1, p. 8 and Table 3.2, p. 9.

[34] *Ahmedabad Municipal Corporation Revised Development Plan 1975–1985*, Vol. I, p. 36.

[35] *Statistical Outline of Ahmedabad City 1984–85*, Table 3.25, p. 69. According to data for 1961, 17.3 per cent of the migrants came from Mehsana district, 8.45 per cent from Kaira (Kheda) district and 28.96 per cent from other districts of Gujarat. See *Ahmedabad Municipal Corporation Revised Development Plan 1975–1985*, Vol. I, p. 63. In 1971, the mother tongue of 70.75 per cent of the city's population was Gujarati, and of 11.65 per cent was Urdu. Only 8.64 per cent of the population's mother tongue was Hindi. *Ibid.*, Table 2.9, p. 52.

[36] *Statistical Outline of Ahmedabad City 1994–95*, Table 3.1, p. 8 and Table 3.2, p. 9.

[37] *Statistical Outline of Ahmedabad City 1984–85*, Table 3.1 and 3.2. The significant decline in population within the Fort Walls occurred between 1981 and 1991, when the population decreased from 474,223 to 398,410.

[38] For descriptions of Ahmedabad as divided into two or three main areas see Burman, 'Social Profile', p. 34; Burman, 'The Two Banks of the River', *Economic and Political*

of the city was an ongoing process, which was informed by the dynamics of the social and economic transformations.

The making of three cities

The walled city, with its twelve gates and numerous mosques, temples and towers, was founded in 1411 by Ahmad Shah on the eastern bank of the Sabarmati river. Despite its dilapidated condition, the Indian Islamic architecture and the houses decorated with woodcarvings attest to its affluent past. The old city is divided into pols, the traditional residential patterns of the walled city of Ahmedabad.[39] These are narrow streets lined with buildings, occasionally so narrow that it is difficult for two people to pass with ease. Most of these pols have strong gates at their entrances as a measure of protection, which make them self-contained. In the past, and to a lesser extent today, a pol provided various infrastructure facilities for its residents. The pols form a hybrid of the street and the inner home. Some of the household activities, such as the washing of clothes, utensils and part of food preparation, used to take place on the wide platform of the house threshold (*otla*), and could be seen from the outside.[40] From the early eighteenth century a pol's residents were mainly of one caste. A pol dweller could not sell his house to an outsider without first offering it to the pol's residents. There was no residential segregation according to class. The rich families lived in the pols among their poor caste fellows.[41] In the walled city, communities of upper castes, Dalits and Muslims lived separately but very close to each other – in mixed but not intermixed localities.

The first to move beyond the walls with the growth of the city's population were the wealthy mill-owners. They built bungalows in the northern suburb of Shahibag. From the early 1920s, wealthy members of upper-caste groups began moving to the western side of the river, where they constructed housing societies. These small cooperative apartment

Weekly, 18 September 1976, pp. 1519–20. For the view of three Ahmedabads see Achyut Yagnik and Anil Bhatt, 'The Anti-Dalit Agitation in Gujarat', p. 51; Nandy *et al.*, *Creating a Nationality*, pp. 110–11; interview with Ashok Shrimali, 14/11/97; Yagnik and Sheth, *The Shaping of Modern Gujarat*, pp. 229–30.

[39] In the 1980s a study of the old city estimated about 500 pols in thirteen wards of the walled city. Anjana Desai, *Environmental Perception: The Human Factor in Urban Planning*, Delhi: Ashish Publishing House, 1985, p. 24. There were 356 pols in 1872. Gillion, *Ahmedabad*, p. 25.

[40] George Michell and Shelal Shah (eds.), *Ahmedabad*, Bombay: Marg Publications, 1988, p. 157.

[41] Gillion, *Ahmedabad*, pp. 25–6; Ravindra G. Sing, *Traditional Urban Indian Neighbourhoods: A Case Study of 'Pols' in Ahmedabad*, Ahmedabad: School of Planning, 1981, p. 42.

buildings, alongside bungalows, became the new residential pattern in the area.[42] Urbanisation processes on the western side started at that time with the acquisition of agricultural land for urban use from the former Sabarmati, Navrangpura and Naranpura villages.[43] The first housing society was established in 1924. In the early 1950s, 110 cooperative housing societies were registered in Ahmedabad and their number had increased to 1,419 by the end of the 1960s, and to 2,154 by the mid-1980s.[44]

Access to the improved housing opportunities and services developing on the western side of the river had been largely limited to the upper-caste and upper-income groups. In order to take part in a cooperative housing society scheme it was necessary to have shared capital and secured funding. Between 1941 and 1965, 8,502 members were enrolled in the housing societies, 28 per cent of whom were Brahmins, 24 per cent Banias and another 28 per cent Patels.[45] By occupation, 27 per cent of the members were in business, 57 per cent in services, and the majority of women were housewives. Many of the residents of the housing societies acquired higher education and an improved income.[46] Residents of the old city who moved to the western side of the river, particularly in the 1960s and 1970s, were perceived as the rising new middle class. Most of the houses constructed between 1968 and 1975 consisted of three or four rooms, which was characteristic of a middle-class residence.[47]

Residents of the old city who moved to the western side reproduced their caste residential patterns.[48] The housing societies that developed from the 1920s were often named after the caste of their members or given the name of a prominent member of the caste.[49] Various social groups from the old city, often even from specific neighbourhoods, moved to particular localities on the western side. Patels from Vadigam in the old city, for example, moved to the Usmanpura area; other Patels

[42] Most of the old city wall was demolished in 1924. Gillion, *Ahmedabad*, pp. 150, 170.

[43] Darshini Mahadevia, *Globalisation Urban Reforms and Metropolitan Response: India*, Delhi: School of Planning, Centre for Environmental Planning and Technology, Ahmedabad in association with Manak, 2003, pp. 186.

[44] *Ahmedabad Municipal Corporation Revised Development Plan 1975–1985*, Vol. I, p. 80; *Statistical Outline of Ahmedabad City 1994–95*, Table 10.17, p. 157.

[45] Lower castes formed about 11 per cent of the members of the societies and Muslims less than 2 per cent. See *Ahmedabad Municipal Corporation Revised Development Plan 1975–1985*, Vol. I, p. 81.

[46] *Ibid.* Also see Desai, *Environmental Perception*, p. 38.

[47] *Ahmedabad Municipal Corporation Revised Development Plan 1975–1985*, Vol. I, p. 81.

[48] Also see Yagnik and Sheth, *The Shaping of Modern Gujarat*, p. 229; Sujata Patel, 'Urbanization, Development and Communalisation of Society in Gujarat', in T. Shinoda (ed.), *The Other Gujarat*, Mumbai: Popular Prakashan, 2002, p. 213.

[49] For example: Brahmin Mitra Society, Sardar Patel Society, etc. *Interview* with Achyut Yagnik, director, Ahmedabad: Centre for Social Knowledge and Action (SETU), 20/11/97.

moved to Navrangpura, while Jains settled mainly in Paldi, and Vaishnav in Ambawadi.[50] The patterns of population movement within the city became common knowledge among the inhabitants of Ahmedabad. This form of everyday knowledge endured even with the expansion of the city in other directions and the migration of population from other places. Thus, for example, it became known that 'in the western side of the city the Patels are from central and north Gujarat and in the eastern industrial area they are from Saurashtra'.[51]

The migration of labour to Ahmedabad, with the developing textile industry, created a growing need for inexpensive housing. From the early 1920s, the mill-owners started building chawls for their workers outside the old city walls next to the mills on its eastern side. A chawl is 'a row of rooms with either no sanitary conveniences or with community facilities'.[52] The chawls became a new residential pattern in the developing industrial eastern area of Ahmedabad. The growth rate of the chawls was the highest between 1921 and 1946, when the textile industry prospered. Most of the chawls were constructed before 1948 and were privately owned.[53] About 71 per cent of the chawl dwellers had migrated to Ahmedabad from rural areas in different parts of Gujarat and 29 per cent came from other states.[54]

Nevertheless, rapid migration of labour to the city created a persistent housing shortage, which resulted in the construction of slums alongside the chawls. These hutment colonies, or *kuccha* dwellings, had no adequate sanitary facilities. The slums were concentrated around the mills on the eastern side of the old city beyond the railways.[55] The accelerated growth of slums in that part of the city took place between 1960 and the early 1970s, when Ahmedabad's population increased but there was no territorial expansion.[56] Between 1961 and 1971 slums accounted for almost 45 per cent of the growth of households in the city.[57] In 1976, 81,255 slum dwellings were counted in Ahmedabad, housing 22 per cent of the

---

[50] Many interviewees, both in the old city and in the western side, described these residential patterns. Also see Desai, *Environmental Perception*, p. 33.

[51] *Interview* with Gordhanbhai Jhadaphia, BJP MLA, Bapunagar, Ahmedabad, 16/12/97.

[52] *Ahmedabad Municipal Corporation Revised Development Plan 1975–1985*, Vol. I, p. 82.

[53] Meera Mehta, 'Urban Housing Processes and the Poor: A Case Study of Ahmedabad', *Nagarlok*, vol. 14, no. 2, April–June 1982, p. 108.

[54] Manesh Bhatt and V. K. Chawda, 'Housing the Poor in Ahmedabad', *Economic and Political Weekly*, 8 May 1976, p. 709.

[55] The number of slums in the old city was not high because this area was already very dense. In the western side of the river the density of slums was low.

[56] About 46 per cent of the slums were erected before 1963 and about 24 per cent between 1968 and 1972. *Report on the Census of Slums Ahmedabad City 1976*, Ahmedabad, Ahmedabad Municipal Corporation, 1976, Table 3, p. 7.

[57] Mehta, 'Urban Housing Processes', p. 109.

city's population, a figure that remained constant throughout the 1980s.[58] About 83 per cent of the slums' residents were members of lower- and backward-caste groups, and 15 per cent were Muslims.[59] The majority of the slum dwellers, 83.2 per cent, had migrated to Ahmedabad in search of work from other parts of Gujarat.[60] About 45 per cent of the workers in the slums were engaged in the manufacturing and repairs industry, the vast majority of them in the textile industry.[61]

The slums and chawls on the eastern side of the old city, as well as the housing societies and bungalows on its western side beyond the river, changed the city's social and economic landscape. Ahmedabad gradually evolved into three cities in substance and meaning. The region on the western side of the Sabarmati became the city of the 'savarna' and the economically prosperous. On the eastern bank, the walled city with its old residential and commercial areas became known as 'Ahmedabad proper' by the city's residents. The river forms a natural dividing line between the two. The third Ahmedabad is situated in the eastern industrial belt of the city, beyond the railways. The 'have-nots' reside in both the Ahmedabads on the eastern bank of the river. The bridges over the Sabarmati river and the railway draw informal borders and map Ahmedabad as three different cities, a distinction that is expressed by the city's residents in their language. People from different neighbourhoods were sometimes typecast: 'often we say that this man must be from Khadia and this man must be from Ellisbridge or Navrangpura'.[62] Each of the Ahmedabads has its own history and was established and developed over different periods. They differ in their architecture, social composition, the lifestyle of their residents and the economic activities that dominate them. The western city is mainly a residential domain of the upper castes/classes. It has modern commercial areas, and businesses of white-collar professionals. Ahmedabad proper, within the walls, is a bazaar, a huge market intermixed with the highly dense dilapidated residential neighbourhoods of the pols. The skyline of the eastern belt, the predominant industrial labour area, is dominated by the chimneys of the textile mills.

---

[58] *Census of Slums*, p. 5. These slum dwellings constituted about 30 per cent of the city's total houses. *Ahmedabad Municipal Corporation Revised Development Plan 1975–1985*, Vol. I, p. 69. For estimates in the mid-1980s see Renana Jhawala and Usha Jumeni, 'Ahmedabad 2001: Planning for the Poor – A Focus on Self-Employed Women', *Nagarlok*, vol. 20 no. 4, October–December, 1988, p. 74.

[59] About 21 per cent of the slum dwellers were members of the scheduled castes. See *Census of Slums*, p. 16.

[60] *Ibid.*, Table 12, p. 15.   [61] *Ibid.*, Tables 18, 19, pp. 21–2.

[62] Kirit N. Raval, 'Law and Order in Ahmedabad', *Is Ahmedabad Dying?*, Ahmedabad: CEPT Ahmedabad and Gujarat Institute of Civil Engineering and Architects, 1987, p. xi.

The distinct social geographies and patterns of settlement that developed in the city informed peoples' perceptions of their social disposition as well as of the status of other groups. The dwellers of the pols conceived of themselves until the mid-1980s to be indigenous Ahmedabadis and middle-class. They referred to the residents of the chawls as labour (*majdoor*). The chawl dwellers also perceived themselves as labouring people.[63]

The gradual making of the three cities of Ahmedabad between the 1920s and 1980s reflected growing class segregation and fissures among castes. These developments resulted in changes in the interrelations between caste and class, engendering increasing identity uncertainties and tensions among Hindus. These tensions were inscribed upon the developing urban face of Ahmedabad. The city therefore constituted a derived text from which social conflicts could be inferred. The growing uncertainties among Hindus were exacerbated and given a new impetus by the economic circumstances of the 1980s.

De-industrialisation

For more than a century the textile mill industry had been the backbone of Ahmedabad's economy and the key to its expansion. With its related vocations and commerce, it had become the principal means of livelihood for most of the city dwellers, and for the many new migrants. This situation changed at the beginning of the 1980s, when a crisis in the industry resulted in the closure of mills. Between 1979 and 1984, 12 of the 65 mills in the city were shut down; 9 of the mills were closed over six months between 1983 and 1984.[64] At the time, the textile mills were estimated to provide direct employment to about 150,000 workers and indirect employment to another 100,000 in related vocations such as subcontractors and suppliers – a total of 37 per cent of Ahmedabad's working population. By 1985 as many as 50,000 labourers had lost their jobs in the mills.[65] Nonetheless, despite the downsizing, increased

---

[63] These views were reiterated by the various interviewees in the old city and the eastern area.

[64] 'Ahmedabad Municipal Corporation at a Glance', Table VII, in *Is Ahmedabad Dying?*, p. 4; B. B. Patel, *Workers of Closed Textile Mills*, New Delhi: Oxford and IBH Publishing, 1988, p. 1.

[65] Figures compiled from *Statistical Outline of Ahmedabad City 1984–85*, Table 3.6, Table 12.7; and *Statistical Outline of Ahmedabad City 1994–95*, Table 3.15. Also see Renana Jhabvala, *Closing Doors: A Study on the Decline in Women Workers in the Textile Mills of Ahmedabad*, Ahmedabad: SETU, 1985, p. 5; Patel, *Workers of Closed Textile Mills*; Shah, 'Caste Sentiments, Class Formation and Dominance in Gujarat', p. 95; Sujata Patel, *Contract Labour in Textile Industry of Ahmedabad*, Ahmedabad: SEWA, 1984, p. 7; Patel,

productivity through newer technologies in small powerloom factories meant that there was hardly any decrease in the output and consumption of textiles.[66]

The increasing diversification to powerloom factories was related to broader processes of de-industrialisation as well as to changes in the textile market that took place throughout India after independence.[67] From 1960, in contrast to the large-scale integrated production systems of the composite mills, which had dominated the economy of Ahmedabad for a century, there was a significant growth in small-scale disintegrated industries.[68] These developments were fostered by state industrial policies. Already in the late 1950s, Ahmedabad Municipal Corporation (AMC) had begun establishing industrial estates so that entrepreneurs with little means could obtain built-up sheds or developed plots with infrastructure facilities such as electricity, water, drainage and roads.[69] In 1961, for example, AMC built an industrial estate in Bapunagar, on the eastern side of the city, with eighty-eight sheds. In 1974, 1,500 workers were employed in seventy-four small industries such as powerlooms, textile processing, the manufacture of chemicals, machine tools and textile machinery on the estate.[70] The government also provided subsidies for employers to construct housing for their employees. In Bapunagar, for example, the government subsidised the construction of 5,008 tenements during the early 1960s.[71] The number of small-scale industries registered with the Commissioner of Industries in Ahmedabad rose from 660 in 1961 to 1,951 in 1965, 3,940 in 1970 and 6,914 in 1975.[72] Some of these small industrial units employed less than ten

'Nationalisation, TLA and Textile Workers', *Economic and Political Weekly*, 7 December 1985, pp. 2154–5; *Request for Assistance from the National Renewal Funds for Ahmedabad Textile Mills*, Ahmedabad: Textile Labour Association (TLA), 1993, p. 3.

[66] Powerloom firms mainly weave manmade cloth with higher productivity.

[67] Tirthankar Roy, 'Development or Distortion? "Powerlooms" in India 1950–1997', *Economic and Political Weekly*, 18 April 1998, pp. 897–911; 'Economic Reforms and Textile Industry', *Economic and Political Weekly*, 8 August 1998, pp. 2173–6; Amitabh Kundu, 'Urbanisation, Employment Generation and Poverty under the Shadow of Globalisation', in Indira Hirway, S. P. Kashyap and Amita Shah (eds.), *Dynamics of Development in Gujarat*, Ahmedabad: Centre for Development Alternatives, 2002, p. 124.

[68] Powerloom factories 'can be defined by de-integration of process'. See Roy, 'Development or Distortion?', p. 897.

[69] Under the Gujarat Industrial Development Corporation several industrial sheds with these infrastructure facilities have been constructed. *Ahmedabad District Gazetteer*, p. 352. Also see *Times of India* (henceforth *TOI*), 28 July 1969.

[70] *Ahmedabad District Gazetteer*, pp. 356–7.   [71] *Ibid.*, p. 366.

[72] *Ibid.*, p. 346. The number of registered small-scale industrial units in Gujarat increased from 15,879 at the end of 1970 to 178,627 at the end of 1995. See Pravin Visaria and Sudershan Iyengar, 'Economic Prospects', *Seminar*, 470, October 1998, p. 25.

persons and were therefore not even registered as industrial units. Over
this period, between 1960 and 1975, factory employment in Ahmedabad
was stagnant.[73]

The intensifying crisis in the textile mills, particularly the closure of
mills between 1984 and 1985, as well as the structural changes in the
economy, severely affected the working class in the city, causing a significant decline in their income and high rates of unemployment.[74] The
wages of workers who found casual jobs or became self-employed fell
drastically from an average of Rs.25 and 50 per day, which they used
to earn in the mills, to an average of Rs.11 and 15 per day.[75] Some
workers experienced even greater hardship. Lavjibhai Bhurabhai Parmar, for example, had worked in Monogram mills for fourteen years,
earning Rs.600 per month. After his mill was shut down, he started a
boot-polishing stool, earning Rs.5–6 a day. His uncle and two sons were
also unemployed mill workers.[76] Valirambhai, a dismissed worker from
Abhay Mill, started selling eggs in his locality, earning Rs.2 for the sale
of twenty-five eggs.[77] A significant percentage of the laid-off mill workers
remained unemployed.[78] De-industrialisation processes, particularly the
shift to powerloom factories, resulted in the systematic abuse of working
conditions. Since protective labour laws did not apply to a factory that
employed a small number of workers, labourers were far more exploited.
Workers experienced a shift from relatively secure terms of employment
to a precarious and unprotected form of contract labour.

To some extent, therefore, the textile mill-owners purposely presented
a picture of economic stagnation with a view to easing the diversification to small factories and to reducing expenditures on the management
of labour. Indeed, 'to utilise low wages or bypass capacity restrictions
some mills subcontracted with powerlooms for cloth that was sold on
mill brand'.[79] The mill-owners' formal reason for closing the mills was

---

[73] *Statistical Outline of Ahmedabad City 1984–85*, Table 12.1, p. 213; Patel, *Workers of Closed
Textile Mills*, p. 11.

[74] Many lost their jobs because of the technological advance of powerloom over manual
spinning and weaving. The same productivity would be attained with a smaller labour
force.

[75] Patel, *Workers of Closed Textile Mills*, pp. 30–44. The provision of a minimum wage did
not apply in the case of textile mills. See Patel, *Contract Labour*, p. 22.

[76] Manish Jani, *Textile Worker: Jobless and Miserable* (a report based on interviews with
workers of textile mills closed in Ahmedabad), Ahmedabad: SETU, 1984, pp. 3–4.

[77] *Ibid.*, p. 12.

[78] A study of 5,773 displaced mill workers, conducted in 1984, found that only 44 per
cent of these workers reported to have had some economic activity during the weeks the
research took place. Patel, *Workers of Closed Textile Mills*, p. 22.

[79] Roy, 'Development or Distortion?', p. 901.

that due to financial difficulties they could not pay the electricity bills and the power in the mills was cut off.[80] Workers believed this was only an excuse: 'the mill has to pay Rs.40 a day to the worker whereas the small factory pays Rs.10 to 12 for the said job. Who will continue this business with less profit?'[81] A representative of the mill-owners approved this line of reasoning. 'The mills had lots of government restrictions, social obligations, an enforced kind of production to protect the lower strata in the society. This had started to cripple the industry. In the powerloom sector there are no such obligations.'[82]

The condition of labour was further aggravated by the salient discrepancy between the economic and social experiences of some workers before the crisis in the mills and their new circumstances. During the growth of the textile mill industry, some groups among the workers, lower castes in particular, had been able to advance their economic and social position. The wages of the mill workers, which ranged from Rs.600 and Rs.1,200 per month, were secure and labour laws protected their terms of employment. The mill workers benefited from provisions similar to those of government employees. Moreover, the Textile Labour Association (TLA), which was strong during the heyday of the mill industry, supported lower-caste workers.[83] Union representatives regularly visited the chawls and assisted with civic amenities.[84] Some members of the scheduled castes attributed the improvement in their social position to the efforts of TLA leaders:

When I was young, we openly used to be called 'dhed' by the higher caste. We always had to eat separately and they tried to avoid touching us. When we went to meetings in TLA, the Patels and other high caste would sit far from us . . . [But] the leaders . . . would always sit and eat with us . . . [and] openly voiced their belief against untouchability and led actions for its removal.[85]

---

[80] This story was reiterated in interviews with many unemployed mill workers. Also see Jani, *Textile Worker: Jobless and Miserable*, pp. 8, 11, 21.

[81] *Ibid.*, pp. 4–5.

[82] *Interview* with the Principal Secretary of Ahmedabad Textile Mill-Owners Association, N. V. Ranganathan, Ahmedabad, 15/12/97.

[83] Mahatma Gandhi founded the TLA in 1918. TLA leaders were well entrenched within the Congress and the nationalist movement at that time. In the 1937 Congress ministry in Bombay, for example, Gulzarilal Nanda, the general secretary of the TLA, became the labour minister. See Jan Breman, *The Making and Unmaking of an Industrial Working Class: Sliding down the Labour Hierarchy in Ahmedabad, India*, New Delhi: Oxford University Press, 2004, p. 71; Ajay Oza, 'Majur Mahajan Asserts Its Identity', *Economic and Political Weekly*, 13 November 1971, pp. 2303–4.

[84] *Textile Labour Association, Ahmedabad, Annual Report 1974 & 1975*, Ahmedabad: Gandhi Majoor Sevalaya, Bhadra, 1977, p. 49.

[85] Jhabvala, *Closing Doors*, pp. 34–5 (an interview with a scheduled caste worker, Kankuben, who referred to the 1940s).

The mill workers also enjoyed housing benefits. Initially the migrant labourers, mainly Dalits and Muslims, were housed in the chawls. From the 1960s, some mill workers were able to rent and later purchase flats in various building schemes of the Gujarat Housing Board in the eastern part of the city. Mill workers could obtain housing loans more easily from the labour union bank and avoid higher interest on borrowings from private moneylenders.[86] By the 1980s, most of the senior textile workers lived in houses that they had acquired through government housing schemes.[87] Those with fewer means remained in the chawls.

Confronted by the closure of mills and estranged by the mill-owners, workers might have been expected to unite and resist. It might even be supposed that residential segregation and the formation of working-class neighbourhoods would be conducive to a class conflict. Yet, caste and communal conflicts emerged instead. The structure and mechanisms of industrial relations that had emerged in the Ahmedabad textile mill industry were impediments to a labour struggle. An industrial relations act created institutional and legal constraints on workers' range of responses to industrial disputes. The division of labour within the mills and the labour union formed an additional barrier for workers' consolidation. Finally, the shift in the structure of the economy and the new policies, which enhanced economic deregulation, further reduced the power of the workers.

Industrial relations in the Ahmedabad textile industry narrowed workers' options for struggle. The industrial relations were based on the principle of arbitration. The weapon of strike was only to be used as a last resort.[88] The TLA was the sole representative of the textile workers. Other unions were excluded from the bargaining process. The TLA's status as the sole representative union of the workers was instituted by the Bombay Industrial Dispute Act (BIDA), 1938.[89] In the context of the crisis in the textile mills during the 1980s, workers felt that the union was no longer effectively representing their interests. In spite of the closure of mills in the mid-1980s, the TLA continued adhering to the principle of arbitration. In the view of some workers, 'the mill owners demolished the composite textile mills, and the TLA was an agent of the mill owners'.[90]

---

[86] Breman, *The Making and Unmaking of an Industrial Working Class*, pp. 124, 88.
[87] Jhabvala, *Closing Doors*, p. 5.
[88] Khandubhai K. Desai (MP), *Textile Labour Association Ahmedabad: An Indigenous Experiment in Trade Union Movement*, Ahmedabad: Textile Labour Association, 1976, p. 6.
[89] According to the Act the union with the largest membership in the workforce would represent the workers.
[90] *Interview* with Pravin Rashtrapar, 29/11/97, Ahmedabad. Also see Jani, *Textile Worker: Jobless and Miserable*, pp. 8–9.

Workers complained that '[o]ur TLA is sleeping'.[91] The union's policy is to 'remain peaceful and get starved'.[92] Although workers were entitled to minimum rights, the textile mills were closed down in disregard of the procedures laid down in the Industrial Dispute Act.[93] 'Throughout the city ... there is what we find a planned subversion of the legal system and not merely isolated violations of labour laws.'[94] Since the TLA was the sole representative union, other labour unions could not fight at the time for the workforce on the basis of the Bombay Industrial Relation Act.[95] A poem by a jobless worker, Jivan Thakore, expressed these feelings:

> Cruel hands of the mill-owners
> have snatched away livings . . .
> Havoc is played here.
> 'Servants' doing services are sleeping
> Rights of labourers are drowned
> Future seems dark . . .
> Havoc is played here . . .
> Eunuchs are sitting with a sword
> Eagles are hovering around Mill temple
> God is dead.
> Havoc is played here[96]

The division of labour in the textile mill industry was also to the detriment of a workers' struggle. In the mills specific social groups composed the workforce in the different departments.[97] The majority of the workers in the spinning department, for example, were scheduled castes. Muslims dominated the weaving departments, where Kadva Patels also worked.[98]

---

[91] Jani, *Textile Worker: Jobless and Miserable*, p. 5.   [92] *Ibid.*, p. 9.

[93] Sanat Mehta (MP), *Plight of Textile Workers* (based on the speech made in the Lok Sabha, 14 May 1997), Baroda: Gujarat Foundation for Development Alternatives, p. 2.

[94] Girish Patel, in *Is Ahmedabad Dying?*, p. xvii.   [95] Patel, *Contract Labour*, p. 89.

[96] Jivan Thakore, 'Eagles Hovering around Mill Temple', in Jani, *Textile Worker: Jobless and Miserable*, p. 26. Also cited in Breman, *The Making and Unmaking of an Industrial Working Class*, p. 169.

[97] Burman, 'Social Profile', pp. 36–7; Howard Spodek, 'From Gandhi to Violence: Ahmedabad's 1985 Riots in Historical Perspective', *Modern Asian Studies*, vol. 23, no. 4, 1989, p. 779. Also see Zenab Banu, *Politics of Communalism: A Politico-Historical Analysis of Communal Riots in Post-Independence India*, London: Sangam Books, 1989, p. 140; Sujata Patel, *The Making of Industrial Relations: The Ahmedabad Textile Industry 1918–1939*, Delhi: Oxford University Press, 1987; Patel, *Contract Labour*, pp. 6–22; T. S. Papola and K. K. Subrahmanian, *Wage Structure and Labour Mobility in a Social Labour Market: A Study in Ahmedabad*, Ahmedabad: Sardar Patel Institute of Economic and Social Research, 1975; Mridul Eapen, 'The New Textile Policy', *Economic and Political Weekly*, 22–29 June 1985, pp. 1072–3.

[98] *Interviews* with Executive Committee member of the TLA, Fushabhai Parmar, 24/3/98, Ahmedabad; Secretary, TLA, M. G. Parmar, 24/3/98, Ahmedabad. Also see Patel, *Contract Labour*, p. 13; Spodek, 'From Gandhi to Violence', p. 779; Manju Parikh, 'Labour–Capital Relations in the Indian Textile Industry: A Comparative Study of Ahmedabad and Combators', unpublished Ph.D. thesis, University of Chicago, 1988, p. 98.

New recruits for a particular department in the mill were frequently members of the same caste.[99] Most of the jobs were secured through other workers, mainly relatives of the job seeker.[100] The division of labour along caste lines often overlapped with inter-class segregation. For example, only scheduled castes worked in the spinning shops, which was the most laborious and one of the lowest paid positions in the Ahmedabad mills.[101] The structure of the TLA, which was organised as a craft-based federation, mirrored the division of labour in the industry. Each department in the mill had a separate union, with representatives on the council of the federation of unions.[102] The division of labour extended in some ways beyond the workplace. In the chawls, for example, Muslims and scheduled castes lived in separate rows of rooms.

To some extent, therefore, the mill workers thought of themselves, as their employers did, in terms of caste rather than class. 'The main problem was that labour has not taken itself as labour but was identified as caste, because of the way capital set up labour by caste.'[103] Even the re-employment of displaced mill workers during the crisis in the mills occurred through the help of caste-fellows and relatives.[104] Unemployed Muslim workers claimed that 'for Muslims, it was very difficult to get work in some mills. Everywhere, one will find nepotism, casteism, communalism. In mills, there will be back-door recruitment. So only relatives will have jobs.'[105] The organisation of labour within the industry and the structure of the union served as a divisive force among workers. These divisions among labour and the industrial relations that had evolved in Ahmedabad contributed to the containment of a potential class conflict at the time.[106] The new economic policies, affecting Ahmedabad in the

---

[99] *Interview* with Jayesh R. Parikh, TLA Research Department, 24/3/98, Ahmedabad; Spodek, 'From Gandhi to Violence', p. 779; Breman, *The Making and Unmaking of an Industrial Working Class*, pp. 17–18, 26, 154.

[100] T. S. Papola and K. K. Subrahmanian, 'Structure of a Local Labour Market: A Study in Ahmedabad', *Economic and Political Weekly*, Annual No., February 1973, p. 291; *Interview* with Ashok Shrimali, Ahmedabad, 24/11/97.

[101] *Interview* with Executive Committee member of the TLA, Fushabhai Parmar, 24/3/98, Ahmedabad. Also *Interview* with Secretary, TLA, M. G. Parmar, 24/3/98, Ahmedabad; Jani, *Textile Worker: Jobless and Miserable*, p. 7.

[102] See *The Textile Labour Association, Ahmedabad: Constitution*, Ahmedabad: Textile Labour Association, 1993, p. 3. Some scholars saw this union structure as such that promoted unity and 'social harmony' among the workers. See, for example, Spodek, 'From Gandhi to Violence', p. 779 and Varshney, *Ethnic Conflict and Civic Life*, p. 233.

[103] *Interview* with the President of Gujarat Majdoor Panchayat, P. Chidambaram, Ahmedabad, 20/12/97.

[104] *Interview* with Ashok Shrimali, 14/11/97, Ahmedabad.

[105] Jani, *Textile Worker: Jobless and Miserable*, p. 11.

[106] The division of labour along caste lines was a historical product of the development of the local textile industry. In the pre-colonial economic structure of the city there had been no strict religious social and occupational separation in the workplace. Gillion, *Ahmedabad*, p. 23.

mid-1980s further operated to the disadvantage of the dismissed mill workers.

In June 1985 the Indian government announced a new textile policy, which privileged small-scale production and which would have accelerated the loss of jobs in the textile mills.[107] As the textile mills declined there was a rapid development of the petrochemicals, cement, chemical, engineering and high-tech industries.[108] However, despite this industrial growth in Ahmedabad between 1980 and 1985, there were fewer jobs for the displaced mill workers, mainly because the new industries required skilled workers.[109] The government of Gujarat began initiating new policies of deregulation at the time. In the wake of the crisis in the textile mills there was a general decline in manufacturing in the city and a significant increase in the tertiary sector and in primary activities.[110]

The workers not only felt estranged by the mill-owners and the union, but perceived the government to be 'in collusion' with their employers and the TLA.[111] In their view, the government and the union neglected the workers and helped the mill-owners to divest themselves of their liabilities and responsibilities. 'This is all politics! Neither Government, nor the owners or Union . . . nobody bothers about workers.'[112]

The collapse of the Ahmedabad textile mill industry, as well as the broader processes of de-industrialisation, affected social relations in the city, resulting in the growth of tensions between various groups and identity concerns among Hindus. Dismissed mill workers belonging to upper-caste, lower-caste and Muslim groups competed for employment in a limited market crowded with job seekers. Many mill workers who did well during the prosperous years of the mills suddenly experienced economic and social hardships.

Some workers among the scheduled castes did particularly well during the growth of the textile industry. They were able to provide their children with opportunities for better education, and the level of literacy among

[107] *The Hindu*, 20 July 1985.
[108] Amitabh Kundu, 'Urbanisation, Employment Generation and Poverty', pp. 123–4; Harish Khare, 'An Unending Struggle for Gujarat's Political Soul', *Seminar*, 470, 1998, p. 21; Breman, *The Making and Unmaking of an Industrial Working Class*, p. 144.
[109] See Indira Hirway, 'Dynamics of Development in Gujarat: Some Issues', in Indira Hirway, S. P. Kashyap and Amita Shah (eds.), *Dynamics of Development in Gujarat*, Ahmedabad, Centre for Development Alternatives, 2002, p. 21.
[110] *Statistical Outline of Ahmedabad City 1994–95*, Table 3.17, p. 34; Amitabh, 'Urbanisation, Employment Generation and Poverty'.
[111] Jani, *Textile Worker: Jobless and Miserable*, p. 8. The living conditions of the workers in the city intensified as a result of a price rise of 3.1 per cent for basic commodities between April and June 1985.
[112] *Ibid.*, p. 9.

them increased.[113] Among the dismissed scheduled caste workers below the age of 25 there were no illiterates. Young scheduled caste workers, as well as the children of scheduled caste workers, performed better in education than workers belonging to backward castes and Muslims, and were on a par with the upper castes.[114] Some workers among the lower castes felt a loss of their life achievements:

These workers had been able to get rid of the oppression of the landlords and upper caste and were able to come to a city and earn something. On their own, they were in a position to educate their children to some extent. They have to go back to the villages . . . The villagers will mock at them and again they will have to suffer under the feudal ruthless oppression.[115]

The sense of downward mobility experienced by workers, along with the growing social tensions, was compounded by the spatial division of the city. The sense of economic and social decline that afflicted upper-caste dismissed mill workers from the old city, for example, was intensified by the comparison with their economically better-off caste-fellows who were moving to the western side of the city. Their frustrations led to increasing identity concerns since they could no longer easily justify their self-ascribed middle-class status.

The de-industrialisation of the mid-1980s precipitated the decline of some upper-caste groups and undermined processes that advanced weaker groups of the society. The resulting changes in the interrelations between caste and class were exacerbated by the developing land and housing policies, as well as the politics that emanated from these policies. Land policies, which aimed to improve the access of disadvantaged groups to housing, in reality advanced more prosperous groups. The land and housing policies increased the vulnerability of the weak social groups and their dependence on various kinds of political patronage.

Housing

The housing patterns in Ahmedabad were shaped in the context of the growing population, rapid urbanisation and shortage of land and housing. The chawls and slums were initially built in response to the arrival of migrant labour, at a time when the textile mill industry was growing. The

---

[113] During 1977–78 the percentage of post-matric scholarship awards to scheduled caste students in Gujarat was higher than the percentage of their population in the state. *Report of the Commissioner for Scheduled Castes and Scheduled Tribes 1978–79*, New Delhi: Government of India (through the Minister of Home Affairs), pp. 7–8.

[114] Patel, *Workers of Closed Textile Mills*, pp. 19, 46; Shah, 'Polarised Communities', p. 32.

[115] Jani, *Textile Worker: Jobless and Miserable*, p. 18.

mill-owners built the chawls around the mills to provide housing for their workers. Until the late 1960s the majority of slums were constructed on private lands.[116] After the formation of Gujarat, government authorities became more involved in the housing market. State policies were designed to address land and housing shortages, on the one hand, and to resolve problems of inadequate sanitary facilities in low-income dwellings, on the other.

From the 1960s, the Gujarat Housing Board (GHB) began developing areas in the surroundings of Ahmedabad, and established several housing schemes for lower-income groups.[117] Between 1961 and 1971 the proportion of dwellings in Ahmedabad increased by 20 per cent, but the population grew by almost 38 per cent.[118] The estimated shortage of pucca (cement housing) houses in Ahmedabad in 1970 was highest among the lowest-income groups and reached 88,900 dwelling units.[119]

In the mid-1970s, about 40 per cent of Ahmedabad's population resided in hutments and chawls.[120] The living conditions in the chawls steadily deteriorated because of increasing overcrowding and neglect by landlords. This process started after the chawls came under the Rent Control Act (1939), which made investment in low-income rental housing less profitable than it used to be.[121] Gradually, the chawls became more like slums. Hutments were built in the open spaces around the original chawl and little room was available for necessary civic amenities.[122] Until 1971 the AMC took action against chawl owners who did not provide sewerage and water closets. Since this led to lengthy litigation, with poor results, the AMC started sewerage works at public expense without notifying the owners. Despite these efforts, by the mid-1980s many residents still did not have running water in their homes, and the chawls remained dilapidated, overcrowded and poorly equipped.[123]

---

[116] *Statistical Outline of Ahmedabad City 1984–85*, Table 11.8, p. 197.

[117] The various housing schemes of the GHB were set for low-income groups, middle-income groups and for industrial purposes. See *Ahmedabad Municipal Corporation Revised Development Plan 1975–1985*, Vol. I, pp. 45, 82 and 149.

[118] *Ahmedabad Municipal Corporation Revised Development Plan 1975–1985*, Vol. I, p. 70.

[119] *Ibid.*, Vol. II, p. 11. Also see Patel, *Workers of Closed Textile Mills*, p. 12.

[120] *Statistical Outline of Ahmedabad City 1984–85*, Table 11.19, p. 209.

[121] Mahadevia, *Globalisation Urban Reforms*, p. 188. On the effects of the Rent Control Act on the deteriorating conditions of old buildings, on the reductions in rental housing construction and the freezing of municipal revenue from property, see *National Commission on Urbanization: Interim Report*, New Delhi: Government of India, Ministry of Urban Development, January 1987, pp. 26–7, 60–1.

[122] *Ahmedabad Municipal Corporation Revised Development Plan 1975–1985*, Vol. I, p. 83; C. N. Roy, *Liberalisation and Urban Social Sources: Health and Education*, Jaipur and Delhi: Rawat, 2003, pp. 208–9.

[123] Roy, *Liberalisation and Urban Social Sources*, p. 9; Kirtee Shah, Ahmedabad Study Action Group, in *Is Ahmedabad Dying?*, Ahmedabad: CEPT Ahmedabad and Gujarat

The growth of slums in Ahmedabad from the mid-1970s was not simply a result of migration and increasing population. The growth rate of
slum households in the early 1980s was 'more than double the rates of in-
migration'.[124] This could have been the result of the worsening economic
conditions of low-income groups. It was, however, mainly the effect of
the failure of the AMC and the government to resolve the problem of
housing supply. Between 1974 and 1976, out of 14,067 building plans
pending before the Ahmedabad Municipal Corporation Town Development Department, only 10,871 were approved. Consistently, at the end
of every year there was a backlog of building plans for authorisation.[125]
In the face of the housing shortage and projected population growth,
the AMC's Revised Development Plan in 1975 advised that the government acquire as much open area as possible.[126] It was in this context of
rapidly growing slums and persistent shortage of housing, particularly for
low-income groups, that the Urban Land (Ceiling and Regulation) Act
(ULCRA), 1976 was introduced.

The ULCRA was intended to ensure government access to vacant
land for purposes of redistribution in order to reduce social and economic inequality, as well as to prevent a concentrated ownership of urban
property and speculation and profiteering.[127] Under the Act, no person
was permitted to hold and/or transfer more than 1,000 sq. m of land.
The government was empowered to acquire the surplus land from its
holders, and to offer the excess land for the use of public bodies such
as the Gujarat Housing Board, the Gujarat Slum Clearance Board, the
AMC, Ahmedabad Urban Development Authority, or any other public
sector bodies.[128] Clauses 20 and 21 of the Act granted an exemption
with regard to surplus land that was to be used for public interest, and
group housing, such as the non-profit cooperative housing societies, or
for building housing for the 'weaker sections of society'.[129] Those seeking an exemption had to submit building plans to the relevant authorities
prior to 1980. However, these exemption clauses, which were intended

Institute of Civil Engineering and Architects, 1987, p. 20. The same situation prevailed
in many of the chawls in Ahmedabad during the late 1990s, when this research was
conducted.
[124] Mehta, 'Urban Housing Processes', p. 111.
[125] *Statistical Outline of Ahmedabad City 1994–95*, Table 10.19, p. 159.
[126] *Ahmedabad Municipal Corporation Revised Development Plan 1975–1985*, Vol. I, p. 84.
[127] See *National Commission on Urbanization: Interim Report*, p. 22. Also see Deo Vinayak
Narhar, 'Urban Land Policy: Evaluation of Urban Land (Ceiling and Regulation)
Act 1976', Unpublished Ph.D. thesis, School of Planning, Ahmedabad, May 1982,
p. 59.
[128] Kiran Vadhva, 'Private Sector and Urban Housing: A Case Study of Ahmedabad',
Nagarlok, vol. 18, no. 3, July–September, 1986, p. 74.
[129] *National Commission on Urbanization: Interim Report*, p. 51.

to advance the public interest, particularly the conditions of low-income groups, were exploited by big landowners, developers and builders and in effect inhibited the implementation of the ULCRA and operated against its objectives. Rather than accomplishing redistribution of land and providing inexpensive housing for the benefit of the 'weaker sections', the Act brought about a decrease in the supply of land and housing in the city and an increase in demand and prices.[130]

Between 1975 and 1980 there was a dramatic rise in the price level of urban land in Ahmedabad, with a significant increase immediately after the enactment of the ULCRA. For example, average land prices in Navrangpura, on the western side of the city, increased 500 per cent over the four years following the passage of the ULCRA; in the inner city average prices increased by 900 per cent.[131] Developers bought land in the periphery of the city in anticipation of the Act.[132] With its introduction about three quarters of the land in the periphery of the AMC came under the Act's authority and were stayed for any further development by the government.[133] This affected construction activity, and over this period there was a decline in the construction of new dwellings in Ahmedabad.

Builders who sought an exemption from the Act submitted building plans designated for the purpose of housing low-income groups. In practice, however, the price of building materials and construction costs increased so significantly that only high-income groups could afford to take advantage of the dwellings purportedly earmarked for 'weaker sections' of the society. Landowners and builders manipulated these development plans. They purchased land under the pretext of housing 'weaker sections', while their intended customers were really higher-income groups.

The landowner suggested a plan for the land for the poor strata and the government would give permission and exemption from the Act. On paper the plan would be according to the conditions of exemption, but in reality the houses could not be afforded by the poor.[134]

---

[130] For an analysis of the impact of the ULCRA in Mumbai see Harini Narayanan, 'In Search of Shelter: The Politics of the Implementation of the Urban Land (Ceiling and Regulation) Act 1976 in Greater Mumbai', in Sujata Patel and Jim Masselos (eds.), *Bombay and Mumbai: The City in Transition*, New Delhi: Oxford University Press, 2003, pp. 183–206.

[131] *National Commission on Urbanization: Interim Report*, p. 56. For data on the rise in land-value in Ahmedabad between 1940 and 1965, see Manesh Bhatt, 'Housing Problem of a Growing Metropolis', *Economic and Political Weekly*, 22 April 1972, p. 850.

[132] From the early 1960s onwards the issue was discussed in the Congress Party. Narayanan, 'In Search of Shelter', p. 185.

[133] Mahadevia, *Globalisation Urban Reforms*, pp. 158–9.

[134] *Interview* with Girish Patel, Ahmedabad, 7/4/98.

By 1986, building schemes that were meant for low-income groups were affordable only to middle- and upper-middle-income groups. Builders also exploited a clause in the ULCRA, which permitted the transfer of 2,000 sq. m in cases of built-up land, a term that was very loosely defined and could easily be manipulated.

One purpose of the Act was to secure the lands on the fringes of the city and to reserve them for public housing schemes of the AMC and the GHB. Although by the mid-1980s 58 hectares of the excess vacant land were taken into possession by the government, only 2.79 hectares (5 per cent) were allotted for residential use.[135] However, by means of the exemption provisions developers obtained large tracts of land on the periphery of Ahmedabad. They entered into *banakhata* (deposit on the promise of future sale) with farmers on behalf of different cooperative housing societies, or under schemes for housing 'weaker sections of the society', and sometimes they pressured the farmers to sell their lands.[136] The main beneficiaries of the ULCRA, therefore, were the developers.[137]

Extensive litigation over the potential surplus lands prevented the government from obtaining these lands.[138] The cumbersome procedures and the time the authorities needed for clearing the proposed schemes also contributed to the uncertainty in the market with regard to the availability of land. Developers nonetheless found various ways of bypassing the Act's constraints:

The developers avoid taxes at various stages of their operation, pay corruption money to the officials to get their jobs done. They, however, do not look at these activities as either illegal or anti-social . . . the developers belong to the new class of rich . . . These people are making things happen. They have had to fight to rise up from the bottom and they have learnt to manoeuvre the system of licences and permits and negotiate through the labyrinthine bureaucracy.[139]

The ULCRA as well as other related legislation had broader ramifications for the deterioration of governance practices and public life in Ahmedabad. The National Commission on Urbanisation Interim Report commented that exemptions have been granted 'most liberally by the government of Gujarat, and that large vacant areas would almost never come into

---

[135] *National Commission on Urbanization: Interim Report*, p. 49.

[136] Banakhata is an agreement prior to the sale of land, wherein some money is given to the seller, but the property is not yet transferred. See Hirway, 'Dynamics of Development in Gujarat', p. 15; Mahadevia, *Globalisation Urban Reforms*, pp. 158–9.

[137] See Vadhva, 'Private Sector and Urban Housing', p. 66. Also see Narayanan, 'In Search of Shelter'.

[138] *Interview* with Girish Patel, Ahmedabad, 7/4/98.

[139] Gurcharan Das, 'A New Rich Class is Born', *TOI*, 1 December 1985, quoted in Vadhva, 'Private Sector and Urban Housing', p. 66–7.

public ownership'.[140] These policies led to illegal acquisition of lands by encroachment and to the politicisation of these processes.[141] Before the introduction of the Act, most of the slums in the city, about 78 per cent, had been erected on private land, with the remainder on municipal and government land.[142] After 1960, slums provided the immediate solution for the housing shortage in the city. In the wake of the Act landowners were reluctant to allow the erection of slums on their plots. Since the very limited available land for new migrants belonged either to the government, or to AMC, there was a growth in illegal appropriation of plots in the form of squatter settlements. Gradually, a new class of 'land-grabbers' emerged. People encroached illegally on the AMC's lands, allowed slum hutments and collected rents from their dwellers. These slumlords were able to keep the land and sustain the slums through the nexuses they created with the AMC authorities and local politicians. In some cases slumlords even became municipal councillors. Through their connections with local politicians they provided basic sanitary facilities to the slum dwellers, and in return they ensured these politicians' electoral support. In practice, slumlords obtained ration cards for the slum dwellers, which entitled them to the Public Distribution System (PDS). The ration card was also a means of registering a citizen on the electoral roll.

You create a slum in the 1970s, call it Indira or Sanjay Nagar; Congress is happy; politicians through the nexus with the slumlords promise themselves vote banks. Each slum has its political patron. Slowly, within these processes the monitoring system on Corporation land and its use collapses.[143]

At the same time the ULCR Act had a different effect on some of the existing old slums. As a result of the growing demand for land and the price-rise, the slum landowners realised that they would get higher returns on the land if the slum dwellers could be evacuated. Previously, the land had had no commercial value and it had been profitable to let the slum exist and collect low rent from the inhabitants. In the meantime, slum dwellers who paid rent for a long time acquired legal rights over the land and the landowners were restricted from removing them. Consequently, slum landlords 'had to resort to other methods'.[144] In some cases, the

---

[140] *National Commission on Urbanization: Interim Report*, p. 24.
[141] Also see Howard Spodek, 'Crises and Response: Ahmedabad 2000', *Economic and Political Weekly*, 12 May 2001, p. 1631. On similar effects of the Act in Mumbai see Narayanan, 'In Search of Shelter'.
[142] *Census of Slums*, Table 2, p. 7.
[143] *Interview* with Achyut Yagnik, director, Centre for Social Knowledge and Action (SETU), Ahmedabad, 8/2/97.
[144] Barjor Mehta, 'Urban Housing Objective Realities for the Poor', unpublished Ph.D. thesis, School of Planning, Ahmedabad, 1980, p. 14.

landowners terrorised the slum dwellers, and riots sometimes became a means of forcing them to leave. Eventually, such incidents encouraged further land encroachment and the creation of new slums.

The ULCRA, which was designed to meet land and housing shortages and advance weaker groups in the society, in practice reduced the number of housing facilities for these groups. Much of the excess land was either unavailable for development due to litigation or obtained by developers by subterfuge. Large-scale corruption prevailed as a result of builders' attempts to attain illegal exemptions.[145] Efforts by landowners to circumvent the Act nurtured slumlordism and illegal developments in the land and housing market. Policies that were designated to benefit low-income groups were exploited by members of middle- and upper-class groups. Thus, the land and housing policies, which had been intended to improve the conditions of the poor, in effect exacerbated their conditions and resulted in growing class segregation and tensions in Ahmedabad.

Land and housing policies, as well as processes of urbanisation and de-industrialisation, informed the dynamics of interrelations between caste and class that developed in Ahmedabad by the 1980s. Tensions and identity concerns among Hindus resulted in their wake. These processes and their effects were driven to a large extent by state policies. Progressive state interventions for the benefit of lower- and backward-caste Hindus in educational institutions and government jobs were another particularly fraught policy area that produced growing uncertainties within the Hindu moral order. From the 1980s, these reservation policies became the driving force of increasing social conflicts. It was these caste conflicts that preceded the rise of communalism in Ahmedabad and elsewhere in India from the mid-1980s. The next chapter analyses the linkages that emerged between the state reservation policies and communalism and sets the political context in which the caste-reservations crisis and communalism grew.

---

[145] *National Commission on Urbanization: Interim Report*, p. 24.

2   The politics and discourse of reservations and caste

Reservation policies for lower and backward castes became a major source of conflict among Hindus from the end of the 1970s in Gujarat as well as elsewhere in India. The riots in Ahmedabad in 1985 erupted over the decision of the Gujarat government to increase the quotas reserved for backward castes in educational institutions and government jobs. This conflict between forward- and backward-caste Hindus over social and economic reforms for the benefit of backward castes turned into communal violence between Hindus and Muslims. This occurred despite the fact that the local Muslims had no part in the reservation dispute, there was no prior religious tension between the two communities, and religion was not a category qualifying a person for reservation of places in educational and governmental institutions. This chapter examines how and why caste disputes over government preferential policies for the benefit of the lower- and backward-caste Hindus escalated into tensions between Hindus and Muslims.

Reservations provided growing opportunities for the lower and backward castes in representative bodies, professional courses and government jobs. The access of lower and backward castes to a higher social echelon through reservations was perceived as potentially undermining the superior status of upper castes. Reservation policies, therefore, generated uncertainties within the Hindu moral order and resulted in the growth of tensions between forward- and backward-caste Hindus. These policies entangled caste and class issues and were shaped on the basis of caste and class deliberations. Policy makers, politicians and the judiciary, in their designation and discourse of reservations, addressed issues of equality on the basis of caste and class considerations as if they were synonymous with the rights of religious minorities. In so doing, they constituted a link between caste, class and communalism, enabling caste conflicts to develop and deepen communal rivalries. The first part of this chapter unravels the processes by which reservations and communalism became inextricably linked. The second part sets the political context in which caste-reservation conflicts and communalism emerged in the 1980s.

The growing caste reservations and communal tensions in the 1980s, the chapter argues, were driven by changes in the Hindu caste regime. The analysis in both parts emphasises the role of policy makers and the judiciary in the linking of reservations and communalism, and establishes the role of various state apparatuses as well as political parties in the constitution of castes and caste prejudices through the shaping of reservation policies and electoral politics.

Reservations: between caste and class

The constitution of India granted the scheduled castes (SCs) and scheduled tribes (STs) reserved quotas of 14 per cent and 7 per cent, respectively, in the Lok Sabha and the states' legislative assemblies, government jobs and educational institutions. The purpose of reservations was to ensure the participation and access to public resources of groups that had been historically discriminated against on the basis of their low-caste status.[1] Reservation policies aimed to promote equality, eradicate caste and secularise society. The constitution stipulated the reservation provisions in proportion to the share of the SC and ST groups in the total population. Reservations in representative bodies for the SCs and STs were set in the constitution for a limited period of twenty years.[2] In 1969 the government of India extended them for another ten years, and since then the parliament has periodically renewed these quotas.[3] Reservations in government jobs and educational institutions had no time limit.[4] Caste was the primary basis for the designation of the SCs. The constitutional (scheduled castes and scheduled tribes) orders of 1950 established state-specific lists, which identified the castes and tribes that fell into these categories. The government used the SC and ST lists of the Government of India Act, 1935, which were based on the 1931 census. These lists were revised in 1956 'to remove anomalies arising from the linguistic reorganisation of the states, and in 1976 to remove intra-state discrepancies in the identification of certain groups as SCs and STs'.[5]

---

[1] See Marc Galanter, *Competing Equalities: Law and the Backward Classes in India*, Berkeley: University of California Press, 1984, p. 122.

[2] Durga Das Basu, *Commentary on the Constitution of India*, 5th edn, Calcutta: S. C. Sarkar and Sons, 1965, p. 149.

[3] The Constitution (Twenty-Third Amendment) Act, 1969, http://indiacode.nic.in/coiweb/amend/amend23.htm.

[4] *Report of the Commissioner for Scheduled Castes and Scheduled Tribes 1978–79*, New Delhi: Government of India (through the Minister of Home Affairs), p. 14.

[5] Rohini Pande, 'Can Mandated Political Representation Increase Policy Influence for Disadvantaged Minorities? Theory and Evidence from India', *The American Economic Review*, vol. 93 no. 4, September 2003, p. 1138. Also see Francine R. Frankel, *India's*

Reservations introduced a tension in the constitution between a commitment to equality, on the one hand, and the scheduling of special quotas for some groups, on the other. This posited constraints on the workings of the state from the outset.[6] The first challenge took place soon after the enactment of the constitution. In *The State of Madras v. Champakam Dorairajan*, 1951, a student sued the state for its reservations policy on the grounds that it discriminated on the basis of caste in violation of Article 29(2). The court ruled in favour of the plaintiff.[7] Even though the parliament subsequently amended Article 15 of the constitution to ensure that the state could make special reservation provisions, compensatory policies for the SC and ST groups continued to be challenged in the courts.

Reservation for the backward castes was a more ambiguous matter. The Constituent Assembly Declaration of Objectives, 13 December 1946, required adequate safeguards to be made for 'Other Backward Classes' similar to the ones granted to the SC and ST groups.[8] Article 16(4) of the constitution secured the provision for reservations of posts for 'any backward class of citizens'. But there was no clear and acceptable criterion for defining who the Other Backward Classes/Castes (OBCs) were. The term 'backward classes/castes' was a procedural rather than a social category, which the British had used since the late nineteenth century to describe a list of groups, also called illiterate and indigent classes, entitled to allowances for study in elementary schools.[9] In the 1920s and 1930s a backward caste movement succeeded, particularly in south India, in gaining British support for caste quotas in admission to colleges and civil service jobs.[10] On that basis, reservations for backward-caste Hindus had already existed in the southern states before independence.[11] Article 340(1) of the constitution stipulated that the president could appoint commissions for determining the criteria for identifying

---

Political Economy 1947–1977: The Gradual Revolution, Princeton: Princeton University Press, 1978, p. 79, n. 21.

[6] Francine Frankel points out the difficulty of 'carry[ing] out social and economic reforms through measures that were consistent with the fundamental rights of individuals guaranteed by the constitution'. Frankel, *India's Political Economy*, p. 79.

[7] Sunita Parikh, *The Politics of Preference: Democratic Institutions and Affirmative Action in the Unites States and India*, Ann Arbor: University of Michigan Press, 2000, p. 160; D. J. De, *Interpretation and Enforcement of Fundamental Rights*, New Delhi: Eastern Law House, 2000, p. 232; Basu, *Commentary on the Constitution of India*, pp. 126–7.

[8] *The Constituent Assembly Debates*, Manager of Publications, Delhi, New Delhi: Government of India Press, vol. 1, no. 5, 13 December 1946, p. 57.

[9] Galanter, *Competing Equalities*, p. 154, n. 1.

[10] *Ibid.*, p. 159; Parikh, *The Politics of Preference*, pp. 171, 173; Sagar Preet Hooda, *Contesting Reservation*, Rawat Publications, New Delhi, 2001, pp. 54–9.

[11] Galanter, *Competing Equalities*, p. 159; Parikh, *The Politics of Preference*, pp. 171, 173.

socially and educationally backward groups. The main question at the heart of the designation of reservations for these groups was whether caste or class should be the defining criterion for backwardness.

The first Backward Classes Commission, headed by Kaka Kalelkar, was appointed in 1953 to determine the criteria for the identification of groups, other than the SCs and STs, that should be treated as socially and educationally backward.[12] The Commission submitted its report in 1955, recommending the use of caste categories for the identification of backward classes.[13] The Commission report was somewhat undermined by the late addition of a letter by its Chairman, Kalelkar, in which he distanced himself from the Commission's recommendation to use caste criteria. The government did not accept the Commission's criteria for an all-India backward-caste list. The Ministry of Home Affairs, appending a memorandum of action to the report in 1956, argued that the use of caste category 'may serve to maintain and even perpetuate the existing distinctions on the basis of caste'.[14] The report was tabled before the parliament but was not discussed until 1965. In the absence of clear criteria for defining backwardness at the national level, the states were free to designate their own reservation policies for the backward classes. While granting the states the discretion to choose their own criteria for defining backwardness in 1961, the Ministry of Home Affairs, in its letter to the state governments suggested that 'it would be better to apply economic test than to go by caste'.[15]

From the outset, the lack of clear guidelines for implementing reservations for the backward classes/castes rendered these policies, where they existed, open to contestation in the courts. The judiciary gradually began playing a role in the shaping of reservations as well as in the debates over these policies. From the early 1960s the courts favoured the use of economic criteria for the implementation of reservations. In *Balaji* v. *The State of Mysore*, 1963, the Supreme Court established that

---

[12] The Commission's other terms of reference were to prepare a list of the socially and educationally backward classes in accordance with defined criteria; recommend steps to improve the conditions of these groups; and present the report to the president. Basu, *Commentary on the Constitution of India*, p. 156.

[13] The Commission composed a list of 2,399 backward castes. Government of India, *Report of the Backward Classes Commission*, 1980 [Mandal Commission], Vols. I and II, p. 2.

[14] Quoted in *ibid.*; Government of Gujarat, *Report of the Socially and Educationally Backward Classes [second] Commission*, Gujarat State, 1983 [Rane Commission], Vol. I, p. 29. Also see De, *Interpretation and Enforcement*, p. 407; Basu, *Commentary on the Constitution of India*, pp. 156–7; Christophe Jaffrelot, 'The Rise of the Other Backward Classes in the Hindi Belt', *Journal of Asian Studies*, vol. 59, no.1, February 2000, p. 88.

[15] *Report of the Backward Classes Commission* [Mandal] pp. 2, 4; *Report of the Socially and Educationally Backward Classes* [Rane], Vol. 1, p. 29.

'the classification of backwardness cannot be made solely on the basis of caste'.[16] This led the Mysore government to establish an economic test for backwardness, on the basis of occupation and income.[17] In 1963 the central government abandoned the use of the states' lists of OBCs for the post-matriculation scholarships and began using income criteria instead. Two years later, in the context of the All-India Backward Class Federation (AIBCF) struggle for the implementation of reservations on the basis of caste, the parliament discussed the Kalelkar report, ten years after it was submitted.[18] The AIBCF grounded its demand on the Kalelkar Commission's recommendations as well as on Article 340 of the constitution, which represented a commitment to apply reservations to communities. Once more, the parliament did not make a clear decision on the issue and it remained open to the states to designate their own policies.[19] The question of reservations for the backward castes at the national level was again raised at the end of the 1970s. On 1 January 1979 the Janata government pursued its pre-election pledge and appointed the second Backward Classes Commission, headed by B. P. Mandal. The Commission submitted its report in 1980 when the Congress Party, led by Indira Gandhi, was in power. The Mandal report embraced caste as the basic unit in all considerations of distributive justice. It suggested a reservation of 27 per cent for the OBCs at the national level. The report would wait a decade before V. P. Singh's government announced the implementation of its recommendations.

Until then, between the mid-1960s and early 1990s, various states established commissions to identify their backward castes/classes.[20]

---

[16] Basu, *Commentary on the Constitution of India*, p. 129. In *Chirtalekha v. The State of Mysore*, 1964 the court supported economic criteria, but also argued that caste 'may be a relevant circumstance in ascertaining' the 'backwardness of a class of citizens'; cited in *Report of the Socially and Educationally Backward Classes* [Rane], Vol. I, p. 20 and *Report of the Backward Classes Commission* [Mandal] p. 26. In the *Balaji* case (also cited in the above sources) the Supreme Court also set a ceiling of 50 per cent on the number of reserved seats.

[17] De, *Interpretation and Enforcement*, p. 233; Parikh, *The Politics of Preference*, pp. 161–3.

[18] The All-India Backward Class Federation was founded on the day the constitution came into force.

[19] Basu, *Commentary on the Constitution of India*, p. 130.

[20] Backward classes commissions and committees were established, for example, in Kerala in 1961, 1964 and 1967; in Jammu and Kashmir in 1967, 1969, 1976; in Tamil Nadu in 1969, 1982; in Punjab in 1965; in Karnataka in 1960, 1972, 1983, 1989; in Gujarat in 1972, 1982; in Andhra Pradesh in 1968, 1970 and 1982; in Bihar in 1971; in Maharashtra in 1961; in Uttar Pradesh in 1975; and in West Bengal in 1980. By 1980, when the Backward Classes Mandal Commission submitted its report, ten state governments had set up fifteen Commissions or Committees for the identification of the backward castes/classes. *Report of the Backward Classes Commission* [Mandal], pp. 5–11. For an extensive discussion of the evolving reservation policies in various states, see also Christophe Jaffrelot, *India's Silent Revolution: The Rise of the Lower Castes in North India*, London: Hursh & Company, 2003, pp. 237–53.

Overwhelmingly, the recommendations of these commissions and government policies that emanated from their reports granted reservations on the basis of caste.[21] The attempts during the early 1960s to apply economic criteria to reservations were gradually abandoned. Occasionally, eligibility for some of the reservation quotas combined caste with a number of economic criteria. The union government did not intervene. Disputes over the policy and its implementation were frequently resolved in the courts. The pattern had been that state governments prepared lists of castes or communities that should be entitled to reservations. These caste lists or the reservations policy were subsequently challenged in the courts. In most cases, the states' High Courts or sometimes the Supreme Court had struck down the criteria for the definition of backwardness or the reservations policy which the state established. The courts rejected the initial backward classes lists and reservations policy that states set up mainly on the grounds of lack of evidence regarding the social and educational backwardness of the scheduled groups, or because the state used caste as the sole criterion for backwardness or because the court found the reservation rules and the beneficiary groups to be obsolete. The state government would subsequently appoint a new commission or committees to redesign its list of the backward classes and the reservations policy.[22] State governments appointed numerous commissions also to respond to the demands of dissatisfied groups who wanted to be included in the state's backward classes list. From the mid-1970s the question of reservations for backward castes gained more prominence on the political agenda. In 1978 thirteen out of twenty-four states of the union implemented or expanded reservations for backward classes.[23]

In Gujarat, a government headed by the Congress Party appointed the Baxi Backward Classes Commission in 1972 to identify socially and educationally backward communities that would qualify for preferential treatment similar to that being granted to the scheduled castes and scheduled tribes.[24] The Commission submitted its report in 1976, when the Congress Party was in power, identifying 82 castes and groups as backward. Two years later, the Janata government accepted the Baxi

---

[21] *Report of the Backward Classes Commission* [Mandal], pp. 5–11. Also see *Report of the Socially and Educationally Backward Classes* [Rane], Vol. I, p. 47.

[22] In some cases, as in *S. V. Balaram* v. *State of Andhra Pradesh*, 1972, the identification of backwardness on the basis of caste was upheld by the court. See *Report of the Backward Classes Commission* [Mandal], pp. 27–8; De, *Interpretation and Enforcement*, pp. 234–5.

[23] Galanter, *Competing Equalities*, pp. 87, 184.

[24] In Gujarat the SCs and STs were granted 7 per cent and 14 per cent reservations, respectively, according to their share in the total population of the state. For the development of reservations for the backward classes in Gujarat also see Parikh, *The Politics of Preference*, pp. 179–81.

Commission's recommendation and established reservations of 10 per cent for these communities.[25] In 1982, a new Commission, Rane, was set up to look into the case of groups that had not been listed as backward by the Baxi Commission. The government decided to appoint a second Commission after some castes, which the Baxi Commission considered but did not recognise to be socially and educationally backward, as well as groups that were not represented before the Baxi Commission, demanded to be treated as socially and educationally backward.[26] The Rane Commission submitted its report in October 1983. It suggested adding an 18 per cent reservation to the existing 10 per cent for the Socially and Educationally Backward Classes/Castes (SEBC). In contrast to the Baxi Commission, it based its recommendation on occupation and income as the criteria for backwardness, rather than caste.[27]

The Gujarat state government ignored the Rane Commission Report for fourteen months. When the government finally declared its intention to implement the report in January 1985, shortly before the forthcoming assembly elections were announced, it reversed the Rane Commission's recommendations. The government insisted that caste and not class should be the criterion for backwardness. Consequently, a committee under the chairmanship of Haruhai M. Mehta (MP) was appointed in order to look into the claims of 239 castes to be identified as socially and educationally backward and to add the new beneficiary castes to the existing 82 groups listed by the first Gujarat Backward Classes Commission, Baxi. The Government's rationale for altering the Commission's criteria was that it was not within the Rane Commission's terms of reference to consider the criteria for backwardness that was set by the Baxi Commission.[28] It was this decision by the Gujarat government to increase the reserved quotas for the SEBC in government jobs and educational institutions that was the immediate cause of the outbreak of

---

[25] Only 5 per cent reservation was implemented for class I and class II jobs.

[26] *Report of the Socially and Educationally Backward Classes* [Rane], Vol. I, p. xvi.

[27] The Rane Commission suggested 63 occupations and an annual income ceiling of Rs.10,000 as criteria for being listed as SEBC. *Ibid.*, pp. 70–80. According to the Commission, discarding caste as a basis for reservations would help in 'accelerating the process of establishing casteless and egalitarian society by eliminating main causes of antagonism . . . between different castes', *ibid.*, p. 54. Also see I. P. Desai, 'Should "Caste" be the Basis for Recognising Backwardness?' in *Caste, Caste Conflict and Reservations*, Ajanta, Surat: Centre for Social Studies, 1985, pp. 61–101; also in *Economic and Political Weekly*, 14 July 1984, pp. 1106–16.

[28] *The Hindu*, 16 March 1985. Moreover, the government had received a letter of dissent from Mr G. L. Bhagat, who resigned from the Rane Commission a few days before its Report was submitted, because he found its recommendations 'not in accordance with the Constitution'. *Report of the Socially and Educationally Backward Classes* [Rane], Vol. I, p. 126.

anti-reservation caste riots in Ahmedabad in February 1985. This reservation dispute was transformed from a debate over caste and class into communalism.

From caste and class to communalism

The main question underlying reservation policies was whether caste or class should be the criterion for determining backwardness. State Commissions, policy makers and the Judiciary, in dealing with this question, as well as in their designation of reservation policies, conflated the issues of social and economic benefits for the lower and backward castes with religious minority rights.

The Constituent Assembly, for example, debated reservations in 1946 in the context of discussions on minority rights. The Advisory Committee on Minorities and Fundamental Rights of the Constituent Assembly in its 1947 report recommended reservations in legislative institutions for Muslims, Sikhs and Christians, but after partition the proposal was not pursued.[29] In *Balaji* v. *The State of Mysore*, 1963, the Supreme Court's ruling deliberated that there might be backward communities among Muslims or Christians, who did not 'recognise castes in the conventional sense known to Hindu society'.[30] When the head of the first Backward Classes Commission, Kalelkar, disclaimed in 1955 the Commission's recommendation to use caste criteria for determining backwardness, he linked his objection to the ramifications it might have on religious minorities and their rights:

My eyes were however opened to the danger of suggesting remedies on caste basis when I discovered that it is going to have a most unhealthy effect on the Muslim and Christian sections of the nation . . . [T]he bulk of the Muslims and Christians in India are converted from the Hindu fold. This conversion was encouraged by the fact that Islam and Christianity were fundamentally opposed to caste. The 'lower castes' in the Hindu fold left their traditional religion . . . because they felt assured that in that way they would be free from the tyranny of caste and caste prejudices. The Government of India recognized certain castes among the Hindus as backward and offered . . . privileges to these communities. This led Muslims and Christians also to assert that although their religion was fundamentally different, and that theoretically it is opposed to caste, in practice their society was

---

[29] Theodore Wright, 'A New Demand for Muslim Reservations in India', *Asian Survey*, vol. 37, no. 9, 1997, p. 853; Parikh, *The Politics of Preference*, pp. 157–8; D. L. Sheth, 'Reservation Policy Revisited', in Gurpreet Mahajan (ed.), *Democracy, Difference and Social Justice*, New Delhi: Oxford University Press, 2000, p. 498.

[30] *Report of the Socially and Educationally Backward Classes* [Rane], Vol. I, pp. 19–20, 26; De, *Interpretation and Enforcement*, p. 234; Basu, *Commentary on the Constitution of India*, p. 129.

more or less caste-ridden . . . Muslims came forward to prove that except for the four upper castes, namely Sheikh, Syed, Moghul and Pathan, all the other Muslim castes were inferior and backward. They told the Ministry of Education and the Backward Classes Commission that caste is rampant among them . . . Indian Christians were prepared in many places to assert that they were still guided by caste not only in the matter of untouchability but in hierarchy of high and low. Their social and religious leaders in their anxiety to secure some Government help for their own people supported the contention that caste was rampant among Indian Christians also.[31]

Some state-level Backward Classes Commissions also cautioned that using caste criteria for the definition of backwardness would risk excluding socially and educationally backward classes among non-Hindus.[32]

Although religious minorities were excluded from the reservation provisions, religious criteria became inherent in the process of designation of the beneficiary groups. In the shaping of reservations and in the legal discourse on their implementation, governments and the courts related the eligibility of a social group to preferential treatment to its position within Hinduism. For the purpose of reservations, the SCs and STs were defined as 'those groups who *because of their low ritual status in the traditional Hindu hierarchy* and their spatial and cultural isolation were subjected to imposition of disabilities and lack of opportunity'.[33] The primary criterion for reservations was untouchability, which was defined as inherent in Hinduism.[34] The Constitution (Scheduled Castes) Order of 1950 provided that 'no person professing a religion different from Hinduism shall be deemed a member of a Scheduled Caste'.[35] The judiciary enforced this designation on the grounds that 'acceptance of a non-Hindu religion operates as a loss of caste'.[36] The Indian government made an exception in 1956, when untouchable castes among the Sikhs were recognised and

[31] Kaka Kalelkar, 'Backwardness, Caste and the Question of Reservations' (excerpted from the *Report of the Backward Classes Commission* headed by Kaka Kalelkar, Government of India Publication, 30 March 1955), in Gurpreet Mahajan (ed.), *Democracy, Difference and Social Justice*, New Delhi: Oxford University Press, 2000, pp. 453–4. These points were also discussed in the Kalelkar Commission Report. See excerpt quoted in the *Report of the Socially and Educationally Backward Classes* [Rane], Vol. I, pp. 24–6.

[32] See, for example, excerpts from the 1972 Havanur Backward Classes Commission in Karnataka in the *Report of the Socially and Educationally Backward Classes* [Rane], Vol. I, pp. 24–5.

[33] Galanter, *Competing Equalities*, p. 122 (emphasis added).

[34] See Marc Galanter, 'The India Constitution and Provisions for Special Treatment', in Gurpreet Mahajan (ed.), *Democracy, Difference and Social Justice*, p. 570; Sheth, 'Reservation Policy Revisited', pp. 501–2.

[35] Basu, *Commentary on the Constitution of India*, p. 158; Galanter, *Competing Equalities*, p. 144.

[36] Galanter, *Competing Equalities*, p. 315. The judiciary made this reasoning in some cases of scheduled castes who converted from Hinduism and lost their reservation rights. The court explained that religious discrimination was not exercised in these cases because non-Hindus have no caste. *Ibid.*, pp. 313, 319.

included in the SCs list.[37] Similarly, in some cases, e.g. in *Gopalkrishan v. The State of Maharashtra*, 1987, the Bombay High Court ruled that a scheduled caste member who converted to Buddhism will continue to be treated as a member of the SCs on the grounds that he 'continues to be subjected to social ostracism'.[38] In the designation of reservation policies the government and the courts conceived caste as a constituent of Hinduism. Consequently, religion was inextricably made an intrinsic criterion for compensatory policies for weaker groups of the society.

The question whether caste or class should be the criterion for determining backwardness was sometimes posited and contemplated in the debates on reservation policies as a choice between religiosity and secularism. Opponents of the use of caste as the basis for classifying backwardness for social policy argued that employing caste criteria would undermine secularism. In this view caste was perceived as integral to religion, and class as a secular social category. In order to promote the secularisation of the society and the state, therefore, backwardness and the eligibility for reservations should be determined by class.[39] Counter-arguments suggested or implied that precisely caste-based reservations were necessary for the development of secularism. 'If you really want to have secularism you need to have interaction between the upper castes and the lower castes and reservation on the basis of caste would create the involvement of people from different social groups work[ing] together.'[40] In this view, the beneficiaries of reservations would become part of the middle class, and this was a secularising process.[41] Reservations on the basis of caste would weaken caste consciousness since they would sever

---

[37] Basu, *Commentary on the Constitution of India*, p. 158.

[38] De, *Interpretation and Enforcement*, p. 425.

[39] Most famously, this position was held by I. P. Desai, who was an academic but also a member of the Rane Commission, and previously associated with the work of the Baxi Commission. See Desai, 'Should "Caste" be the Basis for Recognising the Backwardness?', pp. 61–101; Girish Patel, *Lok Adhikar Sangh Fact Finding Committee Report Ahmedabad Riots*, Ahmedabad: SETU, p. 44; Galanter, *Competing Equalities*, p. 73; *Report of the Socially and Educationally Backward Classes* [Rane], Vol. I, p. 47. Mitra makes this argument even though he recommends reservations on the basis of caste. Subrata Mitra, 'The Perils of Promoting Equality: The Latent Significance of the Anti-Reservation Movement in India', *Journal of Commonwealth and Comparative Politics*, vol. 25, no. 3, 1987, p. 303. Various submissions before the Supreme Court in *Indra Sawhney v. Union of India*, 1993, which is known as the Mandal case, rejected the Mandal Commission's use of caste for the determination of backwardness because 'a secular society can never countenance identification of backward class on the basis of caste'. De, *Interpretation and Enforcement*, p. 373.

[40] Ghanshyam Shah, Lecture delivered at the 'Western Region Jesuits' Meeting', SETU Archive paper 234.5/2.

[41] See an interview with Ghanshyam Shah, 'Special Report on Reservation', *The Herald Review*, vol. 1, no. 28, 17–23 March 1985, pp. 38–9. Also see Dharma Kumar, 'The Affirmative Action Debate in India', *Asian Survey*, vol. 32, no. 3, March 1992, p. 298.

the link between caste and occupation.[42] Caste barriers could be defeated only by constructed social interaction between castes through caste reservations. In both views caste lay at the heart of Hinduism and the guiding task in the shaping of reservation policies was the eradication of caste and the promotion of secularism.

Secularism constituted not only an underlying concern in the designation of caste reservations but also a founding ethos of the Indian state. Communal conflicts and their growth from the mid-1980s challenged India's secularism. Caste reservations and communal conflicts were therefore inextricably linked to each other. Moreover, in the debates about whether caste or class criteria should be the determining category for backwardness, preference for caste was justified by arguing why class should not be the determining principle. Similarly, arguments in favour of a class criterion urged the discarding of caste classifications as a policy guideline. Alternatively, caste and class were used interchangeably. In various court and backward classes commissions discussions, caste was endorsed as 'a class of citizens'.[43] Hence, caste, class and communalism became intertwined in the very discourse of reservations. Debates over India's secularism and communalism formed a subtext in deliberations over caste and class as the defining criteria in the designation of reservations.

In the 1950s and 1960s policy makers used the terms 'communal criteria' or 'communal units' as synonyms for caste in their discussions of reservations. The Ministry of Home Affairs resolution on reservation in September 1950, for example, referred to 'the policy of the government of India in regard to communal representation'.[44] In the early 1960s the Ministry of Education suggested 'employing economic rather than communal categories' for reservations.[45] During the parliamentary discussion of the Kalelkar Commission report in 1965, the speaker of the house rejected the use of 'communal criteria' for identifying the backward classes.[46]

---

[42] Mitra, 'The Perils of Promoting Equality', p. 307.
[43] The Supreme Court formulated this observation in *Rajendran* v. *State of Madras*, 1968. *Report of the Socially and Educationally Backward Classes* [Rane], Vol. I, p. 20. At the time of the First Amendment to the constitution Dr Ambedkar said that 'backward classes are nothing else but a collection of certain castes'. Quoted in De, *Interpretation and Enforcement*, p. 375.
[44] A resolution of the Ministry of Home Affairs No. 42/21/49, dated 13 September 1950. Quoted in Bhagwan Das, 'The Reservation Policy and the Mandal Judgment', *Social Action*, vol. 43, October–December 1993, pp. 427–38. This also recurred in government reports, newspapers and general literature on the subject.
[45] Marc Galanter, 'Who Are the Other Backward Classes?', *Economic and Political Weekly*, 28 October 1978, p. 1816.
[46] Basu, *Commentary on the Constitution of India*, pp. 156–7.

There was no clear or acceptable criterion for defining backwardness at the national level. During the 1970s, backward caste lists 'included converts from SC to non-Hindu religions and several states used this category to provide some concessions to sections of their Muslim population'.[47] This was the case, for example, in Bihar and Kerala. Similarly, in Gujarat, the eighty-two backward class groups identified by the Baxi Commission included eight Muslim groups as well as Christian converts from the SCs.[48] State government attempts to include Muslims and converts from the SCs in their backward classes lists became more prevalent in the mid-1990s.[49] Policy makers, by conflating religion with issues of social and economic reforms for the benefit of lower and backward Hindu groups on the basis of caste or class, created a link between caste-reservation conflicts and communalism. The shaping and implementation of reservation policies also resulted in the construction of castes.

The making of caste (1)

Through reservation policies states officially recognised some groups as backward castes, a status that qualified them for preferential treatment in government jobs and educational institutions. These groups often became the subject of investigation for state commissions, such as Baxi and Rane in Gujarat. In popular usage the backward castes that received reservations in Gujarat were even called the Baxi groups. The very process of forming reservation policies therefore led to a social construction of the backward-caste communities.[50] State reservation policies set boundaries defining a group's scope for mobility and access to public resources. In this process, caste became a basic category in the construction of citizenship.

The demands of some dissatisfied caste groups to be recognised as backward castes by the state in order to qualify for reservations redefined the caste social order and contributed to an ongoing process of caste formation. The recurrent practice of appointing commissions to identify

---

[47] Galanter, 'Who Are the Other Backward Classes?', p. 1812, fn. 45.

[48] See I. P. Desai, 'Anti-Reservation Agitation and Structure of Gujarat Society', *Economic and Political Weekly*, 2 May 1981, p. 822; Achyut Yagnik and Anil Bhatt, 'The Anti-Dalit Agitation in Gujarat', *South Asian Bulletin*, vol. 4, no. 1, Spring 1984, p. 46.

[49] *India Today*, 15 and 30 November 1994; Laura Dudley Jenkins, 'Becoming Backward: Preferential Policies and Religious Minorities in India', *Commonwealth and Comparative Politics*, vol. 39, no. 1, July 2001, pp. 32–50; Wright, 'A New Demand for Muslim Reservations in India', pp. 852–8.

[50] For the construction of group identities through reservations also see Dudley Jenkins, 'Becoming Backward: Preferential Policies and Religious Minorities in India', pp. 45–6; Zoya Hasan, *Quest for Power: Oppositional Movements and Post-Congress Politics in Uttar Pradesh*, Delhi: Oxford University Press, 1998, pp. 142–6, 165.

new backward classes/castes was one of the state mechanisms that contributed to the making of castes. The existence of castes, therefore, was subjected to political contestation. Paradoxically, while the formal aim of reservation policies was to overcome caste, the state designation of and debates over reservations actually made caste categories all the more significant.

Prior to the dispute over whether caste or class should be the determining criterion for backwardness lay the controversy over whether reservations were desirable at all. The detractors of reservation policies claimed that reservations degraded merit considerations and impaired the effectiveness of public institutions.[51] The debate over this question contributed to turning caste social inequalities into natural ones, thereby perpetuating caste prejudice. In 1999, the Supreme Court ruled, for example, that candidates for reserved categories would not be able to benefit fully from specialised training in medical studies, which were 'designed to produce high-calibre well-trained professionals for the benefit of the public'. Such decisions assumed that reserved category students were inherently less capable.[52]

While reservation policies aimed to eradicate caste by providing a means of mobility to groups that were disadvantaged on the basis of their caste status, they also reinforced the construction of castes and caste bigotry. This intrinsic tension within which various state apparatuses acted in their designation and implementation of reservations provoked antagonism, particularly between forward- and backward-caste Hindus. Moreover, the state's 'ever changing reservation policy created a sense of insecurity' among those who were excluded from the benefit.[53] The state governments' habit of repeatedly appointing commissions of inquiry to identify backward classes/caste groups, first ignoring and then partly implementing their recommendations, placed the forward castes in a constant state of uncertainty.

The expansion of reservations for the backward castes in educational institutions and government jobs, as well as preferential policies for the

[51] See Galanter, *Competing Equalities*, pp. 73–6. Also see Jonathan P. Parry, 'Two Cheers for Reservation: The Satnamis and the Steel Plant', in Ramachandra Guha and Jonathan P. Parry (eds.), *Institutions and Inequalities*, Oxford: Oxford University Press, 1999, pp. 129–31; Kumar, 'The Affirmative Action Debate in India', p. 300–1.

[52] *Economic and Political Weekly* (editorial), 14–20 August 1999. An earlier court judgment also ruled that at super-speciality or post-doctoral courses merit alone should count. De, *Interpretation and Enforcement*, pp. 244–5.

[53] Judge V. S. Dave, *Report of the Commission of Inquiry: Into the Incidents of Violence and Disturbances which Took Place at Various Places in the State of Gujarat since February, 1985 to 18th July, 1985* (henceforth *COI*), Ahmedabad: Government of Gujarat, April 1990, Vol. II, p. 7.

SCs and STs, became the main reason for intensifying conflicts between forward- and backward-caste Hindus from the mid-1970s.[54] From that period, there was a general rise in recorded acts of violence against the SCs in India. In 1976, 6,197 'atrocity cases' against SCs were reported; 10,879 cases were reported in 1977; and their number increased to 15,053 in 1978.[55] Anti-reservation caste riots erupted in Bihar in 1978 and 1980 as a result of the government decision to implement the Mungerilal Commission's recommendation for reservations of government jobs for the backward castes in the state.[56]

In Gujarat, riots erupted in December 1980 against reservations in post-graduate medical courses. The anti-reservation agitation was initiated in Ahmedabad by students in B.J. Medical College. In a memorandum they submitted to the government, the students demanded the withdrawal of reservations in promotion, known as the roster system; the removal of the carry-forward reservations policy, whereby reserved positions that were not filled would be kept for the following year; a reduction of the reserved quotas for SC and ST candidates; and an increase in the unreserved seats at the post-graduate level.[57] Although the government agreed to abolish the carry-forward reservation system within a week, the students nonetheless intensified their protest, demanding the abolition of all reservations. Large-scale atrocities, particularly against Dalits, continued throughout the 102 days of the riots.[58]

Caste-reservation conflicts intensified from the late 1970s even though the reservation quotas were not filled. The appointment of SCs and STs for posts and services under the central government fell far below the statutory provisions.[59] In 1966, out of an all-India total of 9,605 reserved vacancies for the SCs, less than half (4,179) were filled. In Gujarat, only

---

[54] See Sunita Parikh, 'Affirmative Action, Caste, and Party Politics in Contemporary India', in John David Skrentny (ed.), *Color Lines: Affirmative Action, Immigration, and Civil Rights Options for America*, Chicago and London: University of Chicago Press, 2001, pp. 297, 333.

[55] *Report of the Commissioner for Scheduled Castes and Scheduled Tribes 1978–79*, p. 2.

[56] Harry D. Blair, 'Rising Kulaks and Backward Classes in Bihar', *Economic and Political Weekly*, 12 January 1980, p. 66; Pradip Kumar Bose, 'Mobility and Conflict: Social Roots of Caste Violence in Bihar', in Dipanikar Gupta (ed.), *Social Stratification*, Delhi: Oxford University Press, 1991, p. 381; *Report of the Backward Classes Commission* [Mandal], p. 7.

[57] The roster system was introduced in Gujarat in 1976.

[58] See [non-official report] Indian Research Society for Welfare of Backward Classes, *Research Project on Atrocities on Harijans for 102 Days in Gujarat*, Research Project No. 10, IRS, Ahmedabad, p. 34; Desai, 'Anti-Reservation Agitation', p. 822; Yagnik and Bhatt, 'The Anti-Dalit Agitation in Gujarat', pp. 45–60; Achyut Yagnik, 'Spectre of Caste War', *Economic and Political Weekly*, 28 March 1981, pp. 553–5; Mitra, 'The Perils of Promoting Equality', pp. 299–302.

[59] *Report of the Commissioner for Scheduled Castes and Scheduled Tribes 1966–67*, New Delhi: Government of India, 1968, p. 15.

53 of the 134 reserved vacancies for the SCs were filled.[60] In the same year, only 1,299 of an all-India total of 4,688 reserved vacancies for the STs were filled, while in Gujarat, members of STs filled 41 of their 164 reserved vacancies.[61] The 1968–9 Report of the Commission for Scheduled Castes and Scheduled Tribes concluded that 'despite the working of the reservation orders for the last seventeen years, both Scheduled Castes and Scheduled Tribes are inadequately represented in Class I, II and III. The position of SCs and STs in Class IV also is far from satisfactory.'[62] By 1971 there was only a marginal improvement in the number of filled reserved places, even though the quotas did not reach the rates granted in the constitution.[63] In Gujarat, in the years 1979–84, just before the anti-reservation riots of 1985 erupted, there were 875 reserved places in medical colleges, of which only 37 had been filled.[64]

An explanation for this paradox – why reservations became a source of violent conflicts even though the quotas were not filled – can be found in the political developments in the 1970s and 1980s. The political context in which the caste reservation crisis emerged intensified the growing uncertainties within the Hindu moral order. It was the resulting tensions among Hindus and their experiences of the changes in caste in politics that engendered the growth of communalism in the 1980s.

The political context of reservations and communalism

From the 1970s, increasing politicisation and social mobility of some groups among the lower and backward castes, and the growing attention invested in them by political parties, created a sense of insecurity among forward castes. Conversely, some groups among the lower and backward castes who experienced political and social mobility were disturbed by the discrepancy between the promises made to them by the parties and the actual political events and direction of state policies.

Gradual processes of political and social mobility among the lower and backward castes had been under way since independence in Gujarat as well as elsewhere in India. These developments became more visible from

---

[60] *Ibid.*, p. 103.   [61] *Ibid.*, p. 106.

[62] *Report of the Commissioner for Scheduled Castes and Scheduled Tribes 1968–69*, Government of India, Manager of Publications, Delhi, 1969, p. 36. Galanter indicates that there is a 'chronic overstatement of the effects of reservation'. Galanter, *Competing Equalities*, p. 560.

[63] *Report of the Commissioner for Scheduled Castes and Scheduled Tribes 1978–79*, p. 13; Also see Santosh Goyal, 'Social Background of Officers in the Indian Administrative Service', in Francine R. Frankel and M. S. A. Rao (eds.), *Dominance and State Power in Modern India*, Vol. I, Delhi: Oxford University Press, 1989, Appendix II, p. 426.

[64] Yagnik and Bhatt, 'The Anti-Dalit Agitation', p. 47. Also see *COI*, Vol. I, pp. 55, 86, 197–200 and Vol. II, pp. 7–8.

the early 1970s when the Congress Party began directly appealing to the SC, ST and backward-caste groups. In 1969 the Congress Party split into Congress(I) and Congress(O). Indira Gandhi, in her quest for a new support base for her Congress(I) faction, directed the party's attention to the deprived groups which constituted a majority of the society and had considerable electoral potential. The Congress(I)'s campaign slogan before the 1971 general elections was *Garibi Hatao* (abolish poverty). Its election manifesto contained a commitment to form a Backward Class Commission and implement reservation policies for the backward castes. In Gujarat, Indira Gandhi even promised the leaders of the Kshatriyas, through her personal envoy, that they would be considered as backward by the Backward Class Commission that her government would appoint.[65] After Congress(I) won the elections, the party's strategy at the national level informed the political developments in Gujarat.

After the 1972 elections in Gujarat, in which Congress(I) won 140 of the 168 seats in the state assembly,[66] the party began giving more consideration to the lower and backward classes. The Congress government in the state, led by Ghanshyam Oza, appointed the Baxi Backward Classes Commission. Jinabhai Darji, who was a prominent Congress politician from a backward-caste background, was elected to the Gujarat Congress presidency. He actively promoted the party among the backward classes and appealed particularly to Dalits and Muslims. The emerging dynamics of party politics in Gujarat between 1972 and 1975 temporarily abated these processes, as a result of the operation of countervailing social forces, as well as the unfavourable economic circumstances.

Ghanshyam Oza was an Indira Gandhi camp follower and a cabinet member in Delhi. He was appointed to the Chief Ministership through Indira Gandhi's intervention in the local Gujarati contest over the position. Despite his appointment the struggles for leadership among Gujarat party leaders continued. Eventually, by June 1973, one of the main contestants for leadership, Chimanbhai Patel, succeeded in obtaining the signatures of 70 legislators on a memorandum of no confidence in Oza. Patel 'sequestered some 70 Congress MLAs at a farm near Ahmedabad for five days until they all emerged in victorious support of his candidacy . . . [T]he general belief was that [the meetings] had been the occasions for the purchase of MLA support.'[67] Patel's political manoeuvre

---

[65] Ghanshyam Shah, 'Agitations in Gujarat', *Seminar*, vol. 375, November 1990, p. 54.

[66] *Statistical Report on General Election, 1972 to the Legislative Assembly of Gujarat*, Election Commission of India, New Delhi, http://eci.gov.in/infieci/key_stat/keystat_fshtm (2 October 2004).

[67] Howard Spodek, 'Crises and Response: Ahmedabad 2000', *Economic and Political Weekly*, 12 May 2001, p. 1631.

was perceived to be a sort of coup.[68] The Chief Minister resigned and Chimanbhai Patel was elected in his place.

At that time, Gujarat experienced a shortage of food and grains and rises in the prices of basic commodities, in particular, of edible groundnut oil.[69] Since groundnut oil was one of the essential staples used by Gujaratis and its consumption was an index of family well-being, the rise in its price was a significant cause of discontent among the middle and upper classes.[70] The situation deteriorated further following the international oil crisis of 1973.[71]

The economic distress of the time was viewed not simply as a downward trend in response to objective circumstances, but largely as stemming from the vested interests of politicians and certain groups.[72] Chimanbhai Patel promised to curb the price-rise, and the price of groundnut oil did briefly go down. However, following a meeting between the groundnut oil dealers, who were strong supporters of Patel, and the Chief Minister in October 1973, prices shot up again. Patel was reported to have said to the oil dealers: 'you know my interests and I know your interests. You will protect my interests and I will protect your interests.'[73]

These political and economic developments bred growing social unrest. In February 1973, 50,000 farmers marched from Baroda to Gandhinagar to protest against the government's decision to impose a levy on rice and groundnuts. In July that year an anti-price-rise campaign was launched by the opposition party Congress(O), which led to three days of violent incidents in Ahmedabad. In January 1974 the NavNirman agitation against corruption and for social justice began when students and professors at Gujarat University in Ahmedabad launched protests against the increase in the cost of college hostels. The agitation continued for more

[68] *Interview* with Girish Patel, 7/4/98; 'A Second Sardar Patel' ('From our correspondence'), *Economic and Political Weekly*, 21 July 1973, p. 1273.

[69] The price of edible groundnut oil rose from Rs.4.50 per kg. in December 1972 to Rs.7.00 per kg. in January 1973. Dawn E. Jones and Rodney W. Jones, 'Urban Upheaval in India: The 1974 Nav Nirman Riots in Gujarat', *Asian Survey*, 16 November 1976, p. 1017. Also see Frankel, *India's Political Economy*, p. 524; Ghanshyam Shah, 'Anatomy of Urban Riots: Ahmedabad 1973', *Economic and Political Weekly*, Annual No., February 1974, p. 234.

[70] *Interviews* with Manish Jani, student leader of the NavNirman, 4/3/98, Ahmedabad; Girish Patel, 7/4/98, Ahmedabad.

[71] See John R. Wood, 'Extra-Parliamentary Opposition in India: An Analysis of Populist Agitations in Gujarat and Bihar', *Pacific Affairs*, vol. 48, no. 3., Fall 1975, p. 315; Shah, 'Anatomy of Urban Riots', p. 234.

[72] See Frankel, *India's Political Economy*, p. 524; B. B. Patel, 'Price Spread and Farmer's Share: Oil and Groundnut in Gujarat', *Economic and Political Weekly*, 17 July 1971, p. 1435; 'Politics of Groundnut' ('From our correspondence'), *Economic and Political Weekly*, 16 October 1971, p. 2187. *Interview* with Manish Jani, Ahmedabad, 4/3/98.

[73] Ghanshyam Shah, 'The Upsurge in Gujarat', *Economic and Political Weekly*, August 1974, p. 1433.

than ten weeks. In the course of these agitations 103 people died.[74] The struggle in Ahmedabad initially reflected a consolidation of middle-class grievances and did not include participation by mill workers.[75] Under the growing pressure of the students and the opposition parties, Chimanbhai Patel resigned on 9 February 1974. Yet, the students' agenda for social justice was slowly taken over and reoriented by the opposition parties, particularly the Jan Sangh, the predecessor of the Hindu nationalist Bharatiya Janata Party (BJP), and Congress(O).[76] Thereafter, the opposition parties demanded the dissolution of the assembly. Even Chimanbhai Patel persuaded members of Congress(I) to resign.[77] In March 1974 the Gujarat assembly was dissolved and the central government imposed presidential rule on Gujarat.

Before the new assembly elections in 1975 Chimanbhai Patel and Vallabhabhai Patel, a prominent Saurashtrian farmers' leader, formed a regional party, the Kisan Mazdoor Lok Paksha (KMLP). The party, which drew support from Patel farmers, won 12 of the 182 seats in the assembly, and because the major contestants did not win enough seats to form a government, became a key factor in the coalition formed by the Janata Front. Congress(I) had been reduced from 140 to 75 seats in the Gujarat assembly and did not participate in the government.[78] In June 1975 Indira Gandhi declared an internal emergency, which abrogated the power of the states. Over the next two years many political activities came to a standstill. In January 1977 she repealed the emergency and announced elections. The Janata Front won the elections in Gujarat as well as at the centre. The government at the centre appointed the second Backward Classes Commission under the chairmanship of Mandal. In Gujarat, the Janata government implemented the Baxi Commission recommendations for reservations for the backward castes. The collapse of the coalition at the centre and subsequently at the state level at the end of 1979 brought new general elections in 1980, in which Congress(I) returned to power on the basis of a greater appeal to the backward classes.

[74] See *ibid.*, pp. 1429–54; Wood, 'Extra-Parliamentary Opposition', pp. 313–34; Frankel, *India's Political Economy*, p. 527.

[75] See Jones and Jones, 'Urban Upheaval in India: The 1974 Nav Nirman Riots in Gujarat', pp. 1013–14.

[76] The students' leader, Manish Jani, recalled that 'the movement was taken from our hands. We were shocked, asking ourselves how did it happen.' *Interview* with Manish Jani, Ahmedabad, 4/3/98. Also *Interview* with Girish Patel, Ahmedabad, 21/1/98, 7/4/98; Wood, 'Extra-Parliamentary Opposition', p. 319; Jones and Jones, 'Urban Upheaval in India: The 1974 Nav Nirman Riots in Gujarat', pp. 1014, 1023.

[77] The Congress expelled Patel from the party for six years for this action.

[78] *Statistical Report on General Election, 1975 to the Legislative Assembly of Gujarat*, New Delhi: Election Commission of India, http://eci.gov.in/infieci/key_stat/keystat_fshtm (2 October 2004).

Madhavsinh Solanki led Congress(I) to victory in the 1980 elections, securing 141 out of the 182 Gujarat assembly seats.[79] This was the first election contested in the state by the BJP, which won nine seats.[80] Congress(I), whose electoral slogan in the state was 'power to the poor', contested the state elections on the basis of the KHAM strategy, a caste alliance that it had established in the mid-1970s, with the idea of promoting itself as the advocate of the oppressed groups.[81] KHAM was the acronym for Kshatriyas, Harijans, Adivasis and Muslims, who together formed about 55 per cent of the population of the state.[82] Most of the caste groups in this alliance were either entitled to or being considered for reservations. The members of the KHAM alliance were identified on the basis of class by employing categories of caste and religion. This was an alliance of economic classes that could potentially upset the social and political order. There was a prevalent perception among both political parties and segments of the public, albeit poorly substantiated, that Muslims formed a vote bank with a high turnout.[83] The political success of the KHAM alliance resulted in the exclusion of some groups among the upper castes, particularly the Patels, from positions of power, and generated anxiety among some upper-caste groups at this challenge to their political dominance;[84] thirteen out of the twenty-two ministers in the new cabinet were from the KHAM groups.[85]

The increasing economic and social mobility among lower and backward castes, which had been developing in Gujarat since the 1960s, also contributed to undermining the upper castes' confidence in their dominant position within the social order.[86] In Ahmedabad, some groups

[79] *Statistical Report on General Election, 1980 to the Legislative Assembly of Gujarat*, New Delhi: Election Commission of India, p. 9, http://eci.gov.in/infieci/key_stat/keystat_fshtm (2 October 2004).

[80] *Ibid.*, the BJP was founded on 5 April 1980 by the ex-Jan Sangh members of the Janata Party. See Christophe Jaffrelot, *The Hindu Nationalist Movement in India, and Indian Politics 1925 to the 1990s*, Delhi: Viking, 1996, pp. 313, 315.

[81] *India Today*, 1–15 November 1979, p. 31.

[82] John R. Wood, 'Congress Restored? The "Kham" Strategy and Congress(I) Recruitment in Gujarat', in John R. Wood (ed.), *State Politics in Contemporary India: Crisis or Continuity?*, Boulder and London: Westview Press, 1984, pp. 197–227.

[83] Yogendra Yadav, 'Understanding the Second Democratic Upsurge: Trends of Bahujan Participation in Electoral Politics in the 1990s', in Francine Frankel, Zoya Hasan, Rajeev Bhargava and Balveer Arora (eds.), *Transforming India: Social and Political Dynamics of Democracy*, New Delhi: Oxford University Press, 2000, pp. 132–3.

[84] In 1975, the Patels held 24 per cent of the assembly seats and the Kshatriya 16 per cent. By 1985 the former held only 18.2 per cent of the seats and the latter held 24.6 per cent. See Pravin Sheth, *Political Development in Gujarat*, Ahmedabad: Karnavati Publications, 1998, p. 28; Atul Kohli, *Democracy and Discontent*, Cambridge: Cambridge University Press, 1990, p. 246.

[85] Mitra, 'The Perils of Promoting Equality', p. 298.

[86] Bose, 'Mobility and Conflict', p. 369; Ghanshyam Shah, 'Polarised Communities', *Seminar*, vol. 470, October 1998, p. 33.

among the Dalits had been able to improve their economic situation. Some had been able to improve the quality of their housing conditions and to provide their children with better schooling. On the basis of their economic conditions some groups among the Dalits had become part of the urban middle class.[87] By the 1980s, the SCs in Gujarat had reached the national average level of literacy, and reservations had also increased the numbers of professionally trained graduates among them. In primary and secondary education the SC children competed with Patels.[88] The reservation quotas had not been achieved, but the growing number of scheduled caste and scheduled tribe government employees, especially in the lower-ranked positions of the civil service – classes III and IV – made their presence more visible.[89]

The frustrations of upper castes over reservations and the political achievements of the lower and backward castes were expressed in the anti-reservation caste riots that erupted in Ahmedabad in December 1980. The riots started only six months after the electoral success of the lower and backward castes in the state assembly elections. The students in Ahmedabad, who had started the agitation against reservations in post-graduate medical courses, 'enacted a public marriage ceremony between the "reservationist" bride and the "government" groom'.[90] They also performed a symbolic operation 'on a clay model of a Dalit student's brain in order to show that it contained nothing but sawdust'.[91] Government and other public service employees joined the anti-reservation struggle, demanding the abolition of reservations in promotions.[92] Dalits were the main target of the violence.[93] Groups like the Vankars, who benefited from reservations and experienced social mobility, suffered most in

---

[87] Shah, 'Polarised Communities', pp. 32, 34; Achyut Yagnik, 'Search for Dalit Self Identity in Gujarat', in Takashi Shinoda (ed.), *The Other Gujarat*, Mumbai: Popular Prakashan, 2002, pp. 23.

[88] Shah, 'Polarised Communities', p. 32.

[89] See *Report of the Commission for Scheduled Castes and Scheduled Tribes April 1984–March 1985*, New Delhi: Government of India, pp. 5,7; *Report of the Commission for Scheduled Castes and Scheduled Tribes April 1985–March 1986*, New Delhi: Government of India, p. 10. For processes of social mobility among the lower and backward castes through reservations in Gujarat also see Ghanshyam Shah, 'Middle-Class Politics: A Case of Anti-Reservation Agitation in Gujarat', *Economic and Political Weekly*, Annual No., May 1987, p. AN-163; Shah, 'Polarised Communities', p. 32; Upendra Baxi, 'Reflections on the Reservations Crisis in Gujarat', in Veena Das (ed.), *Mirrors of Violence*, 1990, New Delhi: Oxford University Press, p. 217; Sheth, 'Reservation Policy Revisited', p. 494; Jan Breman, *Footloose Labour: Working in India's Informal Economy*, Cambridge: Cambridge University Press, 1996, p. 179.

[90] Yagnik and Bhatt, 'The Anti-Dalit Agitation in Gujarat', p. 51.

[91] *Ibid.* Also see, IRS, *Research Project on Atrocities on Harijans for 102 Days in Gujarat*, pp. 46–7.

[92] *Ibid.*, pp. 36–7.

[93] Desai, 'Anti-Reservation Agitation and Structure of Gujarat Society', p. 822.

the riots.[94] The main agitators were groups among the Patels. In Ahmedabad, Patels from Saurashtra, who had prospered as a result of the land reforms and arrived in the city in the 1970s as new entrepreneurs, were disturbed by the increasing social mobility of some Dalits and by the success of Congress(I) on the basis of the KHAM alliance.[95] The SCs medical students started a counter-campaign to protect reservations, even managing to mobilise to their struggle 7,500 mill workers who observed a two-day strike in mid-February 1981.[96] The anti-reservationists continued their agitation and even sought to promote an anti-reservation campaign in Delhi. The agitation gradually subsided in mid-April after the High Court rejected the anti-reservationist petitions and the national parliament 'reaffirmed its faith in the reservation system'.[97]

From the viewpoint of some Dalits, the anti-reservation riots indicated that 'the idea of KHAM in Gujarat failed. Although Solanki formed a government in 1980 with no Patels, in the end, all parties were controlled by high caste leaders. The KHAM success was only political but not social; it was for personal political benefits.'[98] In theory, the KHAM caste alliance as well as reservation policies aimed to advance the social, economic and political position of the lower and backward groups. In practice, however, there was a growing discrepancy between the rhetoric of reservations and electoral politics and the subsequent policy outcomes. The Congress(I) ministry, led by Madhavsinh Solanki, did not pursue economic reforms for the benefit of the poor. On the contrary, from 1980 the government launched liberal economic policies and adhered to the demands of the industrial lobby with the view that 'only industrialisation would create jobs for the masses'.[99] 'Entrepreneurs could manage concessions in policy, tax breaks, and land at throw-away prices for the asking.'[100] Solanki acknowledged that 'KHAM became a trade word; it was in our mind as a support base. It was used to exclude people from Congress'.[101] One of the founders of the KHAM strategy admitted that 'we didn't believe in caste, we just used it'.[102]

[94] Pradip Kumar Bose, 'Social Mobility and Caste Violence: A Study of the Gujarat Riots', *Economic and Political Weekly*, 18 April 1981, p. 713.
[95] *Interview* with Gordhanbhai Jhadaphia, BJP MLA, Bapunagar, Ahmedabad, 16/12/97. Also see Kohli, *Democracy and Discontent*, p. 252.
[96] IRS, *Research Project on Atrocities on Harijans for 102 Days in Gujarat*, p. 34.
[97] Yagnik and Bhatt, 'The Anti-Dalit Agitation in Gujarat', pp. 55.
[98] *Interview* with Valgibhai Patel (Dalit Panthers), Ahmedabad, 29/11/97.
[99] *Interview* with Madhavsinh Solanki, Delhi, 16/3/98. Also see Kohli, *Democracy and Discontent*, pp. 260–1.
[100] Harish Khare, 'An Unending Struggle for Gujarat's Political Soul', *Seminar*, vol. 470, 1998, p. 21. Also see Achyut Yagnik, 'Paradoxes of Populism', *Economic and Political Weekly*, 27 August 1983, p. 1507.
[101] *Interview* with Madhavsinh Solanki, Delhi, 16/3/98.
[102] Quoted in Wood, 'Congress Restored? The "Kham" Strategy and Congress(I) Recruitment in Gujarat', p. 212.

At the same time, the quest of Congress(I) for a support base among the oppressed KHAM groups empowered some of the backward classes. The number of Congress MLAs from lower and backward groups increased significantly between 1967 and 1980.[103] The growing participation of lower- and backward-caste groups in the legislature and administration informed the formation of new attitudes and ideas about the operation of politics among these groups. These processes of politicisation did not necessarily improve the economic conditions of the lower groups, but it gradually positioned them beyond the simple category of a 'vote bank'. That was the way they had often been perceived by upper-caste party leaders.

Processes of mobility among the lower and backward castes, as well as deepening upper-caste anxieties over reservations and over the growing political role of these groups, occurred elsewhere in India from the 1970s. In Bihar, Karpoori Thakur was able by the end of the 1970s to unite the backward classes politically on the basis of the reservations policy.[104] Upper castes' frustrations over these developments were manifested in the anti-reservation riots that erupted in Bihar in 1980:

The reservation policy is a symbolic issue that has gripped the imagination of virtually everyone in Bihar who has even the slightest degree of political awareness. Through the reservation issue Karpoori Thakur asserted that . . . the old days of dominance in public affairs from village to the Vidhan Sabha by the 'twice-born' were gone for ever, and that his government would be one based on the support of the Backwards.[105]

In Uttar Pradesh (UP) the emerging Bharatiya Kranti Dal (BKD) Party, which was led by Charan Singh, a member of a backward-caste community, appealed directly to the common economic interests of the peasantry from the backward classes. Already during the 1967 elections the BKD had emerged as the second largest party in the state.[106] Later Singh constructed the AJGAR political alliance, an acronym for Ahir (Yadav), Jat Gujar and Rajput, which covered a wide range of OBC and inter-mediate castes. Upper castes' concerns over reservations and growing

---

[103] *Ibid.*, p. 219. Also see Mitra, 'The Perils of Promoting Equality', p. 298; Kohli, *Democracy and Discontent*, p. 246. Generally, the share of OBC MPs in the Hindi belt had increased by the end of the 1970s. Jaffrelot, 'The Rise of the Other Backward Classes in the Hindi Belt', pp. 93, 98–9; Jaffrelot, *India's Silent Revolution*.

[104] Bose, 'Mobility and Conflict', p. 380. For social mobility processes among STs in Bihar see Stuart Corbridge, 'Competing Inequalities: The Scheduled Tribes and the Reservation System in India's Jharkhand', *Journal of Asian Studies*, vol. 59, no. 1, February 2000, pp. 62–85, particularly p. 76.

[105] Blair, 'Rising Kulaks and Backward Classes in Bihar', p. 66.

[106] Frankel, *India's Political Economy*, p. 386. For an insightful analysis of OBC mobilisation in UP from independence to the early 1990s and the effects of reservations on these processes see Hasan, *Quest for Power*, pp. 121–65.

politicisation among the lower and backward castes received expression in the media in the late 1970s: 'the majority of Caste Hindus grow increasingly jealous and curse the recipient [of reservations] as "Government Brahmins" . . . The alleged rising number of atrocities against Harijans is an off-shoot of this upper-caste jealousy and prejudice against reservation.'[107] In 1979 *India Today* wrote: 'the vaulting ambition of a whole lot of long subdued middle castes, newly awakened to their potential power, now aroused almost to a point of militancy . . . The Harijans are showing signs of a new pride and a new awareness of their rights.'[108]

The making of caste (2)

The construction of political alliances between castes on the basis of shared class considerations was not a new phenomenon in Gujarat politics. Driven by their opposition to the land reforms, rich Patel farmers from central Gujarat and Saurashtrian Rajputs among the Kshatriyas formed the Swatantra Party in 1959. In the 1962 and 1967 Gujarat assembly elections the party gained support from the Kshatriya Sabha.[109] This political caste alliance, which was formed in spite of the deep animosity between the Patidars and the Kshatriyas in Gujarat, resulted in fissures among the Kshatriyas. The lower-status groups of Kolis among the Kshatriyas, who amalgamated into the caste fold in the 1940s in their pursuit of higher status, opposed the alliance with the Patels. Divisions among the Patels occurred because the Patels from Saurashtra, who benefited from the land reforms, did not have common interests with their northern and central Gujarati caste-fellows. In the context of the KHAM alliance and the expansion of reservations for backward castes in the 1980s, a process of reunification between the lower- and upper-caste groups among the Kshatriyas took place. Paradoxically, under these new circumstances the former Kolis, who had identified themselves for already half a century as Kshatriyas, joined the Dalits. Thus, political alliances between castes on the basis of class sometimes unified castes and sometimes produced fissures within them.

The politics of caste in the formation of electoral alliances as well as reservation policies sometimes created conflicting interests within various

---

[107] Galanter, *Competing Equalities*, p. 74 (quoted from the *Sunday Statesman Magazine*, 19 February 1978).

[108] *India Today*, 1–15 January 1979, pp. 31–3.

[109] See N. Sanghavi, *Gujarat a Political Analysis*, Surat: Centre for Social Studies, 1996, p. 262; Sanghavi, 'Fewer Seats, but Congress More Cohesive', *Economic and Political Weekly*, 4 March 1967, pp. 476–9; Ghanshyam Shah, *Caste Association and Political Process in Gujarat: A Study of Gujarat Kshatriya Sabha*, Bombay: Popular Prakashan, 1975, p. 93.

groups, which hampered their organisation for collective action. Lower- and backward-caste groups sought to alleviate their social caste status, but conversely, in order to secure reservations in government jobs and education, they sought recognition of their low-caste identity. Their formal caste status endowed them with greater political leverage. In some cases even dominant castes, for example the Jats in Harayana, successfully pressured the government for recognition as a backward caste in order to benefit from reservations in government jobs.[110]

The political dynamics of caste reservations and the formation of electoral alliances highlighted the social boundaries that made the caste groups rather than the characteristics that were assumed to constitute castes. This had two conflicting results: on the one hand, the experience of castes in Gujarat politics demonstrated that in politics, caste boundaries were always negotiable, and that the cultural or religious properties that constituted caste could not be easily defined. On the other hand, because caste was used as a natural building block in the designation of reservation policies and in the formation of electoral alliances, it was also essentialised. Both these processes, as well as their innate contradictions, which lay at the basis of caste politics and collective action by various groups, contributed to the persistence of caste prejudice. The perpetuation of caste prejudice became a means of mitigating the discrepancies between the political rhetoric of equality and redistribution, which underlay reservation policies and electoral politics in Gujarat in the 1980s, and the enduring reality of inequalities. Consequently, prejudiced perceptions of caste and other social groups informed the attitudes, as well as practices, of various state apparatuses towards these groups. This also made it all the more difficult for upper castes to overcome their status anxiety over reservations.

The discrepancies between the political rhetoric and evolving policies and governance practices reflected the contradictions that plagued the functioning of the state institutions. Reservation policies aimed to promote equality, secularism and the eradication of caste. In the designation of reservations, policy makers imagined the society on the basis of caste; they were guided by a decision to negate social categories, which their policy reconstituted. The formation of caste electoral alliances on the basis of class by political parties from above, on the one hand, and groups' attempts to increase their political leverage on the basis of caste, on the

---

[110] Hooda, *Contesting Reservation*, p. 59. Laura Dudley Jenkins argues that group-based policies influence group identity claims. These claims, in turn, 'prevent the reification of state categories'. Dudley Jenkins, 'Becoming Backward: Preferential Policies and Religious Minorities in India', pp. 32–3.

other, magnified these contradictions. In these processes, the state institutions and social groups both transformed and constituted one another.

In the designation and discourse of reservations various state apparatuses addressed the redistribution of material, social and ideological resources for the benefit of the lower and backward castes as if these were synonymous with the rights of religious minorities. In the shaping of party politics, religious minorities were lumped together with the lower and backward castes for the purpose of the redistribution of political resources. Attempts to promote secularism yielded scepticism about the secular ethos, which officially constituted the state and the bedrock for its key policies. In both the designation of reservations and party politics between caste and class, the politics of redistribution created a link between politics for the benefit of the lower and backward castes/classes and communalism. The state reservation policies established Hindu identity in relation to caste. The experience of caste in politics as a fluid social category and practice further perplexed the notion of a Hindu identity. Communalism and a Hindu identity grew, therefore, in the interstices between the dynamics of caste and class. The historical conjunction between caste conflicts and communalism occurred in Ahmedabad in the mid-1980s.

In Ahmedabad, the caste-reservation crisis and the success of the KHAM strategy coincided with the transformations in the interrelations between caste and class, which were driven by the social and economic dynamics in the rapidly growing city. In 1985, just as the Congress won the Gujarat assembly elections on the basis of the KHAM alliance with a greater victory than before, anti-reservation riots erupted in Ahmedabad. This caste riot turned into large-scale communal violence between Hindus and Muslims. This was unexpected, as Gujarat politics in the 1970s and 1980s had displayed no evidence of endemic or even newly developing Hindu–Muslim strife. How and why, then, did caste disputes over reservations turn into communal conflict between Hindus and Muslims? How was the link between caste reservations and communalism, which was established in the discourse of reservations, expressed on the ground? The second part of this book continues exploring these questions through a detailed investigation of the Ahmedabad riots of 1985. It elaborates on the context in which the caste-reservation and communal conflicts emerged and upon which a communal Hindu identity began forming from the mid-1980s. The next part of the book also unravels the dynamics by which the state's communalised attitudes and practices began to consolidate.

Part II

The 1985 Ahmedabad riots: the historical conjunction between caste conflicts and communalism

Outlining the riots – the plot[1]

Seven months of ferocious large-scale riots in the city of Ahmedabad started in February 1985 with the death of a bus passenger who was burnt alive as a group of protesting students set fire to a State Transport bus, along with the injuring of eight policemen during a violent demonstration. The riots erupted over the decision of the Gujarat state government to increase the reserved quotas for backward-caste Hindus in educational institutions and government jobs from 10 per cent to 28 per cent. Upper-caste Hindus started the agitation against the state policy. Startlingly, within a month, the intra-Hindu caste dispute turned into communal violence between Hindus and Muslims. Communal uproar spread throughout the city. The army was called in, but the waves of outrage continued. The police force also became embroiled in the agitations. The spree of violence persisted with unprecedented stabbings, and the looting and burning of houses and shops. Most of the victims were Muslims. Bomb blasts hit the city. The newly elected Chief Minister resigned because of the government's inability to bring the situation under control. Moreover, the state was paralysed by a massive government employee strike. Finally, after seven months of anti-reservation agitation and catastrophic communal violence the riots gradually abated.

When the new reservation policy was announced by the Gujarat government in January 1985 there was at first no overt reaction from the

[1] The plot of the riots is based on Justice V. S. Dave's *Report of the Commission of Inquiry: Into the Incidents of Violence and Disturbances which Took Place at Various Places in the State of Gujarat since February, 1985 to 18th July, 1985* (henceforth *Commission*, and *COI* in references), Ahmedabad: Government of Gujarat, April 1990; reports in the *Times of India* (*TOI*), January–August 1985; *The Hindu*, January–August 1985; *India Today*, January–August 1985; newspaper cuttings from the *Indian Express*, *The Hindustan Times* and *Patriot*, February–July 1985; and *The Shattering of Gujarat*, a background paper for private circulation, Series 1985, No. 2, Bombay: BUILD Documentation Centre, 1985 (the diary of the events in this source was compiled from the *TOI*, *Indian Express*, *Hindustan Times*, *Tribune*, *Telegraph*, *Free Press*, *Journal*, *Hindu*, *Newstimes* and *Sunday Observer*.

upper castes.[2] Anti-reservation action took shape only in mid-February, when the students of L.D. Engineering College in Ahmedabad held their first meeting and decided to agitate against the reservation of places in the engineering and medical colleges. The students decided to boycott the preliminary examinations, which were scheduled for 18 February. Within a few days the students formed an All-Gujarat Educational Reform Action Committee (AGERAC), as well as a student central anti-reservation body, Akhil Gujarat Navrachna Samiti. The students decided to embark on an indefinite strike and to boycott examinations until the government repealed the new reservation quotas. The government's response was to shut down the universities and schools.

Initially, the confrontation was concentrated around the universities and schools. The principal protagonists were upper-caste students and the agitation was limited to the western side of the city. The riots began with protest rallies and school boycotts, but soon took a violent turn in the form of stoning and arson, causing widespread damage to government and municipal property, mainly buses.[3] The AGERAC called for a *bandh* (shutting down of businesses, shops and offices) in Ahmedabad on 25 February, which was observed in the old city, but had no effect in the predominantly working-class areas on the eastern side of Ahmedabad. It also gained the support of some Bar Associations and the doctors of Ahmedabad. Almost all the house surgeons in the city went on a token strike the next day. Moreover, the AGERAC submitted a memorandum to the government, demanding the abolition both of the new quotas and of the roster system of reservations in government job promotions. On 28 February, a student protest resulted in the death of the passenger in the burning bus.

During the first week of March, when the Gujarat state assembly elections were held, there was a lull.[4] Congress(I), led by Madhavsinh Solanki, won the elections with a large majority, securing 149 out of the 182 Gujarat assembly seats. Solanki formed a government on 11 March, in which members of the KHAM caste coalition held fourteen of

---

[2] The government decision, as already mentioned, was based on the Rane Commission Report recommendations. The government, however, reversed the Commission's recommendations. It insisted that caste and not class should be the criterion for the identification of backwardness.

[3] According to police records, between 19 and 24 February municipal and state buses were damaged, and passengers and policemen were injured in daily incidents of stone throwing by students. During the first ten days of agitation fifty-four buses were damaged or destroyed. Additionally, the students stoned the bungalows of a few state officials.

[4] On 2 March the AGERAC handed over a memorandum to the State Home Minister, urging the Prime Minister to re-establish merit as the sole criterion for admission to educational institutions.

the twenty cabinet seats.[5] Subsequently, the students revived the agitation by stoning private and public vehicles, damaging fifteen buses and burning two.[6] The Akhil Gujarat Navrachna Samiti called for a Gujarat *bandh* for 18 March. A parents and guardians organisation in support of the students, Akhil Gujarat Vali Maha Mandal, was formed. In the face of the mounting disturbances the government decided on 16 March to defer the new reservation policy for one year, publish the Rane Report, and postpone the examinations in the universities and schools from mid- to late-March.[7] Nonetheless, the students hardened their position and announced that they opposed any kind of reservations. No communal incidents were reported during this period.

On 18 March, during the 'Gujarat *bandh*' day, which was successfully observed, the police recorded fifty anti-reservation agitation offences.[8] The main targets of stone throwing were the police, buses, banks, and municipal and government establishments. On that evening, at the end of the *bandh* day, communal riots erupted, starting in the Dariapur area in the walled city of Ahmedabad near the Hindu locality of Vadigam and the Muslim locality of Naginapol. As the *bandh*'s 'death knell' rang out,[9] a stone hit a Muslim boy on the head while he was playing carrom. He was rushed to a hospital.[10] From that moment, 'the signal was on' and communal violence began.[11] Communal riots lasted throughout the night of 18 March and the following morning and continued with killings, arson and looting in the walled city.[12] In the adjacent localities of Naginapol and Vadigam, Hindus and Muslims threw stones, bottles and glass tubes filled with acid and burning rags at each other.[13] The turmoil spread to the nearby localities of Dabgarward and Kalupur, where there was sporadic shooting and shops and houses were set on fire. Although a curfew was declared at 10:30 p.m., the 'day-long orgy of mob fury' continued.[14]

---

[5] KHAM was the acronym for Kshatriyas, Harijans, Adivasis and Muslims. The Congress(I) contested the state elections on the basis of this caste alliance.

[6] According to police records, between 11 and 17 March such incidents were recorded daily in different areas of the city.

[7] The government took the decision after leading educationalists and social workers in Ahmedabad appealed to the Chief Minister to withdraw the new reservation quotas, and assured him that this would persuade the students to retract the agitation.

[8] *COI*, Vol. III, Annex XXXV, pp. 178–87.

[9] This programme was known as 'Mruyughant': at 8 p.m. people would go to the roofs of their houses and ring bells or make other sounds (with their thali dishes), heralding the death of reservations.

[10] *COI*, Vol. I, p. 226. Also see pp. 64, 214, G.W.-12, p. 93, S-144, p. 149.

[11] *Ibid.*, p. 226. Also see pp. 205, 228; *The Hindu*, 30 March 1985.

[12] *COI*, Vol. I, p. 226.   [13] *Ibid.*, G.W.-12, p. 93, G.W.-13, p. 97, S-144, p. 149.

[14] *TOI*, 20 March 1985.

The army was called in on 19 March, and the walled city was placed under curfew. Yet during the next three days the city witnessed a rise in both communal and anti-reservation incidents. The burning and looting of shops and clashes between various groups occurred mainly in the walled city and in the Naranpura areas of western Ahmedabad.[15] Thereafter the violence subsided. The Prime Minister, Rajiv Gandhi, came to Ahmedabad on 23 March. He accused the opposition parties, which had lost the elections, of being responsible for the events.[16] On this occasion the police arrested three student leaders of the AGERAC for abetting communal violence. They were later detained under the National Security Act (NSA) 1980. The rest of the month was relatively quiet, and by 2 April the army had withdrawn and the curfew had been lifted.

Nonetheless, the fight against the new reservation policy continued with the persistent boycotting of schools, colleges and examinations. Various professional associations supported the struggle and went on a sympathy strike, protesting against the arrest of the student leaders. At this stage a counter-, pro-reservation reaction emerged.[17] Pro-reservation organisations such as the Baxi Commission Action Committee and the Anamat Andolan Pratikar Manch (Opposition Front against Reservation Agitation), which had been established in March, launched a demonstration for the implementation of the new reservation quotas. Meanwhile, the state government employees initiated a new anti-reservation front against the roster reservation system of promotion.[18] One thousand of them were arrested in the nearby capital of Gandhinagar when they tried to hold a rally, demanding the publication of the Sadwani Commission report on reservations in promotion.[19]

There were also increasing tensions between the anti-reservationists and the police. On 4 April, the 'police bursted [sic] tear-gas shells and resorted to lathi [truncheon] charge' to disperse an anti-reservation protest in the Asarwa Chakla (crossroad) area. The demonstrators claimed that 'the police went on rampage damaging homes and beating up women'.[20] At a state level meeting on 7 April, the student bodies

---

[15] See *COI*, Vol. III, pp. 184–98, 298–312.   [16] *The Hindu*, 30 March 1985.

[17] It started when the CPI (ML) General Secretary, Santosh Rana, declared that the party would start a movement against any change in the reservation policy and would also demand the implementation of the Mandal Commission recommendations.

[18] Under the roster reservation system, government workers belonging to the SCs and STs receive preferential treatment in promotion.

[19] The Sadwani Commission was appointed after the anti-reservation riots of 1981 to study the roster system of promotion. The Commission submitted its report in September 1981. The government did not accept its recommendations, and instead appointed a cabinet subcommittee to consider the Sadwani report. By the time riots erupted in 1985 the subcommittee had not yet finished its work. *COI*, Vol. I, p. 200.

[20] *The Shattering of Gujarat*, p. 7.

demanded that the government take action against the policemen responsible for these actions. They decided to continue boycotting the examinations until the government released the detained students and called
for the abolition of the roster reservation system of promotion by 1989.[21]
With the arrival of members of an SCs association, the Gujarat Pach-
hat Samaj, the meeting turned into a clash between anti-reservationists
and pro-reservationists. This period also witnessed several confrontations
between forward-caste Hindus and SCs. At Meghaninagar, for example,
violence erupted because upper castes claimed that SCs had desecrated
a statue that they had garlanded.[22] Pro-reservationists threatened to call
for a separate Dalitstan in Gujarat if the anti-reservation movement was
not disbanded.[23] Grievances against the police gained further momen-
tum during the second week of April. The police detained seventy-five
lawyers of the lower court in Ahmedabad who had attempted to march
to the collector of the city to submit a memorandum protesting against
police atrocities at Asarwa, on the eastern side of the city, five days earlier.
They were later released. Lawyers from Gujarat also decided to submit
a memorandum to the Prime Minister, requesting a change in the state
leadership.[24]

During the following upsurge of violence in April much of the protest
centred on police atrocities against agitating students and citizens. In
mid-April, the situation intensified as confrontations between the police
and residents occurred in various localities. Cases of police shooting and
killings increased, and there were repeated clashes between Hindus and
Muslims. In Saraspur, on the eastern side of the city, violent clashes
between residents and the police occurred on 13 April. Upper-caste Hindus complained that police had entered a temple and broken a door. An
indefinite curfew was imposed on that part of the city since, as the media
explained, 'the police were engaged in ding dong battle all morning'.[25]
Despite the curfew, violent incidents intensified and spread across the city
over the next two days. In Saraspur, furnishings in a local school were
set on fire. In Astodia, in the old city, some people tried to break into
the Bank of Baroda, damaged electricity and telephone wires and pelted
the police with stones. On the following day police killed two people
and injured six when they opened fire on looters. Similar incidents were
reported from Kalupur, Shahpur and Gheekanta within the walled city,
as well as from localities in the western side of the city.

The Commission of Inquiry characterised the time between 16 and 23
April as 'the darkest period during the course of anti-reservation agitation

---

[21] COI, Vol. I, pp. 214–15.
[22] Ibid., p. 215; TOI, 8 April 1985.   [23] The Shattering of Gujarat, p. 8.
[24] COI, Vol. I, p. 215.   [25] TOI, 14 April 1985.

and communal disturbances in Ahmedabad'.[26] On 16 April, a 'jail *bharo*' agitation, initiated by the Akhil Gujarat Navrachna Samiti, resulted in the arrest of more than a thousand students.[27] The parents and guardians organisation, the Vali Maha Mandal, threatened to launch a disobedience movement. A confrontation between Dalits and Patels occurred in Saraspur, and violent disturbances took place in different parts of the city. The police used excessive force against residents of Khadia in the old city and their property.[28] On that day the army was called into the old city again, where it remained for three months. On the first day that the army took up its position in the city, eight people were killed and twenty injured, many of them in stabbing cases in Dariapur and Kalupur in the old city, while looting and arson continued.[29] The next day, four more people were killed and a dozen others injured in police shooting and stabbing incidents. The newspapers reported that in various localities of the old city 'sporadic communal violence continued'.[30]

On 18 April the government released the detained students. The anti-reservationists, however, took the position that this step would only set the stage for talks, and that the agitation would continue. At the same time, representatives of various backward castes met and formed a state-level body, the Gujarat Anamat Rakshak Vali Mandal (Reservation Protection Guardians Association).[31] As a response to the unrest, the curfew was extended to the predominantly mill workers' areas of Rakhial and Bapunagar, and the government replaced the police with the army to patrol the Khadia–Raipur areas of the city.[32] Despite these steps, police and communal violence escalated in the city.

The situation deteriorated when, on 22 April, the police revolted after the killing of Head Constable Laxman Desai. The same day, the police attacked and set fire to the building of the Gujarat Samachar Press. Large-scale arson, looting, rioting and destruction followed throughout the day and night. Mass-scale communal riots also erupted in the predominantly working-class eastern area, especially in Bapunagar. The principal allegation of the Muslims in the area, who were the main victims of the violence, was that 'Hindus had done all the damages to Muslims' life and property with the aid, assistance and connivance of the police.'[33]

---

[26] *COI*, Vol. I, p. 215. During that time the police recorded 192 incidents regarding anti-reservation agitation and 82 incidents regarding communal riots. *Ibid.*, Vol. III, pp. 216–58, 323–39.

[27] Jail *bharo*, literally 'put inside jail'. The idea was to agitate to provoke mass arrests and thereby overcrowd the jails.

[28] *Ibid.*, Vol. I, G.W.-34, p. 236, p. 242. Also see pp. 237–9.   [29] *TOI*, 17 April 1985.

[30] *Ibid.*, 18 April 1985; *The Shattering of Gujarat*, p. 9.   [31] *The Shattering of Gujarat*, p. 9.

[32] On 21 April several big rallies, protesting against police misconduct, were held in various curfew-free localities.

[33] *COI*, Vol. I, p. 215.

As a result of this turmoil several hundred houses were burnt down and several thousand people, mostly Muslims, were rendered homeless and were forced to find shelter in a relief camp.[34] Subsequently, the army took control of the entire area of Ahmedabad. In the wake of the events of 22 April a group of Ahmedabad intellectuals and social activists established the Nagrik Sangthan (Citizens Organisation), endeavouring to stop the violence in the city. Even the textile mills, which had remained open during the previous months of disturbances, were closed after the rampage of that day.

Although there was a decline in the number of incidents over the next fortnight, various organisations and associations continued protesting against police atrocities, held rallies and strikes, and demanded that the government appoint a commission of inquiry into the events.[35] Sporadic stabbing incidents continued, mainly when the curfew was relaxed. At this time, less than two months after he was elected, calls for the dismissal of Solanki's government intensified. On 29 April, the central government turned down an opposition demand to dislodge the Gujarat government. A week later the police in Ahmedabad thwarted an attempt by the parents and guardians body to organise a demonstration for the removal of Solanki. State employees also revived their struggle and went on strike, demanding the abolition of the caste-based roster reservation system of promotion in government jobs.[36] This strike paralysed government offices as 'ten lakh [one million] workers took leave'.[37] Initially, the government employees defined their leave as a protest against police excesses, but within a day they threatened to continue striking until the government abolished the roster system. The pro-reservationist Akhil Gujarat Baxi Panch demanded action against the striking employees and recruitment of more backward classes into government jobs. The strike was called off on 7 May after the government promised to publish the Sadwani Report and the employees withdrew their demand for the total abolition of reservations in promotion.[38]

In the following week, 8–15 May, communal clashes resumed and intensified after the murder of Police Sub-Inspector Mahendrasingh Rana in the Hindu locality of Bhanderipol in the Kalupur area of the walled city. Over the next few days thirty-three people died and many more were

---

[34] *TOI*, 24 April 1985.
[35] The Ahmedabad Criminal Court Bar Association went on strike for four days in protest against police atrocities. Later it also offered free services to citizens who had been abused by the police.
[36] *COI*, Vol. I, p. 204
[37] *TOI*, 4 May 1985. Other sources estimated that about 700,000 workers went on strike. See *The Shattering of Gujarat*, p. 11.
[38] *TOI*, 1–7 May 1985; *The Shattering of Gujarat*, pp. 12–13.

injured, some as the result of police shooting. Most of the casualties in the walled city were victims of stabbings.[39] Cases of communal arson and stone throwing also continued throughout the month. Meanwhile, talks held between the government and the students and parents organisations on 30 May failed. The pro-reservationists threatened Solanki that they would revolt from 1 June if the new 18 per cent reservation quotas were not implemented. The Gujarat Chamber of Commerce initiated a five-day *bandh* from 5 June as a protest against the government's inability to maintain law and order.

The next round in the riots erupted on 5 June, on the occasion of the Gujarat Chamber of Commerce's *bandh*. Large-scale violence broke out in the walled city, when 200 women tried to stop traffic, protesting against the failure by some to observe the *bandh*. Over the next few days thirty-four people were killed in shootings and stabbings, and many more were injured.[40] The communal clashes, in the form of shop burning and looting, as well as anti-reservation violence, increased.[41] Two major events marked this period. First, eight members of a Hindu family were burnt alive in Dabgarward locality in Kalupur in the walled city on 9 June.[42] Hindus in the area retaliated by setting fire to three houses belonging to Muslims and by burning and looting Muslim shops. At the same time, a significant number of state government employees renewed their strike for the abolition of the roster system. In view of the escalating disturbances, the Gujarat government decided to set up a judicial inquiry to probe all aspects of violence in the state, and Solanki agreed to postpone the increase of reservations for the Socially and Educationally Backward Classes (SEBC) until a national consensus on the issue was reached. The government also extended the academic year and released the student leaders who had been arrested under the National Security Act.[43] Surprisingly, although Solanki agreed to accept the anti-reservationists' demands, they decided to continue their struggle and advanced new claims, demanding that the existing 10 per cent reservations for the SEBC would not continue after 1988.

The second event that intensified the violence during that month occurred on 20 June, when a Hindu religious procession, the Rath Yatra, happened to coincide with the Muslim holiday of Id-Ul-Fitr. The Yatra,

---

[39] On 10 May, for example, the newspapers reported eight stabbing incidents. The next day, police and army fire killed twelve people, and for the first time a few areas on the western side of the city were placed under curfew. In Gomtipur, a labour-dominated area on the eastern side of the city, '5–6 chawls were burnt and seven persons were killed'. *COI*, Vol. I (Case of Central Relief Committee), p. 53.

[40] These figures are based on reports in the *TOI* between 6 and 11 June 1985.

[41] *COI*, Vol. III, pp. 276–84, 396–403.   [42] *COI*, Vol. I, pp. 261–2.

[43] *TOI*, 10 June 1985, 11 June 1985 (editorial).

which took place in defiance of an agreement between the temple organ-
isers and the authorities, turned into communal combat. 'The entire
security and the curfew arrangement in the army controlled area went
haywire.'[44] By the end of that day the death toll of the four-month-old
agitation had reached 173.[45] The next day 'thousands of Muslim women
defied the curfew and came out on the streets in Dariapur-Kalupur area',
protesting against the army's conduct and demanding action against the
Hindu devotees who had led the procession.[46]

Bomb blasts and stabbings continued in the city until the end of
July, further aggravating the situation and raising the death toll. At the
beginning of July the anti-reservation agitators, as well as the opposition Bharatiya Janata Party (BJP), demanded the immediate dismissal of
the Solanki government.[47] The BJP also protested against the government's failure to solve the problems caused by the government employees' strike. The party even launched a 'Madhavsinh hatao' programme
aimed at unseating Solanki, whereupon over 600 BJP workers were
arrested in Gandhinagar.[48] On 6 July Solanki resigned under pressure
from the Congress Party High Command. The party appointed Amarsinh
Chaudhary, an Adivasi, to the Chief Ministership. Chaudhary replaced
five Kshatriya ministers, members of the KHAM alliance, with members
of the Patel and Bania caste groups, trying to form a balance in the government between the backward and upper castes. The Director General
of the Central Reserve Police Force, Julio Ribeiro, took command of the
Gujarat police force.

Nonetheless, the long-awaited dismissal of Solanki failed to quell the
disturbances. More sectors joined the government employees' strike,
nearly paralysing the state administration. The students and parents
organisations announced a three-day 'jail *bharo*' programme, to begin on
19 July, but on 18 July the government and the anti-reservationists finally
reached an accord over the reservation issue. The government agreed
to abandon the 18 per cent increase of reservations for the SEBC and to
establish a commission that would look into the question of the 10 per cent
reservation for backward castes after 1988. The government also agreed
to set up a commission of inquiry into the police atrocities and to release,
without charge, all those who had been arrested in connection with the
anti-reservation agitation.[49] Even though the army had left Ahmedabad

[44] *TOI*, 21 June 1985.
[45] *The Shattering of Gujarat*, p. 19. The figure was compiled from newspapers.
[46] *Indian Express*, 22 June 1985.   [47] *TOI*, 1 July 1985.
[48] *The Shattering of Gujarat*, p. 20.
[49] *Ibid.*, p. 22. The anti-reservation leaders called off their protest only after the Chief
    Minister, Amarsinh Chaudhary, read out the agreement before the state assembly. A
    splinter group of the student body, which did not accept the accord, signed an agreement

the day before, after 117 days in the city, communal clashes persisted in the walled city and the eastern area. In Dariapur in the old city five people were killed by police fire and two were stabbed to death a day after the army left. On 22 July at least eight more people were killed in the area. Curfew was lifted only at the beginning of August. In mid-August the government reached a settlement with its employees, the strike was called off after seventy-three days and the agitation finally subsided.

The exact number of deaths and casualties is difficult to estimate, as neither the Report of the Dave Commission of Inquiry nor the newspapers or other sources presented a complete calculation of these figures. However, from the different sources it seems that approximately 220 people lost their lives. Property worth $1.75 billion was damaged or destroyed. From February to July 1985, the police in Ahmedabad city recorded 662 incidents and offences connected with the anti-reservation agitation and 743 connected with communal incidents.[50] According to the evidence and records presented to the Commission, Muslims were the main victims of the riots: 2,500 of their houses had been damaged, 1,500 shops had been burnt or looted, approximately 100 Muslims had been murdered, 400 stabbed, and hundreds severely injured. Around 12,000 Muslims had been rendered homeless and 900 had been arrested.

The description of the events, both in the newspapers and in the Report of the Commission of Inquiry into the riots, portrayed a spectacle of uncontrolled rage, destruction and at times the utter collapse of the rule of law and social order, particularly in Ahmedabad, but also in other parts of the state.[51] The waves of violence seemed to verge on anarchy. The various groups had to face long periods of curfew, and, at least apparently, the routine of everyday life was paralysed.

The next two chapters present two narrative explanations of the riots. The first captures the official accounts, as depicted in the Commission of Inquiry and government and police sources. The second narrative represents the personal accounts of the people who experienced the riots. The two accounts explore the conjunction between the caste-reservation crisis and communalism.

with the government at the end of the month. *TOI*, 20 July 1985 and 31 July 1985; *The Shattering of Gujarat*, pp. 22–3.

[50] *COI*, Vol. III, Annextures XXXVII and XXXVIII, pp. 439–40.

[51] The riots that erupted in Ahmedabad also affected the rest of Gujarat, with violent incidents occurring in other districts, mainly in Baroda (Vadodra) and Surat. See *COI*, pp. 158–91. An examination of the events in other areas in Gujarat is beyond the scope of this study.

3   The official account

> A sultan once saw a rabbit turn on an attacking dog, where the Kankaria
> lake now stands and this convinced him that it would be the ideal site
> to build a city – a place such as this, where even something as timid
> as a rabbit could fight a dog. That was the day that Ahmedabad was
> conceived in a vision of violence.[1]

Agitation against reservations policy for backward-caste Hindus in
Ahmedabad in 1985 escalated into communal violence between Hindus and Muslims. Religious issues, however, were ephemeral at the start
and throughout the riots. This fact makes it difficult to identify religion as
the primary source of the conflict. Moreover, a range of conflicts evolved
within the riots. Upper castes confronted the government in the streets
over the issue of reservations. Then communal riots erupted. The state
employees began a struggle against reservations in promotion of SCs and
STs. Some violence took place to settle scores and local enmities, which
were unrelated to the reservation and the communal riots. The police
agitated. There was a struggle to dismiss the government, which had just
won a clear majority in the elections. Since such diverse groups of people
participated in the riots, the collective violence cannot be ascribed to a
single group, class or religious community. The 1985 riots brought about
rapid shifts in social alliances, demonstrating the flexibility and fluidity
of caste and communal identities.

Two immediate puzzles emerge from the Ahmedabad riots of 1985.
First, how did the anti-reservation agitation turn into communal riots?
Second, what might explain the incapacity of the state to maintain law and
order and to contain the violence? This chapter presents the answers given
by the official views of the events, which attributed these events either to
a culture of violence or to manipulations of communal politicians. The
way bureaucrats, administrators, police officers, party and public representatives explained the riots, and the way the state's Dave Commission
of Inquiry related to these accounts and inferred its conclusions represent

[1] Esther David, *The Walled City*, Madras: Manas, 1997, pp. 189–90.

what will be termed the official views of the events. The official account corresponds to the conventional explanations of communal violence in both popular and scholarly writings. An examination of the events from the viewpoint of various government officials and policemen reveals the degree of incoherence and rivalry between various state bodies. In their practices, the various state apparatuses were informed by similar *a priori* notions, group prejudices and ahistorical understanding about various social groups and the relations between them. These shared beliefs mitigated the disparities and competing interests within the state and formed a common denominator, which held together the narrative of the official views. By capturing the official views of the events, the analysis throws light on the origins of the communalisation of the state. The conduct of the state apparatus responsible for maintaining law and order during the riots of 1985, as well as the views expressed in the state inquiry into the events, reveals the dynamics by which the violence endured and the state's communalised practices developed.

In the Dave Commission's official view, as expressed by the Police Commissioner and subsequently adopted by the Commission, Ahmedabad city and its residents were prone to violence: 'The entire walled-city is, thus, even now a volcanic crater ready to erupt a mass of communal lava. It is [a] highly volatile pocket where aggression by one community over the other is a cult developed . . . when members of both the communities attack one another under the façade of self defence.'[2] The Commission explained that,

by the end of 19th century, Ahmedabad came to be known as [the] Manchester of India and several textile mills had come up. Hence the labour from far and near migrated to Ahmedabad and it started assuming a cosmopolitan character and ever since then *the people of Ahmedabad became agitational minded.*[3]

The Commission reinforced this reasoning by suggesting that the city had had an old legacy of communal trouble ever since 1714, when riots had erupted during the Holi festival. It added that the Court's decision to open the Babri Masjid in Ayodhya in October 1984 had widened the gulf between Hindus and Muslims, but also affected Gujarat.[4] Thus, the Commission implied that Ahmedabad city and its people were culturally violent.[5]

---

[2] *COI*, Vol. I, p. 70. Also see G.W.-52, p. 52 and p. 141.

[3] *Ibid.*, p. 72 (emphasis added). Moreover, the Commission found 'it essential to mention that they [people of Ahmedabad] are also masterminded in spreading rumours'. *Ibid.*, p. 73.

[4] *Ibid.*, pp. 226, 269.

[5] *Ibid.*, pp. 225–6. These views were often repeated in the testimonies of state officials in the Commission's report.

Historical records provide no evidence for a history of sustained sectarian animosity between Hindus and Muslims in Ahmedabad.[6] Gillion's study of the history of the city argues that 'the communal problem has fortunately played only a small role in the history of Ahmedabad'.[7] From 1714 until 1969 Hindu–Muslim riots were recorded in the city in 1941 and 1946.[8] During partition, less than a year after the 1946 incidents, there were no riots in Ahmedabad. Even the Justice Reddy Commission of Inquiry into the Ahmedabad Communal Disturbances of 1969 argued that after partition:

> The people of Gujarat in general and those of Ahmedabad, in particular, were not prone to communal passions or excitement – both the Hindu and the Muslim community lived by and large in amity except in a few places here and there which had their own special reasons for communal disturbances.[9]

Paradoxically, the Dave Commission's attempt to introduce a historical perspective stands in contrast with its own reasoning about how 'the people of Ahmedabad became agitational minded'. It was precisely the expansion and growth of the city since the 1860s, the waves of migration of various populations, and thus the changes in its social composition, that made it implausible to delineate a uniform character of Ahmedabad dwellers as naturally prone to violence. Moreover, until the 1950s and 1960s most of the labour had come to the city from Ahmedabad district and the surrounding area. These processes heralded social conflicts and indeed had important effects on the city's social dynamics. But they contradict the Commission's own argument. The Commission presented an elaborate account of the cultural propensity of Ahmedabad's people to violence, but did not consider the social and economic circumstances of the events of 1985.

---

[6] See *Ahmedabad District Gazetteer*, Ahmedabad: Government of Gujarat, 1984, pp. 107–8 (generally, pp. 70–141).

[7] Kenneth L. Gillion, *Ahmedabad: A Study in Indian Urban History*, Berkeley and Los Angeles: University of California Press, 1968, p. 171. Yagnik and Seth argue that there was 'a steady distancing of the communities [Hindus and Muslims]' from the last decade of the nineteenth century. Achyut Yagnik and Suchitra Sheth, *The Shaping of Modern Gujarat: Plurality, Hindutva and Beyond*, New Delhi: Penguin Books, 2005, pp. 225, 193–224.

[8] *COI*, Vol. I, p. 69. Referring to the riots of 1941 in Ahmedabad in a letter to Dr Abraham Paul, Mahatma Gandhi wrote that 'it is likely that the riots had economic causes rather than religious'. *Collected Works of Mahatma Gandhi*, Vol. LXXX, p. 298. For more details on the 1941 riots see Yagnik and Seth, *The Shaping of Modern Gujarat*, pp. 219–20. In 1946 communal riots erupting on the Rath Yatra day were triggered by a scuffle between Muslim gymnasts who observed the procession and belittled the performance of the Hindu gymnasts. *COI*, Vol. I, pp. 69–70.

[9] Judge J. Reddy, *Report of the Commission of Inquiry: Ahmedabad Communal Disturbances (1969)*, Ahmedabad: Government of Gujarat, 1970, Chapter XVIII, p. 212.

Although the immediate cause of the eruption of the riots was the decision of the government to raise the quota of reservation for the backward castes, the Dave Commission considered the reservation issue, and the violence it generated, as a device, or a strategy, for accomplishing political goals. It commented on the opportunistic timing of the Congress government's announcement of the new policy.[10] The Commission insinuated that Solanki, who had contested the elections on the basis of the KHAM strategy, had wanted to expand and consolidate his support base, and thus to obtain electoral benefits in the forthcoming elections.[11] This point was substantiated by the way the Rane Backward Classes Commission Report, which formed the basis for the Gujarat government's new reservation policy, had been shelved for fourteen months.[12] The government had decided to implement it just prior to the elections. Solanki had reversed the Rane Report's core recommendation, insisting that caste and not occupation and income be the criterion for reservation. The Education Department had not been consulted about the decision to implement the Rane recommendation. This raised doubts about the sincerity of the government's policies on social justice and reservation in universities.[13] The Dave Commission of Inquiry into the riots of 1985 bolstered its claim that the Congress government was opportunistic over reservations by pointing out that the issue had been left unresolved for so long. After each commission on reservation submitted a report, its recommendations were either partly concealed, or shelved, but never fully implemented, and then, a new commission was invariably nominated. The Commission showed that even the existing reserved places for the Socially and Educationally Backward Classes (SEBC) were not fully utilised.[14]

The main allegations of political manipulation as a driving force behind the riots were levelled at the opposition. According to the state counsel and police, from the very early stages, the Akhil Bharatiya Vidyarthi Parishad (ABVP), a student wing of the BJP, had taken command of the agitation. The Commission of Inquiry argued that 'they were master minded in planning and its execution and, therefore, they simultaneously started damaging public property throughout the length and width of Gujarat'.[15] In the Commission's concluding opinion:

---

[10] *COI*, Vol. II, pp. 8–9, Vol. I, p. 223.

[11] 'He [Solanki] took the opportunity of implementing Rane Commission and thereby concentrating on 70% of the votes', *COI*, Vol. II, p. 9.

[12] See the discussion in Chapter 2.

[13] According to the Secretary in the Department of Education, the office was not consulted or informed in advance. *COI*, Vol. I, G.W.-2, p. 86. Also see p. 199.

[14] *Ibid.*, Vol. II, pp. 7–8. Also see Vol. I, p. 200.

[15] *Ibid.*, Vol. I, p. 269. Also see p. 209, G.W.-52, p. 139.

Motives of the agitation . . . [were] opposing the reservation policy but courses of events show that once the planning came in the hands of ABVP supported by BJP and VHP, further joined by Congress dissidents, and some other persons . . . the motive for continuance of the agitation and spreading the communal disturbances became the ouster of Shri Madhavsinh Solanki.[16]

The political dimension of the riots became more visible when, before polling day in Gujarat and after assurances from Prime Minister Rajiv Gandhi that the state's reservation policy would be reviewed after the assembly elections, the student organisation decided to call off the protest. After the elections the protest acquired a political tone, when it was alleged that Congressmen who had not been chosen as electoral candidates, and members of parties who found themselves in the opposition after the elections, lent their support to the upheaval.[17] The anti-reservation agitation could have come to an end on 18 March, when Solanki agreed to accept the students' demands. Yet, the ABVP had called for a *bandh* on that day, 'which resulted in out breaking [*sic*] [of] communal violence'.[18] Almost the same accord would end the riots four months later.

The question of the communal 'twist' that the agitation acquired from 18 March remained unclear. Indeed, communal clashes erupted on the day of the *bandh*, which was organised mainly by the ABVP. But, at that point groups that originally had no part in the student reservation dispute began to engage in the violence.[19] The opposition parties, mainly the BJP, claimed that the government itself was responsible for the eruption of communal riots in order to divert attention from the reservation issue. Rajiv Gandhi, the Congress Prime Minister, and the Gujarat government placed the entire blame on the opposition for the communal unrest in Ahmedabad. Rajiv Gandhi accused 'those who lost at the polls and have taken to the streets to strengthen themselves'.[20] Moreover, according to a Police Inspector from Dariapur, where communal riots first erupted, most of the Hindus in the area were followers of the BJP and members of the RSS.[21] These parties, as well as dissatisfied persons from Congress(I), 'played an important part to turn the

---

[16] *Ibid.*, Vol. II, p. 11. Also see Vol. I, p. 191.

[17] This claim was repeated in various testimonies submitted to the Commission of Inquiry by police and government workers. See, for example, *ibid.*, Vol. I, pp. 53, 60, 95, 101. The Commission also mentioned this factor. See *ibid.*, Vol. II, p. 9.

[18] *Ibid.*, Vol. II, p. 9.

[19] The second account of the riots in the following chapter reveals that many of those who began to take part in the violence were not even fully aware of the reservation issue.

[20] *The Hindu*, 30 March 1985. The same allegation was made by the then Chief Minister, Madhavsinh Solanki. *Interview* with Madhavsinh Solanki, Delhi, 18 March 1998.

[21] *COI*, Vol. I, p. 228.

anti-reservation agitation to communal riots'.[22] The involvement of right-wing Hindu organisations was repeatedly cited in the evidence submitted to the Commission. The Commission's account simply observed that 'the anti-reservation movement took a sudden communal turn'.[23] It emphasised the political factors and, despite the communal shift, argued that the conflict was not over religion, and that 'communalism is not caused by religious difference and that a religious person is not essentially a communal'.[24] But, '[r]eligion is becoming a means to have the power'.[25]

The Commission tried to address the shift from caste agitations to communal riots, but it did not find a meaningful link between the two. Although it considered various political aspects of the riots, the Commission's account for the transition in the riots from anti-reservation to communal agitation yielded to its own prior assumptions. Reviewing the large numbers of mosques and temples in the city, the Commission suggested that 'one is persuaded to feel that people of the town had and has a religious bent of mind'.[26] In addition to adopting an instrumental view about the link between religion and politics, the Commission also contended that 'it cannot be lost sight of that over religious people are prone to drift to be communalised [sic]'.[27]

It is significant that the Commission and the state's apparatuses dealt separately with the anti-reservation caste riots and the communal ones.[28] The dynamic of events was analysed as a zero-sum game: 'whenever there was an increase in the communal riots the incidents of crime due to anti-reservation agitation would come down'.[29] The police registered separately incidents and offences linked to anti-reservation agitation and those linked to communal riots. Before communal riots erupted in the city, the police had mainly classified the 'nature of crowd' in its records of anti-reservation incidents as a 'mob of agitators' and 'mob of anti-reservationists'.[30] After communal violence started, the police used the term 'Hindu agitators' more often and even specified the caste name of the offenders involved in the violence. In their statements, policemen also divided the events into two: 'the first period was about anti-reservation

---

[22] *Ibid.*, G.W.-12, p. 95. Also see the statement by the then Commissioner of Police, B. K. Jha. *Ibid.*, p. 232.

[23] *Ibid.*, p. 214. Also see G.W.-41, p. 129, p. 27. Although all the sources and the Commission were struck by the 'sudden' communal turn, the police recorded an incident 'in connection with communal disturbances [by] a mob of Hindus' as early as 15 March. *COI*, Vol. III, Annex XXXVI, p. 292.

[24] *Ibid.*, Vol. II, p. 14.   [25] *Ibid.*, p. 13. Also see p. 18.

[26] Ibid., Vol, I, p. 52.   [27] *Ibid.*, Vol. II, p. 14.

[28] Notably, most of the analyses of the riots in the newspapers and scholarship also distinguished between reservation and communal issues.

[29] *COI*, Vol. II, p. 10. Also see Vol. I, p. 222.   [30] *Ibid.*, Vol. III, pp. 158–90.

agitation while the second time there were communal riots'.[31] The course of events, as well as the police records of incidents, does not conform to such a division.[32] Remarkably, during the escalation in communal violence, from mid-April, which by that time was prevalent throughout the city, the anti-reservation mêlée, in the form of a caste war, was kept alive.

In its report the Commission made only one reference to the caste factor in the caste-communal riots. It identified connections between the right-wing Hindu groups, their involvement in the anti-reservation and communal agitation and their aspiration to undermine the Solanki ministry, with a specific social group: the 'Patels of Khaira district and north Gujarat'.[33] The Commission suggested that the Patels had lost political power with the rise of the KHAM alliance in the Congress Party. The victory of this coalition in the state election had heightened their frustration.

The incapacity of the government and the police to maintain law and order and to contain the violence became a subject considered by the Commission. According to considerable evidence that was brought before the Commission, the police were accused of inactivity and of committing atrocities against citizens. Police misconduct, therefore, had contributed to the continuation of the violence. Testimonies of both Hindus and Muslims claimed that many acts of arson, looting and killing on the night communal riots erupted in the Dariapur area had occurred in the presence of police forces. According to some evidence, the police themselves were responsible for creating hostility in harmonious neighbourhoods.[34] Moreover, some residents asserted that 'the police did not come to their rescue. On the contrary, policemen told that save yourself [sic].'[35]

The tension between the police and citizens heightened between 13 and 23 April, when the police appeared to become the perpetrators of violence. Affidavits of both Hindus and Muslims from Saraspur complained about the police's use of excessive force and false arrests during that time. One resident stated that he had been on his way back from work and that '[h]e is not even aware of the reasons for his arrest'.[36] In Khadia locality in the old city, residents accused the police of breaking into houses, damaging water taps and electricity transformers, and beating people, even though they had remained at home during curfew.[37]

---

[31] *Ibid.*, Vol. I, G.W.-18, pp.100–1.   [32] *Ibid.*, Vol. III, pp. 187–291, 295–434.

[33] *Ibid.*, Vol. II, p. 9.   [34] *Ibid.*, Vol. I, p. 268.

[35] *Ibid.*, S-80, p. 148. Also see S-70, S-73, S-78, p. 148.

[36] *Ibid.*, p. 236. For evidence of police violence against students during that time see Upendra Baxi, 'Reflections on the Reservations Crisis in Gujarat', in Veena Das (ed.), *Mirrors of Violence*, 1990, New Delhi: Oxford University Press, p. 231.

[37] *COI.*, Vol. I, pp. 237, 242.

About 50 police people armed with rifles, sticks, spades etc. came there. Those people were drunk and agitated. They wanted to show their might and force unnecessarily. They were using filthy language and asked to open the door of the pole. Having not been successful in doing so, they acted barberously [sic], broke open it and entered the pole. They fired at a person who was standing on the roof of his house who died.[38]

On 20 April the Gujarat High Court appointed a two-member fact-finding committee to inquire into the alleged police atrocities in different parts of Ahmedabad after receiving two petitions on the Khadia incidents two days earlier.

On the other side, police testimonies suggested that policemen had been attacked. With regard to the violence in Saraspur, the police recorded that 'the mob pelted stones at police and passing by police vehicles and injured of policemen [sic]'.[39] Policemen also claimed that the local Police Station had been attacked.[40] A Deputy Commissioner of Police argued that from 15 April, before the curfew, violence against the police in Khadia area had intensified. 'The mob used to throw stones, acid, petrol bombs and burning rags from the lanes and roof tops continuously . . . on the police.'[41]

Police violence intensified on 22 April after the killing of Head Constable Laxman Desai. On that day Desai had joined two security men who were accompanying the Inquiry Committee appointed by the Gujarat High Court to investigate allegations of police atrocities in the Khadia area. A Deputy Commissioner of Police who escorted the Committee sent the security men to bring army or police reinforcements to guard its members on their way out of Khadia, since the area had become 'packed with a huge crowd' and was deemed unsafe.[42] The reinforcement team was attacked on its way back to join the committee. Laxman Desai was injured and shortly after died in hospital. As news of his death spread, some of the messages transmitted through the police wireless were: 'Khadia has to be burnt down today . . . Policemen are angry. They want the army to get out of this area. Hand over this area to the police . . . Withdraw army from here . . . We have to attack Khadia. Take revenge . . . Rush to Gujarat Samachar to take revenge. They have incited people against the police. Gujarat Samachar will burn at midnight.'[43]

[38] *Ibid.*, S-190, p. 237.
[39] *Ibid.*, Vol. III, p. 212. The police claimed that three BJP leaders gave inflammatory speeches at Saraspur and instigated the people against the police. *The Shattering of Gujarat*, background paper Series 1985, no. 2, Bombay: BUILD Documentation Centre, 1985, p. 9.
[40] *COI*, Vol. I, G.W.-34, p. 236.   [41] *Ibid.*, G.W.-41, p. 238.   [42] *Ibid.*, p. 239.
[43] *Ibid.*, p. 241. This is part of the transcript of the taped wireless messages. The Commission produced in the report an edited transcript translated from Gujarati.

According to the Commission, the *Gujarat Samachar* daily had published detailed news of the anti-reservation and communal incidents 'with special reference to the conduct of the Police Officers and the Police force'.[44] The newspaper had claimed that 'the local police of Ahmedabad was dancing to the tune of the politicians much particularly Shri Madhavsinh Solanki'.[45] The government and the police, in their testimony before the Commission, alleged that the newspaper reported events in such a way as to 'incite the people's feeling against the Government more particularly against the police'.[46] The tension between the police and the *Gujarat Samachar* management dated back to May 1984, when the newspaper's editor had sent a telegram to the Press Council stating that 'for last several months Gujarat Samachar is not toeing the line of Gujarat government as it wants . . . hence politically planned crowd rushed near Gujarat Samachar Daily on 26th May night. Prevented dispatching its copies. Big police force present stood silent spectator.'[47] Moreover, on 19 March 1985 and 10 April 1985, in the face of threats, the editor wrote a letter to the Ahmedabad Commissioner of Police, asking for protection. The protection was not provided and on 22 April the Press was set on fire. The police did not even record the case.

During the large-scale communal violence that erupted in the eastern side of the city on that day, the police, according to numerous testimonies of Muslim residents, had aided the Hindu rioters and participated in the violence. In Bapunagar, outside 16 Block apartments, the police and their vehicles had stood in front of a 'crowd of 8,000–10,000 persons (Hindus) . . . who were armed with lathel [*sic*] weapons'.[48] When the crowd had started stoning the block, the residents of the locality had asked the police to call in the army, but the police did not do so. 'When the people asked for protection from the police the police instead opened fire on them.'[49] A woman resident described how her son had been shot to death by police.[50] The residents' affidavits claimed that Hindus had set on fire and looted houses, shops and garages in the presence of the police, which did nothing to stop them. Moreover, the policemen had supplied the rioters with petrol from their vehicles and told them that 'they were with them'.[51] On that evening, 'she and other persons ran for life [*sic*] to Aman Chowk', where some Muslims had set up a relief camp.[52] Many Muslims were attacked on their way to the camp. Rickshaw drivers were pulled out of their rickshaws and beaten. One Muslim

---

[44] *Ibid.*, p. 242.   [45] *Ibid.*   [46] *Ibid.* Also see p. 248.   [47] *Ibid.*, p. 243.
[48] *Ibid.*, P.W.1, p. 251. Also see: S-87, p. 253.
[49] *Ibid.*, P.W.5, p. 255, S-83, p. 252.   [50] *Ibid.*, P.W.1, p. 251.
[51] *Ibid.*, P.W.1, p. 252, S-83, S-87, S-116, S-120, S-125, P.W.6, pp. 252–5.
[52] *Ibid.*, P.W.1, p. 251.

described in his testimony how his wife had been murdered in the rick-shaw, in front of her family, while they were on their way to the camp.[53] Nearby, Hindu residents of the two-storey Anand Flats stoned the houses of Muslims in the adjacent Indira Garibnagar. In the early morning of 23 April some Hindus in police uniform set fire to a Muslim betel shop. 'Police fired on Muslims though the rioters were Hindus . . . They [police] were . . . inciting and instigating the persons staying in Anand Flats'.[54] A police inspector estimated that during this incident about 700 Mus-lim houses had been burnt and property worth Rs. 5.3 million belonging to Muslims had been destroyed.[55] Policemen denied that the police had connived with the Hindu rioters, but 'admitted that there was a mass killing of Muslims in this incident'.[56]

The Commission of Inquiry commented that '[r]egarding Indira Garibnagar incident, lesser the said better it is [sic]'.[57] The Commission concluded that the lives of Muslims in the area had been lost and their properties burnt because the police had been inactive and negligent. The events had taken place 'right under the nose of the Police Chowki and in presence of the Senior Officers'.[58] Similarly, the Commission noted that a Hindu family had been burnt alive in Dabgarward on 9 June 'despite a police point placed opposite to this house'.[59] Moreover, the Commission was 'firmly of the opinion that the police force was on the rampage after the murder of Laxmanbhai [Laxman Desai] and it was this *police mob* which set ablaze the Gujarat Samachar press'.[60] Police did not register the case because policemen were involved.[61] The Commission also con-firmed that the police had used excessive force and damaged properties in Khadia.[62] The Report of the Commission of Inquiry concluded that 'some officers . . . remained silent spectators and witnessed the poor and down trodden being beaten and humiliated. There [sic] hutments were set on fire in their presence.'[63] The Commission added briefly that the police also sided with Bungalow and Housing society owners, who were trying to force the poor out of their neighbourhoods.[64]

If, as the Commission explained, Ahmedabad's people were prone to violence and 'agitational minded', then the police conduct is not sur-prising. Moreover, the Commission's view corresponded with police

[53] *Ibid.*, P.W.6, p. 255. Also see S-87, S-125, pp. 253–4.   [54] *Ibid.*, S-114, p. 253.
[55] *Ibid.*, G.W.-33, p. 257, G.W.-41, p. 259.   [56] *Ibid.*, G.W.-33, p. 124.
[57] *Ibid.*, p. 259.   [58] *Ibid.*, pp. 269–70, Vol. II, p. 16.   [59] *Ibid.*, Vol. I, p. 261.
[60] *Ibid.*, p. 249 (emphasis added).   [61] *Ibid.*, pp. 250–1, 249, Vol. II, p. 17.
[62] *Ibid.*, Vol. I, p. 242. Also see *Shri Rasiklal N. Shah and Others* v. *State of Gujarat and Others*, in the High Court of Gujarat, Ahmedabad, Special Criminal Application No. 284, 29/4/1985.
[63] *COI*, Vol. II, p. 10, Vol. I, p. 270.   [64] *Ibid.*, Vol. II, p. 10.

attitudes, as these attitudes were expressed both in the police records and in testimonies by individual policemen. On the evening that communal violence erupted in the old city, policemen testified that they had arrived 'to *pacify the madness of the crowd*'. For that purpose they had used 'several rounds of tear gas shells, and when they were found to be not effective', they had opened fire.[65] The police used similar language in its records of incidents and offences linked with anti-reservation agitation, in which the agitators were repeatedly described as 'a mob', even if they were only eight people, or as a mob that 'formed unlawful assembly'.[66] A special directive issued by Ahmedabad Police Commissioner on 18 June instructed that '[a]ll bad characters and head-strong elements should be rounded up on the midnight of 19/20 June'.[67] The police's indiscriminate characterisation of the people who participated in the violence as 'unlawful' 'madness crowd', and its presumptions that some people were naturally bad, informed police practices. It is likely that precisely these classifications and this language concealed some of the factors underlying the enduring violence, and perhaps even complicated the role of the police. Likewise, the distinction that the police drew between the anti-reservation and the communal riots not only prevented them from discerning a link between these riots, but also contributed to obscuring their understanding of the events and to distorting their conduct.

Police violence was directed intermittently against various social groups, but more frequently against Muslims. In some of the incidents it appeared that police complicity in the violence was not related directly to the anti-reservation or communal riots. Rather, police misconduct, as well as the apparent inability to contain the violence, was linked more closely to various tensions between the police and different groups among the city's residents.

A closer look into the communal violence that erupted in Ahmedabad on 20 June, the day of the Rath Yatra and Id-Ul-Fitr festivities, indicates that at the start the dispute was not between Hindus and Muslims, but between Hindus and the police. The Rath Yatra procession traditionally departed from the Jagannath Temple in the Jamalpur area of the old city of Ahmedabad.[68] During the procession three wooden chariots carrying the figures of Lord Krishna, his sister Subhdra and his elder brother Balbhadra were pulled along a specific route within the walled city. Sadhus, akhadas gymnasts, musical bands, elephants and trucks with devotees accompanied the procession. According to the then Police Commissioner

---

[65] *Ibid.*, Vol. I, G.W.-12, p. 93 and p. 226 (emphasis added).
[66] *Ibid.*, Vol. III, Annex XXXV, pp. 159–291.   [67] *Ibid.*, Vol. I, G.W.-52, p. 264.
[68] There are records of the Rath Yatra procession in Ahmedabad from 1884. *Ibid.*, p. 262.

of Ahmedabad, the trustees of the temple had agreed in early June to his request to cancel the procession that year in the face of the agitation. Nevertheless, since a large number of devotees were expected to visit the temple on the Rath Yatra day, the Police Commissioner instructed, among other precautions, to erect strong barricades to regulate the entry and exit of the devotees. Yet, 'the Rath Yatra procession was forcibly taken out in defiance of the prohibitory orders. All security arrangement made . . . to prevent the Chariots from being taken out went hay-wire.'[69] The Commission presented, on the basis of a video film that documented the events, 'the strategy chalked out before, as to how the orders would be defied and . . . that no police and army could stop the religious procession'.[70] A large number of the temple's long-horned cows were let loose on the numerous policemen, standing at the entrance gate of the temple. Then elephants pushed the police vehicles, which were parked to form an additional cordon to prevent the chariots from leaving the temple. The Commission claimed that 'it could be nothing but a pre-planned training [of] the elephants'.[71] It described 'how jubilant the Sadhus were on defying the orders' and how upon returning from the procession they 'were feeling so jubalant [sic] as if they had won a battle'.[72]

When the Rath Yatra procession began, the Hindu devotees chanted slogans against the government and called for Solanki's dismissal.[73] The procession advanced peacefully until it reached Saraspur, where it traditionally stopped for a brief halt. At this point, the Additional Commissioner of Police asked the temple's trustees not to take the procession through Prem Darwaja into the 'communally sensitive' areas,[74] which the army controlled at the time. Although the temple trustees agreed, the procession went through the gate in spite of the army's efforts to prevent its entry. Hindus began shouting provocative slogans at the Muslims. The customary chant 'Jai ranchor makhan chor' (Oh Lord Krishna, the thief of butter milk), was changed to 'Jai ranchoer mia chor (Oh, Muslims are thieves)' and 'Musliman ka ek sthan, Pakistan ya kabristan' (The Muslims have one place, either Pakistan or the graveyard).[75] Both sides started throwing stones and bricks and the army resorted to firing, killing six people.

In some cases the labelling of the violence as communal or anti-reservation enabled the police to cover up their own complicity in the violence. In Ambedkarnagar, according to the case the Dalit Panther

---

[69] *Ibid.*, p. 264 (affidavit of B. K. Jha, then Police Commissioner of Ahmedabad).
[70] *Ibid.*, p. 266.   [71] *Ibid.*   [72] *Ibid.*, pp. 266–7.
[73] *Ibid.*, p. 265; *India Today*, 15 July 1985.
[74] *COI*, Vol. I, p. 265.   [75] *Ibid.*, Vol. I, p. 266.

Party presented before the Commission, the police had not provided protection when 260 houses of scheduled castes were burnt to ashes on 22 April.[76] The police had registered the incident in its records of offences in connection with anti-reservation agitation.[77] The Commission of Inquiry went to the locality to study the incident and concluded that 'it was a fight for the supremacy of boot-legging which has been given a colour of violence due to anti-reservation agitation'.[78] The children of the residents in the locality were not 'studying in schools or colleges and, therefore, the reservation policy has no meaning for them . . . Certain anti-social elements of both the sides were carrying on anti-social activities including the bootlegging and had the patronage of both the police and the politicians.'[79] This case led the Commission to suggest that:

There is evidence to show that anti-reservation agitation provided an opportunity to some police officers for shirking the responsibilityies [sic] in investigating the cases properly and bringing the crimes to book. The cases have been registered as cases of Arson and Looting by anti-reservationists or pro-reservationists or vice-versa but in fact it all appeared to an eye wash.[80]

Some allegations about the link between the police, politicians and so-called anti-social elements were brought before the Commission. The BJP claimed that 'the police department had become the political arm in the hands of the government' and that Solanki was 'assisted by anti-social elements and associated them with autonomous bodies, assemblies of committees and boards'.[81] According to the case presented by the Nagrik Sangthan, in the Dariapur and Kalupur areas 'hired gundas operated and people were paid a fixed amount for stabbing and another amount for a murder . . . communal trouble was manoeavered [sic] by political leaders by hiring gundas'.[82] This testimony suggested that some anti-social elements received protection for their anti-social activities from political parties, and at the same time assisted the poor. Some analyses of the riots of 1985 similarly suggested that bootleggers, smugglers, drug dealers and local *dada*s took this opportunity to 'plunder and loot'.[83]

---

[76] *Ibid.*, p. 56.   [77] *Ibid.*, Vol. III, Annex XXXV, p. 242.

[78] *Ibid.*, Vol. II, p. 16. Bootleggers are traders of illicit liquor (alcohol is prohibited in Gujarat).

[79] *Ibid.*, p. 11.   [80] *Ibid.*, pp. 10–11.   [81] *Ibid.*, Vol. I, p. 60.   [82] *Ibid.*, p. 58.

[83] Ali Asghar Engineer, 'From Caste to Communal Violence', *Economic and Political Weekly*, 13 April 1985, pp. 628–9. Also Patel, 'Debacle of Populist Politics', pp. 681–2; Howard Spodek, 'From Gandhi to Violence: Ahmedabad's 1985 Riots in Historical Perspective', *Modern Asian Studies*, vol. 23, no. 4, 1989, p. 769; John R. Wood, 'Reservations in Doubt: The Backlash against Affirmative Action in Gujarat', in Ramashray Roy and Richard Sisson (eds.), *Diversity and Dominance in Indian Politics*, Vol. II, London: Sage, 1990, p. 162.

The Dave Commission did not discuss the nature of relations between the police, politicians and anti-social elements. Some of the findings of the Miyanbhai Commission of Inquiry Report on Prohibition Policy in Gujarat shed more light on this issue.[84] According to the *Miyanbhai Report*, bootleggers 'play an important role in the state's political life, especially in the local unit, or state or central government elections. By spending huge funds for religious and social activities, they have expanded their circle of influence among the voters of their own areas . . . candidates standing for elections vie for favour of these persons, so that they would promote them and urge the voters to elect them.' Furthermore, 'the police are hand in glove with the illicit liquor businessmen', and 'bribery and corruption prevail in the executing agencies'.[85] Notably, after the Director General of the Central Reserve Police Force, Julio Ribeiro, took command over the Gujarat police force in July, he stated that 'the police force here has been ruined due to heavy politicisation. Every transfer used to take place at the behest of politicians. Police officers were pressurised to do what politicians wanted.'[86] In his autobiography, Ribeiro stated that corrupt police officers in Ahmedabad regularly received large sums of illegal money from bootleggers. At the station level, police officers were reluctant to carry out Ribeiro's orders to arrest bootleggers who 'were friends of different ministers and [the police officers] would have to face their wrath'.[87]

Police malpractice and its adverse outcomes on law and order became part of the course of events of the 1985 riots. In some cases, the Commission of Inquiry went so far as to refer to the police as a mob. The behaviour of the police as reflected in the preceding account suggests that, at least during the riots, there was not always a clear distinction between violators of the law and its purported guardians. This leads to the question of how law and order were normally perceived and experienced. A Nagrik Sangthan witness to the Commission described the working conditions of the State Reserve Police (SRP): the temporary SRP posts throughout the walled city had been set up in tents, for example, in residential neighbourhoods and at busy intersections. Since the SRP posts did not have sanitary arrangements the policemen depended on the people in the

---

[84] The Miyanbhai Commission of Inquiry, appointed in order to 'examine all the aspects of the present policy of prohibition adopted by the state', submitted its report in 1983. Judge N. M. Miyanbhai, *Report of the Commission of Inquiry into the Prohibition Policy in Gujarat* (henceforth *Miyanbhai Report*), Ahmedabad: Government of Gujarat, 1983.
[85] *Ibid.*, pp. 30, 32.   [86] *India Today*, 31 August 1985.
[87] Julio Ribeiro, *Bullet for Bullet: My Life as a Police Officer*, Delhi: Penguin Books, 1998, pp. 258, 256.

localities for some of their basic needs.[88] Additionally, the SRP were not
provided with means of transport or communication, such as wireless, so
the residents felt less secure with the SRP than they did with the presence
of the army.[89] The functioning of the police was therefore largely determined by the contingencies of the local context in which they worked.
The basic autonomy, which the police required in order to assert authority on behalf of the state and to fulfil its duties, did not properly exist.
Hence, the official meaning and purpose of the rule of law was apparently
distinct from the police's everyday practice in the localities.

While policemen sometimes acted tyrannically during the riots, their
authority was sometimes contested, subjected to scrutiny and undermined by other state bodies and by the people. The army's intervention
challenged police command over parts of the city. The Ahmedabad Police
Commissioner suggested in his testimony before the Commission that the
'[a]rmy should not be inducted for quelling communal riots'.[90] Already at
the beginning of April, after the anti-reservationist students complained
that police had damaged houses and attacked women during a protest in
Asarwa Chakla, Ahmedabad's District Magistrate ordered that all police
documents regarding this incident should be produced before the court.
The court also appointed a court commissioner to record the damage
done to the property of twenty-four families listed in the complaint.

Power struggles also evolved between the Gujarat government and
other state institutions in their efforts to quell the agitation. Inconsisten-
cies between the Gujarat government and the government at the centre
emerged, for example on 16 April, when the army was called into the
old city for the second time. Only six hours before the army took up
its positions, Gujarat Home Minister, Amarsinh Chaudhary, declared
that the government did not want to call in the army. Government decisions were also challenged in the court. During the strike of junior doctors in Ahmedabad the government began interviewing new doctors for
the government civil hospital, but the Gujarat High Court stayed the
process.[91] At the same time, the state government asserted control by
different means. The Gujarat government issued the Anti-social Activities Prevention Ordinance, which empowered it, beyond the National
Security Act, to detain people for a maximum period of one year on the
basis of their past record of anti-social activity, without the necessity of a
witness.[92] Some of Ahmedabad's citizens felt themselves trapped in the

---

[88] *COI*, Vol. III, Annexture VIII, pp. 25–6; Vol. I, p. 57.   [89] *Ibid.*, Vol. I, p. 57.
[90] *Ibid.*, G.W.-52, p. 141.   [91] *The Shattering of Gujarat*, p. 8.
[92] The government issued the Ordinance by 25 May. *The Shattering of Gujarat*, p. 15.

context of inter-contestations within and among the state apparatuses. Thus, the state became partly culpable for the deterioration of law and order.

The persistence of the violence and the occasional collapse of the machinery of law enforcement led the police to shift responsibility for the maintenance of law and order onto the people. A Deputy Commissioner of Police told the Commission of Inquiry that:

[W]hen the genesis of the riot is beyond the control of the police force and is an outcome of surcharged atmosphere, the ultimate answer is that it is only the people of the locality and the respectable persons from both the communities i.e. minorities and Hindus who should take the assistance of the people to make the people understand.[93]

The Commission recommended that '[t]here must be constituted strong Maholla committees of persons considered high-minded and able to influence all sections of the community in that Maholla and whose duty it would be to see that conditions are not created which will disrupt the harmony of the residents'.[94] Similarly, a recent study of communal violence, which also examined Ahmedabad, concluded that the fundamental reason for riots does not lie in the policing or administrative factors. 'It is the environment of a peaceful city that makes the police and administration perform its law-and-order functions better, irrespective of biases or the level of professionalism . . . a communally integrated place is simply better policed and administered.'[95]

Various studies of the Ahmedabad riots of 1985 have concurred with the official views surveyed above, attributing the events, at least partly, to Ahmedabad's proclivity for communal riots and the 'background of a normal structural violence, embodied in every-day life in Gujarat'.[96] Similarly, in consonance with the Commission's account, the reservation issue, which triggered the riots, was generally viewed as a device utilised by Solanki in order to expand and consolidate his support base before the elections and was not explored in relation to the communal escalation in the riots. The persistent violence was seen as a means of destabilising the

---

[93] *COI*, Vol. I, G.W.-41, p. 258.   [94] *Ibid.*, Vol. II, p. 25.

[95] Ashutosh Varshney, *Ethnic Conflict and Civic Life: Hindus and Muslims in India*, New Haven: Yale University Press, 2002, p. 289. Also see pp. 222, 277, 288. This study's view of the means of preventing communal riots is similar to the Commission's suggestions. Varshney's analysis of communal violence in Bhiwandi contradicts his own argument and indicates the important role of the state in maintaining communal peace. *Ibid.*, pp. 293–5.

[96] Baxi, 'Reflections on the Reservations Crisis in Gujarat', p. 215. Spodek discusses the phenomenon of violence in urban areas in general, and claims that in Ahmedabad it has been endemic. Spodek, 'From Gandhi to Violence', p. 766.

newly elected government.[97] Particularly since violence was unleashed against the communities that had won the elections with a large majority, these explanations might imply that the masses were simply manoeuvred by politicians. Contrary to the official views, some scholars have emphasised the economic context of the riots – the increasing unemployment and declining textile mills.[98]

Scholars who examined the caste conflict over the reservations and the mobilisation of sections of the scheduled castes and backward castes in relation to the violence have noted the growing conflict between the Patels and the generally backward Kshatriyas. Some suggested that the powerful landowning Patels, who were politically dominant in the Congress before independence, became hostile to the party which, having adopted the KHAM strategy, excluded them from the centre of political power.[99]

The link between the caste-reservation issue and communalism was not considered. The reservation issue was 'the new frontier in Indian politics in the 1980s'.[100] The anti-reservation disputes from the end of the 1970s in Gujarat and elsewhere in India were related to processes of mobilisation among the lower castes and an expression of antagonisms between castes.[101] At the junction of increasing caste cleavages among Hindus, an all-Hindu communal consolidation began to emerge. The failure to consider a meaningful link between the caste-reservation issue and communalism takes communalism for granted and leaves the shift in the political relevance of social identities that occurred in the mid-1980s unexplained.

On the one hand, the failure of the backward castes to resist the anti-reservationists may suggest that their social mobilisation had been rather limited. On the other hand, if the electoral success of the backward classes did not reflect their social power, and the reservation quotas were not even

[97] Kohli, *Democracy and Discontent*, Cambridge: Cambridge University Press, 1990, pp. 263–4; Sujata Patel, 'The Ahmedabad Riots, 1985: An Analysis', Surat: *Reports-Papers*, Centre for Social Studies, 1985, p. 11; Baxi, 'Reflections on the Reservations Crisis in Gujarat', p. 222.

[98] Patel, 'The Ahmedabad Riots, 1985, p. 96; Patel, 'Collapse of Government', *Economic and Political Weekly*, 27 April 1985, pp. 681–2; Patel, 'Nationalism, TLA and Textile Workers, *Economic and Political Weekly*, 7 December 1985, pp. 2154–5.

[99] See Subrata Mitra, 'The Perils of Promoting Equality: The Latent Significance of the Anti-Reservation Movement in India', *Journal of Commonwealth and Comparative Politics*, vol. 25, no. 3, 1987, pp. 298–303; Ganshyam Shah, 'Strategies of Social Engineering: Reservation and Mobility of Backward Communities in Gujarat', in Ramashray Roy and Richard Sisson (eds.), *Diversity and Dominance in Indian Politics*, vol. II, New Delhi: Sage Publications, 1990, pp. 111–45; Shah, 'Caste Sentiments, Class Formation and Dominance in Gujarat', in Francine R. Frankel and M. S. A. Rao (eds.), *Dominance and State Power in Modern India*, Vol. II, Delhi: Oxford University Press, pp. 59–114; Kohli, *Democracy and Discontent*, pp. 241–51.

[100] Mitra, 'The Perils of Promoting Equality', pp. 308, 293–4.   [101] *Ibid.*, p. 303.

filled, why did forward castes feel so anxious about lower- and backward-caste mobilisation? Indeed, Solanki's ministry did not pursue economic reforms for the benefit of the poor, but accelerated economic liberalisation.[102]

During the 1985 riots, after every government concession towards the anti-reservationists, violence continued. This suggests that the uproar over the increase in the reserved quotas manifested deeper, as well as disparate, social conflicts. The Commission's findings also indicate that some of the violent incidents were actually local riots within the official riot that were unrelated to the reservation dispute or the communal violence.

The official views of the riots disclosed some of the presuppositions and attitudes that parts of the state apparatus held towards various groups in the society – for instance, that some groups, such as over-religious people, were prone to violence. The communal shift in the riots was to be explained both by the police, in their testimonies before the Commission of Inquiry, and the Commission on the basis of an *a priori* Hindu–Muslim divide.[103] Indeed, it seems superfluous to search for the social origins of the riots if the people were considered to be 'agitational minded' by nature. Therefore, it is also not surprising that the state, in its final account, laid responsibility for the prevention of riots on the people.

The official account disclosed how the state apparatuses, rather than operating an 'effective pattern of conflict management' for maintaining institutional and state power in the context of communal violence,[104] formed a fractured body of institutions, which were intermittently challenging one another. This account exposed the limitations of the state: the attitudes of the various state institutions, as well as their indiscriminate language and use of classifications, obscured, sometimes purposefully, the authorities' understanding of the events and hindered their function. In fact, despite different perspectives and inner fragmentation, the state apparatuses established a relatively coherent set of assumptions about the society they governed and particular social groups within it. Drawing on these assumptions, the official views appeared to provide a coherent narrative explanation. Yet, its explanations for the main puzzle of the riots – why the anti-reservation dispute escalated into a communal one – were

---

[102] See *Interview* with Madhavsinh Solanki, Delhi, 16/3/98; Kohli, *Democracy and Discontent*, pp. 241–51; *India Today*, 31 July 1985.

[103] See *COI*, Vol. I, pp. 70, 52; Vol. II, pp. 13–14.

[104] See Paul Brass, 'The Strong State and the Fear of Disorder', in Francine R. Frankel, Zoya Hasan, Rajeev Bhagava and Balveer Arora (eds.), *Transforming India: Social and Political Dynamics of Democracy*, Oxford: Oxford University Press, 2000, p. 65; Brass, *Theft of an Idol*, Princeton, NJ: Princeton University Press, 1997.

not satisfactorily explained. The official account leads to the conclusion that it is not useful to understand the riots as though their impetus lay simply in a Hindu–Muslim conflict. The account of the riots in the following chapter attempts to address the unresolved questions from a different perspective. It examines the tensions among Hindus more closely, on the basis of other sources, in order to understand the conditions under which the communal turn in the riots occurred. It seeks to provide a deeper understanding of the various social categories, their interaction, meaning and effects.

4　The 'living text', or, the riots within the riot

This second account of the riots forms an attempt to find another path of interpretation for the shift in the riots from anti-reservation agitation to communal violence and for the collapse of law and order in the city. It does so by examining the moments of crisis of 1985 at the local level, in relation to the social circumstances of people who experienced the riots and on the basis of their oral accounts of the events. In interviews, people recounted at length their own and their families' circumstances at the time, something the official views did not account for. The chapter also aims to unravel the social contexts within which the shift in the political relevance of identities from caste to communalism took place, from the mid-1980s.

A reading of the events at the local level through the experiences of those who actually participated in them suggests that there can be no single coherent account, or vernacular explanation of the Ahmedabad riots. Oral testimonies suggest that there was much more to the riots than a simple shift from caste-reservations to communalism caused by political manipulation or a historical disposition to violence. Riots had different contents and were experienced differently in the various parts of the city. What are known as the riots of 1985 were in fact made up of numerous smaller riots that broke out among the diverse populations of the 'three cities of Ahmedabad' – the walled city, the eastern industrial belt, and the western city. The implications of peoples' experiences of the riots will inform the analysis of the making of ethnoHinduism in the next part of the book.

The walled city

The Dariapur area, where the communal turn in the riots occurred, is a socially mixed locality within the old city of Ahmedabad, where the communities of upper-caste Hindus, Dalits and Muslims resided in separate localities. It is the densest ward in the city.[1] Vadigam is an upper-caste locality of Patels and Brahmins within Dariapur. Its borders are marked by the circular road between Dariapur gate and Prem Darwaza on one side and by the Muslim vicinity of Naginapol on the other. Nearby, opposite its entrance gate, reside Dalits. The residential and architectural structure of Vadigam is typical of Ahmedabad's old city. Its three-storey houses form a complex surrounding of fortifications, and the massive wooden gate at the entrance, especially when closed, guards Vadigam like a fort. Its inner part consists of a labyrinth of pols. Protected by their own gates, these micro-neighbourhoods make Vadigam a miniature city within the Dariapur area.

Morji Parekh pol within Vadigam consists of a narrow lane shaded by tightly packed dilapidated three- and four-storey houses. In 1997–98, when I conducted my research there, a blackboard that functioned as a public notice board was still set up outside the pol's wide-open wooden gate. Another blackboard and a small temple marked the entrance to the pol. Some of the pol's houses shared a wall with the adjacent Muslim houses of Naginapol. In 1985 it was populated by Brahmins and Patels. For example, Ramesh's Brahmin family came from Kheda district and had settled in Ahmedabad at the turn of the twentieth century. He had worked as a supervisor in the weaving department of Rohit mills, but after 1980 he started a small business in his house. He explained that:

After 1980 problems started between the Majoor Mahajan [TLA] and the mill-owners. So, the mill-owners split the mills and started small factories. First, only *badli* majdoor [temporary workers] worked there and later also those who lost their jobs with the closure of the mills. Their income drastically fell and they had to work 14 hours a day. The mill-owners realised that permanent workers cost them a lot.[2]

Sonaben, a local resident, defined herself as a 'native Ahmedabadi'. Her family had resided in Morji Parekh pol since 1942:

Economically, we were always medium class. Since 1980 I started a small industry of embroidery in the house. After the mills began to close the elder people could not get new jobs and many were unemployed. We had to sustain ourselves. Some became rickshaw drivers and others started small businesses and *paan* shops.[3]

Sunil's family settled in the pol in 1965. This Brahmin family of four brothers and four sisters came to Ahmedabad from another district, where

---

[1] The density in Dariapur in the late 1980s was 92,882 persons per sq. km; see *City Election Wards (Population Area & Density)* [map], Ahmedabad Municipal Corporation, Ahmedabad, 1991.

[2] *Interview* with Ramesh, Vadigam, Ahmedabad, 21/3/98.

[3] *Interview* with Sonaben, Vadigam, Ahmedabad, 26/3/98.

they had a small snack shop, in quest of a better livelihood. The family owned the house in Morji Parekh and the four brothers and their families lived there together, using separate kitchens. Sunil said that 'during the 1980s we and most of the people in Vadigam faced economic difficulties. Some were unemployed. Then many became rickshaw drivers, opened *paan* shops or became hawkers with a *lari* or a *galla*.'[4] The elder brother worked in a mill that was not closed; the other brothers became rickshaw drivers, but only one of them owned a rickshaw. Another resident of Morji Parekh, Dhansukh, was a tailor whose family had moved to the pol in 1967. They paid low rent, since the landlord used to be his client and they had got the house 'through personal relations'. Dhansukh defined his family as lower-middle-class. Like his pol-fellows, he explained that 'after the closure of the textile mills there was a problem of unemployment for a few months, but the main difficulty was the loss of income'.[5]

The upper-caste residents of Morji Parekh, and Vadigam in general, saw themselves as indigenous Ahmedabadies and defined themselves, in 1985, as middle- and lower-middle-class. Typically, the people lived in extended families, each floor allocated to one son and his immediate family, who often used a separate kitchen. Within the Patel caste hierarchy in Ahmedabad, the Patels of Vadigam were considered lower in status. Most people in the locality attested that they were reasonably well-off economically at that time. The majority of them used to work in the nearby textile mills, mainly in clerical jobs or as supervisors in the weaving and spinning departments. Although they were labourers in the textile mills, they saw themselves as middle-class; in conversations they referred to their mill mates from the eastern side of the city as labourers. The collapse of the composite textile mills from the early 1980s and the shifting of industrial activity to the eastern periphery of Ahmedabad severely affected them and the overall economy of the walled city. Many were able to secure jobs in the emerging powerloom factories with the closure of the mills, but their income fell dramatically and they had to work longer hours to sustain their livelihood. Some became rickshaw drivers and others started small businesses. By 1985, the most significant change for them was the decline in their social and economic position.

In interviews conducted in 1997–98, residents of Vadigam, as well as people in other Hindu localities of the old city, did not initially remember the anti-reservation agitation. They only recalled the communal riots.

---

[4] *Interviews* with Sunil and Ashwin, Vadigam, Ahmedabad, 31/3/85. This is also verified by the interviews with unemployed mill workers in Manish Jani, *Textile Worker: Jobless and Miserable* (a report based on interviews with workers of textile mills closed in Ahmedabad), Ahmedabad: SETU, 1984.

[5] *Interview* with Dhansukh, Vadigam, Ahmedabad, 26/3/98.

When they were reminded of the reservation issue, they identified it
as either the '*roti* (bread) riots', or as the upheaval against Gujarat's
government: 'Gujarati people started agitation against Solanki';[6] 'it was
a political game by Solanki'.[7] They claimed that the reservation issue
had no effect on them, as many of the families could not even afford to
educate all their children: 'I could not give education to all the kids for
better jobs.'[8] Most interviewees believed that the riots had erupted as a
result of the Rath Yatra religious procession, even though the procession
had taken place four months after the agitation started and three months
after communal riots first erupted in the city. Alternatively, and often after
realising that this assumption was inaccurate, many residents in the area
explained that the communal riots had started after Muslims had slaugh-
tered a cow of the Saryusdasji Mandir (temple) near Vadigam.[9] However,
this incident was alleged to have taken place two months after communal
riots had erupted in the area. A pamphlet on the incident was circulated
by the Hindu Yuvak Mandal in Ahmedabad during the riots:

**The Cow of the Temple Decapitated: Its Head Thrown in the Temple at
Dariapur**[10]

This horrifying act of desecration was committed by the Muslims on 13–05–
1985. The Saryudasji Temple is situated in the Prem Darwaza, and one of the
cows of the Temple, named 'Jasola' was beheaded by the Muslims from Jijiwada
who left its bleeding head lying at the Temple Gate. They also wrote a message
in its blood, 'the Hindus are Kafirs and pigs'. When the head of the cow was
spotted in the morning, it was being eaten up by street dogs. A complaint was
filed about this in the Dariapur police station, and later three Muslims were
arrested also. But they were released due to influential connections. We Hindus
consider cows as Mothers as sacred too. Muslims have killed one such cow. Now
it is the time to awaken, and to take revenge of this cruel deed of the Muslims by
beating them to death. To kill the demons in the guise of Muslims who perform
such cruel deeds to behead a sacred cow, is our real religion (Dharma) and

---

[6] *Interview* with Sonaben, Vadigam, Ahmedabad, 26/3/98.
[7] *Interview* with Ramesh, Vadigam, Ahmedabad, 21/3/98.
[8] *Interviews* with Bhartiben, Vadigam, Ahmedabad, 31/3/98; Sunil, Vadigam, Ahmedabad,
  31/3/98.
[9] *Interviews* with Ramesh, Vadigam, Ahmedabad, 21/3/98; Bhagirath, Vadigam, Ahmedabad, 26/3/98; Saurabh, Vadigam, Ahmedabad, 26/3/98; Sunil, Vadigam, Ahmedabad,
  31/3/98.
[10] A pamphlet published by the Hindu Yuvak Mandal, a local Hindu youth organisation
  near Sarkhej Roja and circulated in Ahmedabad during the riots, SETU Archive Files,
  Ahmedabad. According to Police records a pamphlet in connection with the slaughter
  of a cow was circulated on 13 May 1985. Judge V. S. Dave's, *Report of the Commission of
  Inquiry: Into the Incidents of Violence and Disturbances which Took Place at Various Places in
  the State of Gujarat since February, 1985 to 18th July, 1985* (henceforth *Commission*, and
  COI in references), Government of Gujarat, Ahmedabad, April 1990, Vol. III, Annex
  XXXVI, p. 376.

sacred duty. There is no sin in killing people like them, even the sacred Gita vouchsafes.

SO FORGET ALL YOUR DIFFERENCES AND UNITE!

Read this pamphlet, give to others to read, print it and make others print it: for it is a sacred duty of a Hindu; by doing his duty he will get his Moksha.

The police records contain an unclear reporting of the disappearance of a cow of the temple: 'a cow of Saryudas temple was missing . . . and on 14–5–1985 one dog came near temple with the mouth of cow in his jaw (mounth) [*sic*]. [T]emple authority identified it and missing cow went in Naginapole and Muslims slaughter the cow and religious pain to Hindus [*sic*].'[11] A Police Inspector mentioned this complaint in his testimony before the Commission of Inquiry.[12] The Commission noted the report of such an incident in a single brief comment, and referred to a similar alleged case as an 'incident of a rumour'.[13] Nevertheless, the story was widely remembered and even retold as a provocation that had triggered the beginning of communal violence in the city. Thus, a sectarian clash between Hindus and Muslims dominated the remembrances of ordinary peoples in the old city. They initially failed to remember the caste dispute.

When reminded of the moment of the turn in the riots from caste-reservations to communalism, people from Vadigam stated that:

On 18 March there was a programme of sounding of Mryutghant [death knell] against reservation. At 8 PM everybody went on the roofs to 'play' their thali dishes. The noise was very loud. At that time police was not in the area, and in its absence the fighting started. It began with stone throwing and then missile, kakada.[14]

The riots started from a mischief between boys, and then it became a snowball. We [people of the pol] functioned as a military, co-operated as an army regiment. At a certain point we have started to dismantle bricks and stones from the road for weapons. The women helped to lift them up to the roofs. The kerosene for the burning rags and cloths was available as many of us were by then rickshaw drivers.[15]

---

[11] *COI*, Vol. III, pp. 374–5.   [12] *Ibid.*, Vol. I, G.W.-12, p. 94.   [13] *Ibid.*, pp. 228, 229.

[14] *Interview* with Sonaben, Vadigam, Ahmedabad, 26/3/98. The same account of the 18 March events was reiterated in interviews with Sunil, Vadigam, Ahmedabad, 31/3/98; Dhansukh, Vadigam, Ahmedabad, 26/3/98; Saurabh, Vadigam, Ahmedabad, 26/3/98. Only one person claimed that 'when the bells were ringing, the people from Naginapol started to throw stones because they thought it was against them'. *Interview* with Ramesh, Vadigam, Ahmedabad, 21/3/98, 22/3/98.

[15] *Interview* with Sunil, Vadigam, Ahmedabad, 31/3/98. Also, *Interview* with Dhansukh, Vadigam, Ahmedabad, 26/3/98

Residents of Morji Parekh pol remembered vividly the fighting with the neighbouring Naginapol and the sense of solidarity in their pol. They also recalled the involvement of politicians and the police in the turmoil:

On the 18th morning, Bajap [BJP] and Vishwa Hindu Parishad [VHP] people came and organised that roof programme. They announced it with a loudspeaker, and wrote a notice in every pol's blackboard and on the main one. Bajap people said that the Muslims are organising themselves against us. They give shelter to foreign elements to fight us. Don't be afraid of them, protect yourself, be prepared.[16]

Then the fights started police gave us support. They came on our terraces and helped us because we were Hindus.[17]

While boasting of the help given to them by the police, some people from Vadigam also cited the police's role in the escalation of the violence:

The local police not only joined, but later they started their own agitation. If police wanted, they could stop it, but they did not because of their personal selfishness, because they were not getting their *hapto* [bribe]. It is a result of deterioration of politics. Even the British government was better.[18]

The description of the events of 18 March by the Muslim residents of the neighboring Naginapol was similar to the accounts given by the Hindu aggressors. Here, the traces of the 1985 riots, as well as of riots that occurred thereafter, were still apparent. The main lane winds past the burnt remains of walls and roofs. Both the place and the people carry the scars. During a visit to the pol I was told that 'this house was burnt, this one six times [over the years], this woman lost her son'.

On 18 March morning Muslims' shops remained open in the area, but it did not cause any problem. At 7 PM, the people of Vadigam started to play their utensils [thali dishes], on their roofs. With the growing sounds, slogans were shouted: 'Muslim should go'; 'this is a Hindu Raj come out and bow down'. Then, stones and burning cloths were thrown from the roofs of Vadigam on the houses of Naginapol. Some of them were set on fire. The escalation took place when a boy playing carrom was hit by a stone near the pol's gate. He ran outside bleeding. [At] his sight and the shouts, Muslims from the bordering Kalupur area began to flow into the pol. By then, the police was already on the roofs of Vadigam – shooting at us.[19]

---

[16] *Interview* with Sonaben, Vadigam, Ahmedabad, 26/3/98. This was reiterated almost in the same words in *Interviews* with Sunil, Vadigam, Ahmedabad, 31/3/98.

[17] *Interview* with Ramesh, Vadigam, Ahmedabad, 21/3/98.

[18] *Interview* with Saurabh, Vadigam, Ahmedabad, 26/3/98.

[19] *Interview* with Rasul, Naginapol, Ahmedabad, 30/12/97.

A pamphlet by an anonymous Muslim stated that:

The Mryutghant was a death bell ring for the Muslim community, as from Vadigam's pols stones and burning rags were thrown on Naginapol. Its buildings and people's belongings were burning. Then, firing from private people and the police started towards the Muslims. That midnight, at the Vadilal Hospital, where the wounded were taken, some Bajap political leaders gave baseless and provoking information to the people about the events. The false information was immediately spread, and the atmosphere became very tensed.[20]

The houses on one side of the Muslim locality of Naginapol share walls with Vadigam, and the houses on its other side border on Jorden Road. Naginapol's one-storey houses look like small hutches leaning on Vadigam's taller houses. Some of them are semi-*pucca*. From Naginapol's lane, Vadigam's terraces look like spires.[21] This topographical structure clarifies part of the dynamics of the violence.

Naginapol residents at the time experienced circumstances similar to those of Vadigam residents. According to the residents of Naginapol, by 1985 the majority of the people in the locality were unemployed mill workers and faced severe economic difficulties. They had worked in the spinning and weaving departments of the mills and many of them became rickshaw wallas, or started petty trading. The people described themselves as poor, struggling to make a living. Even before 1985 the women and children had worked at home, stitching fabrics, in order to sustain the families, earning about Rs.10–20 a day.

The Dalit residential area (*Dalit vas*) in Dariapur, in the vicinity of Vadigam, is not an enclosed neighbourhood. In Ambedkar Street, for example, there is no gate or fort-like structure. To the unfamiliar visitor, some of the Dalit houses appear to be, both inside and outside, in better condition than those of the upper-caste Hindus in Vadigam. Testimonies of people in this locality revealed that the communal riots that erupted in the city were not really spontaneous. About ten days before the Vadigam–Naginapol incidents, rumours were spreading that riots might start, and people had even stored food in advance.[22]

Although the residents of Vadigam saw themselves as agitators against their Muslim neighbours they did not identify any concrete tension with them. Some residents even stated that people from Naginapol and

---

[20] Mujahid (anonymous), 'An Inquiry Report on 1985 Communal Riots in Ahmedabad City, 18th March and After: Real Facts', Unpublished Pamphlet, SETU Archive Files (henceforth 'Mujahid Pamphlet').

[21] In 1997 one four-storey house at the end of the pol lane, where fifty-four people resided, and a towering mosque were built after the riots.

[22] *Interview* with Revaben, Kalupur, Ahmedabad, 25/2/98. During the 1985 riots she lived in Ambedkar Street, Dariapur. Other residents also recalled such rumours.

Vadigam used to work together in the mills and had good relations. Rather than identifying a specific conflict with their Muslim neighbours, Vadigam's upper-caste residents asserted that the government discriminated against them in favour of the Muslims. An upper-caste resident of Vadigam who was arrested under the National Security Act during the riots explained: 'I was arrested because I represented the savarna [upper castes].'[23] Residents of Vadigam argued that:

Congress supported Muslims, so BJP supported Hindus. A few days after communal riots erupted in Dariapur Prime Minister, Rajiv Gandhi, visited the area. Firstly he went to Naginapol, because Solanki supported the Muslims. So, the people of Vadigam closed the gate and did not let him in.[24] In fact, Bajap people instigated the people not to see him.[25] Later, Congress people suggested to arrest Vadigam's people.[26]

Some residents traced the development of these political attitudes back to the end of the 1960s. Ramesh, for example, noted that 'until 1969 Vadigam's people supported the Congress party, but later many converted to the Jan Sangh. In fact, after 1969 political parties had taken much more interest in them.'[27] Ramesh had been a member of the RSS since 1954, but became active in the organisation after leaving the mill. Some upper-caste residents recalled that 'before 1969, Hindus and Muslims were friends . . . Afterward, even Hindus and Muslims who were friends lost trust.'[28]

The Muslim residents in the area insisted that there was no reason for the 18 March attack. They saw themselves as victims of a situation they had no part in. 'The reservation agitation was a Hindu business and Muslims had nothing to do with that. They neither supported nor opposed the anti-reservation campaign.'[29] Dabgarward was a mixed locality in Dariapur, where Hindu Dabgars and Muslims used to live. 'The Dabgars were OBCs on the list for the increase in reservation, but this made no difference to their neighbouring Muslims.'[30] 'The Muslim minority remained neutral during this time, but was watching with worry. When the [upper-caste Hindu] agitators felt that the anti-reservation movement would not be successful and as the state's government failed to control law and

[23] *Interview* with Ramesh, Vadigam, Ahmedabad, 21/3/98. Savarna means 'upper castes'.
[24] *Ibid.*   [25] *Interview* with Sonaben, Vadigam, Ahmedabad, 26/3/98.
[26] *Interview* with Dhansukh, Vadigam, Ahmedabad, 26/3/98.
[27] *Interview* with Ramesh, Vadigam, Ahmedabad, 21/3/98. Most interviewees in Vadigam described the history of their political leanings similarly.
[28] *Interview* with Saurabh, Vadigam, Ahmedabad, 26/3/98. Other residents in Vadigam expressed a similar opinion.
[29] *Interview* with Makbul, Sajjan Jamadar's Moholla, Dariapur, Ahmedabad, 30/12/97.
[30] *Interview* with Shirin, Dabgarward, Dariapur, 4/1/98.

order, they blamed the Muslims.'[31] Similarly, some Muslims explained that 'the communal twist was a planned move by upper caste Hindus because they began to fear, as they were equally beaten by lower castes'.[32] Interestingly, it appeared that Muslims slowly developed a stance against the policy of reservation, which they were excluded from. Several noted that 'whenever we hear the call to abolish reservation, we realise that communal riots are about to erupt'.[33] In the view of some Muslim residents of Dariapur 'the main purpose of the riots was political: to oust Muslims from the Congress'.[34] 'There was no reason for a clash between the communities, politicians took the active part and turned it to communal.'[35] 'It was political parties who employed goondas to begin the killings.'[36]

Residents from all social groups in the Dariapur area explained that it was not the people themselves who started the riots, but policemen, bootleggers and politically involved persons who had incited the people for the sake of their own 'wars'. An incident that heightened violence in the Dariapur area occurred on 8 May, after Police Sub-Inspector Mahendrasingh Rana was shot dead in Bhanderipole. Police testimonies to the Commission of Inquiry suggested that he was a victim of communal clashes between Hindus and Muslims.[37] Local residents claimed that 'the local bootleggers were pressed by the local police to increase their baksheesh payments. So, in order to thwart police's demand, both Hindu and Muslim bootleggers created riots and initiated stabbing incidents.'[38] They elaborated on the dynamics of relations between the police, bootleggers and politicians in the following account. On this occasion, a local tension between the police and some residents in Dariapur over extortion and graft motivated some of the violence in the area:

The local bootleggers were free to run their business of illicit liquor and brown sugar (hashish), protected by police's closed eyes. In fact, police was forcing them to run their business, otherwise they would lose their main income. There is a nexus between bootleggers, police and politicians. Some time prior to the

[31] 'Mujahid Pamphlet', p. 1.
[32] *Interview* with Makbul, Sajjan Jamadar's Moholla, Dariapur, Ahmedabad, 30/12/97.
[33] *Interview* with Inayat, Dariapur, Ahmedabad, 22/2/98. The idea was also restated by Makbul, Sajjan Jamadar's Moholla, Dariapur, Ahmedabad, 30/12/97; Parvin, Shahpur, Ahmedabad, 11/3/98.
[34] *Interview* with Rasul, Naginapol, Ahmedabad, 30/12/97.
[35] *Interview* with Ahmed, Dabgarward, Dariapur, 15/12/97.
[36] *Interviews* with Shirin, Dabgarward, Dariapur, 4/1/98; Ahmed, Dabgarward, Dariapur, 2/1/98.
[37] *COI.* Vol. I, p, 260; G.W.-28, p. 118.
[38] *Interview* with Sunil, Vadigam, Ahmedabad, 31/3/98. This account was reiterated in *Interviews* with Makbul, Sajjan Jamadar's Moholla, Dariapur, Ahmedabad, 29/12/97; Rasul, Naginapol, Ahmedabad, 30/12/97.

riots of 1985 the Police Inspector of Dariapur police station was replaced by another person, who bribed the Home Minister (it was said that he paid Rs.3 Lakh), in order to get that post. It is a common knowledge among policemen and residents in the area that in Dariapur station policemen received high baksheesh payments from the bootleggers, in exchange for their ability to conduct their illegal businesses. As revenge and with the hope to get back his office, the going Police Inspector who lost the post, but had very good connections with the local liquor dealers instigated them to create social havoc.[39]

The background for intricate political stratagems was localised. For example, residents explained that before 1985, when Dariapur–Kalupur had formed one electoral ward, the Member of Legislative Assembly (MLA) Bupendra Kathri, a Hindu resident of Vadigam, had failed to win the financial support of the local bootleggers. In particular, he had been unable to collect money from Latif, an underworld don, who aided the Muslim Congress MLA, Muhammad Hussin Barejya.[40] In certain circumstances, such a story about local political competition could easily feed into the narrative, which suggested that 'Muslims are organising themselves against us.'[41]

Several residents from Vadigam attested that Hindu organisations had provided help both during the economic hardship caused by the mill closures in the city and during the violence and the prolonged curfew, when living conditions had deteriorated. 'We had income problems, but social institutions like the RSS and Vadigam Seva Sangh provided relief to the people of the locality and medical aid when needed. They also gathered Hindu youths and gave them lessons. The VHP helped to find new jobs.'[42] Dhansukh said that he had no customers during that time and was bound to take aid, but 'Hindu organisation and rich Hindus donated money.'[43]

Dalits in the old city recounted similar experiences. In spite of the improvement in their standard of living, the Dalits were not spared economic hardships: 'we had to borrow money from relatives. There was a *dudh* (milk) crisis. Milk and fresh vegetables were rare commodities.'[44] During the riots of 1985 'the BJP and VHP provided relief, money, food

---

[39] *Interviews* with Rasul, Naginapol, Dariapur, Ahmedabad, 30/12/97; Makbul, Sajjan Jamadar's Moholla, Dariapur, 30/12/97.

[40] *Interviews* with Makbul, Sajjan Jamadar's Moholla, Dariapur, Ahmedabad, 28/11/97; Rasul, Naginapol, Dariapur, 30/12/97.

[41] *Interview* with Sonaben, Vadigam, Ahmedabad, 26/3/98.

[42] *Interviews* with Ramesh, Vadigam, Ahmedabad, 21/3/98; 22/3/98.

[43] *Interview* with Dhansukh, Vadigam, Ahmedabad, 26/3/98.

[44] *Interview* with Karsenbhai, Ambedkar Street, Ahmedabad, 28/11/97. Many interviewees mentioned the economic hardship they had experienced at the time.

and legal aid'.[45] Residents of Ambedkar Street testified that some BJP MLAs, who had persecuted them during the riots of 1981, provided aid in the riots of 1985. Many noted that while the police harassed them as usual, Dalits in the old city were seldom attacked by the upper-caste Hindus, in contrast to previous riots. 'They [Dalits] were happy as the BJP protected them from the police.'[46] Some Dalits explained that since the BJP and Hindu organisations continued to display these new attitudes after the riots, a 'Hindu opinion' began to develop among the Dalits of Ahmedabad and the BJP gradually started to win the sympathy of the Dalits living in the inter-mixed localities.[47]

Moreover, some Dalit testimonies indicated that Dalits in the old city who had participated in the Rath Yatra procession in 1985 had even taken part in the agitation and looting that followed it.[48] Contrary to the customary practice of Hindu religious functions, Dalits were allowed to participate fully in the Rath Yatra rite. Bhanu, a Dalit who had participated in that Rath Yatra, expressed how meaningful it had been for the Dalits: 'at that time we felt part of the Hindu community'.[49] In his description of the procession, he stated that:

From Jaganath Temple, in Jamalpur, where the procession departed, until it entered Dariapur, it was peaceful. However, in Saraspur, where the procession halted for a break, a rumour was spread that there is tension in Dariapur, 'so let's be ready'. Stones and bricks were loaded on the trucks. Piles of them were ready there. When we entered Prem Darwaza provocative slogans about Muslim women were shouted, and Caste Hindus were also engaged in throwing stones on the police.[50] Then, opposite Vadigam, persons connected with Latif fired five-six rounds. The procession went on a rampage. The trucks were spreading in different directions. Those who proceeded in the regular route, to Shahpur, looted all Muslims shops there.[51]

At the same time, at least in some areas, genial social interactions between Hindus and Muslims endured or emerged during the riots.

---

[45] *Interviews* with Revaben, Kalupur, Ahmedabad, 25/2/98; Karsenbhai, Ambedkar Street, Ahmedabad, 28/11/97.

[46] *Ibid.*

[47] *Interviews* with Karsenbhai, Ambedkar Street, Dariapur, 29/11/97; Inayat, Ambedkar Street, Dariapur, 22/2/98, 11/3/98. Also *Interviews* with Ashok Shrimali, Navrangpura, Ahmedabad, 14/11/97; Achyut Yagnik, Navrangpura, Ahmedabad, 3/3/98.

[48] *Interviews* with Bhanu, Kalupur, Ahmedabad, 23/2/98; Inayat, Dariapur, 22/2/98.

[49] *Interview* with Bhanu, Kalupur, Ahmedabad, 23/2/98. During the Rath Yatra in 1985 Bhanu was on one of the trucks with devotees, which took part in the procession.

[50] According to other testimonies of people in the area 'when the Yatra entered through Prem Darwaza there were loud shoutings. The slogans were sexually intolerable.' *Interview* with Makbul, Sajjan Jamadar's Moholla, Dariapur, Ahmedabad, 30/12/97; Inayat, Kalupur, Ahmedabad, 25/2/98.

[51] *Interview* with Bhanu, Kalupur, Ahmedabad, 23/2/98.

The main difficulty, according to residents in Dalit localities, was to live through the very constrained routine of curfew and violence:

The most dangerous time was when curfew was released, usually for two hours in the morning. While the women were on the rush to buy commodities, most of the stabbing and acid bulb throwing took place. Muslim women were harassed when they went for shopping in the Hindu localities.[52]

Once a ten-year old Muslim girl came to Ambedkar Street to sell eggs. Hindu youths were surrounding and harassing her. But some women from our locality approached her, helped her to sell the eggs, and to leave the locality safely.[53]

Revaben, from the Dalit locality, joined a local voluntary initiative against communal violence, established at that time. 'We were conducting our own investigations of the ongoing events', finding, for example, that in the Muslim area on Jorden Road, on the border of Kalupur–Dariapur, police shot and targeted Muslims.[54]

Strikingly, in the midst of the fury in Dariapur, some localities in the area remained undisturbed most of the time. Sajjan Jamandar's Moholla is located a few minutes' walk from Vadigam–Naginapol. Its *naka* [entrance] parallels Jorden Road, yet according to its residents it was struck by violence only in June, four months after the riots started, during the incidents that took place on the Rath Yatra day. A resident of the Moholla attributed the relative harmony in his locality to the good relationships between Muslims and Dalits from the nearby Ambedkar Street. 'They [prominent Moholla residents] had good relationships with people from the nearby Ambedkar Street Dalit area, and were visiting each other, providing an example to the youth.'[55] So, even as the riots occurred, people from various groups tried to overcome the rupture of social life and to restore some elements of normality, even in their relations with 'antagonistic' groups.

Despite the long period of curfew and violence, residents from various localities in the old city described good community life within their neighbourhoods. They also explained how they had sustained themselves during the time of violence. 'The people in Vadigam were very cordial with each other. We appointed a Shanti Committee to lift the curfew.'[56] 'In fact, during the curfew we had very good social life. The people were playing together, mainly carrom and cards.'[57] Sonaben narrated that:

[52] *Interview* with Karsenbhai, Ambedkar Street, Ahmedabad, 28/11/97. Many interviewees mentioned that fact.
[53] *Interview* with Revaben, Ahmedabad, 25/2/98.   [54] *Ibid.*
[55] *Interview* with Makbul, Sajjan Jamadar's Moholla, Dariapur, Ahmedabad, 29/11/97, 30/12/97.
[56] *Interview* with Dhansukh, Vadigam, Ahmedabad, 26/3/98.
[57] *Interview* with Saurabh, Vadigam, Ahmedabad, 26/3/98.

While curfew was relaxed we were buying products, however, only women went for the shopping. They had the problem to run the house and look after the children, who, at that time, were not going to school and became like devils. The men played. Still, curfew was like a picnic. Food was not really a problem, because we used to store a one-year stock of all basic ingredients. We were all sitting at the thresholds of the houses, preparing the meals. All we talked about was the riots, and this is how rumours were created: who was killed, stabbed, a mob came to attack. Many times we discovered that these hearsays were only rumours. We were living between tension and laughter.[58]

'The people were harassed, so, for our security we kept weapons for stabbing in the house.'[59] It appeared that the residents effectively provided themselves with a sense of security so as to claim that although 'all fights took place in Dariapur, Vadigam was the safest area in Ahmedabad city'.[60]

Like the experiences of Hindus, Muslim residents of Sajjan Jamandar's Moholla stated that 'in the Moholla, community life was very good and there was harmony. People helped each other, and in everyday curfew time we were playing and gambling.' He added that 'because I was a government employee, and had a permit to go to work during the curfew, I could bring food. Also, we had good contacts with the local State Reserve Police [SRP], so they brought us what was needed.'[61]

Panchbhai pol, a Hindu locality of mainly upper-caste Jains and Banias on the border of Kalupur–Dariapur, was another example of an island of calm within the sea of violence. Viral's family settled in the pol in 1971. They had previously lived in Saraspur in the old city, near the Sindhi market, which was badly affected during the 1969 communal riots, and moved because 'Panchbhai was a Hindu locality and, therefore, safer.'[62] The family owned a jewellery shop in Ratanpol, a commercial area in the old city. Viral estimated that they lost about 50 per cent of their customers as a result of the crisis in the mills at the time. Members of the family recounted that:

It was a difficult time. In the background was an economic crisis. There was an ongoing curfew and we could not get to the shop. Even when curfew was relaxed we could not go because we had to pass through a Muslim locality. [However,] we had good circles in the pol, people helped each other and lent money. Pol's people

---

[58] *Interview* with Sonaben, Vadigam, Ahmedabad, 26/3/98.

[59] *Interview* with Bhagirath, Vadigam, Ahmedabad, 26/3/98.

[60] *Interview* with Ramesh, Vadigam, Ahmedabad, 22/3/98.

[61] *Interview* with Makbul, Sajjan Jamadar's Moholla, Dariapur, Ahmedabad, 29/11/97 and 30/12/97. By 1985 most of the people in this locality, who were ex-composite mill workers, had a job in the powerloom factories. A few worked for the municipality.

[62] *Interviews* with Viral, Navrangpura, Ahmedabad, 11/1/98; Kalupur, Panchbhai Pol, 14/1/98.

arranged their own protection. In shifts we were standing on the terraces, with thali plates, and if we saw suspected people approaching the pol, we were playing the instruments, making alarm noise. Inside the pol we felt free and secured but outside the pol we felt in jail.[63]

During curfew time people were playing cards and watching videos. There was no shortage in basic food, because we used to store wheat, oil, rice, lentil and sugar in quantities enough for one year, and we also had a reservoir for water in the house.[64]

Family members also mentioned that social workers from the area visited the pol every fortnight. Only when they named them did it become clear that they included senior BJP politicians from the area among their social workers.

In other cases, residents referred to people, whom the state apparatus defined as anti-social elements, as social workers. According to various people in the old city, both Muslims and Hindus, Latif and his associates started charitable work during the communal riots and distributed essential commodities to poor people. 'Latif himself brought aid. He came at the gate and brought money, food, and even fresh milk, which was a scarce product during that time. He also supplied medicines. During the riots Latif was our [Muslims'] saviour and pride.'[65] Particularly for Muslims in the old city area, he became a local Robin Hood. 'He donated money for widows, unemployed and helped people with dowry to marry their daughters.'[66] The government, politicians and newspapers defined him as an 'anti-social element', or 'the dreaded underworld don'.[67] Latif gained recognition and legitimacy from the people when two years after the riots, in the 1987 Ahmedabad Municipal Corporation elections, he was elected, as an independent candidate, from five wards in the old city.

In the aftermath of the Ahmedabad riots of 1985, residents who were economically better off, mainly businessmen, left Vadigam and moved across the river to the western side of the city. Those who were not able

---

[63] *Interview* with Viral, Ratanpol, Ahmedabad, 25/12/97.

[64] *Interview* with Surbiben, Kalupur, Panchbhai Pol, Ahmedabad, 14/1/98.

[65] *Interview* with Rasul, Naginapol, Dariapur, 30/12/97. The same narration was repeated by Makbul, Sajjan Jamadar's Moholla, Dariapur, Ahmedabad, 30/12/97; Parvin, Shahpur, Ahmedabad, 11/3/98; Karsenbhai, Ambedkar Street, Dariapur, 29/11/97. Latif was considered to be an underworld don.

[66] *Interview* with Karimbhai, Gomtipur, Ahmedabad, 6/1/98.

[67] *Interviews* with Ashok Bhatt (BJP), Khadia, Ahmedabad, 15/12/97; Anisha Mizra, Council Ahmedabad Municipal Corporation (henceforth AMC), Raikhal, Ahmedabad, 16/12/97; Madhavsinh Solanki, Delhi, 16/3/98. This was also the language used in newspaper reports.

to do so, mainly workers, stayed: 'after the 1985 riots the family wanted to leave, but we did not have the economic capacity to do so'.[68] Many of the Patels who left Vadigam joined Patel societies in Naranpura or Navrangpura in western Ahmedabad. Internal population shifts between localities in the city increased, and divisions along religious lines sharpened. Generally, Vadigam remained an upper-caste locality, but some backward-caste families also moved there. The '*avarna* [low caste] people were absorbed in the locality because they came from Muslim dominated areas, which they had to leave after the riots'.[69] Residents in the old city claimed that even the underworld was divided along religious lines after 1985. Previously, Hindu and Muslim bootleggers had collaborated with each other, but now they worked separately. Moreover, in various localities in the old city people stated that in 1985 there was a political shift in the city from Congress to the BJP. 'Before 1985 there was a mixed voting pattern among the people of Panchbhai, but after 1985 all voted for Ashok Bhatt [BJP].'[70]

Ahmedabad of the chimneys: the eastern industrial belt

The Ahmedabad of the eastern industrial belt, beyond the railways, suffered severe communal violence and mass-scale destruction, which left thousands of people homeless, especially in Bapunagar. This was also how residents in the area recalled the events of 1985. The reservation issue was absent from their accounts. The area of Morarji Chowk, which is known as 'old Bapunagar' and constructed in 1952, was a mixed locality with both Hindu and Muslim residents. 'New Bapunagar', about half a kilometre away, was constructed a few years later. The area was incorporated into the Ahmedabad municipal limits in 1958, and the Gujarat Housing Board (GHB) bought land and built houses in the locality in order 'to help weaker sections of the society'.[71] Most of the houses, however, were subsequently allotted to mill workers for very low rent. A letter from the mill-owner, which confirmed their employment in the mill, qualified them to participate in this housing scheme. From the early 1970s the government enabled the tenants to purchase the property.[72] 'The municipality was not able to control its rent and maintenance. This is also why

---

[68] *Interview* with Sonaben, Vadigam, Ahmedabad, 26/3/98.

[69] *Ibid.*; *Interview* with Ramesh, Vadigam, Ahmedabad, 22/3/98.

[70] *Interviews* with Viral; Surbiben; Lalitaben, Navrangpura, Ahmedabad, 11/1/98.

[71] *Interview* with M. S. Thakkar, AMC Town Planning Officer, Ahmedabad, 6/1/98; Utpal C. Padia, Assistant Municipal Commissioner, Ahmedabad, 3/12/97.

[72] *Interviews* with Gaurang, Navrangpura, Ahmedabad, 6/12/97, Bapunagar, Ahmedabad, 7/12/97; Amina, Morarji Chowk, Bapunagar, Ahmedabad, 27/12/97.

they sold the GHB flats to the tenants by 1980, and moreover, why the municipality did not initiate any housing schemes after 1974.'[73] After the communal riots of 1969 Ahmedabad Municipal Corporation (AMC) allotted temporary accommodation in adjacent plots to the mainly Muslim riot victims, who were rendered homeless.[74] One of these settlements became the Indira Garibnagar slum.

In 1985 'Small' Indira Garibnagar was located down the hill below the Lal Bahadur Sastri (Malek Saban) Stadium. The Hanuman temple and an *akhada* (gymnasium) were situated on the way down to the locality. Bupunagar's water tank towered over the area. The locality bordered on Anand flats, with three- to four-storey GHB housing on one side and Block 16 on the adjacent side. A police *chowki* (post) was situated between Indira Garibnagar and the main road. 'Big' Indira Garibnagar and Morarji Chowk were situated on the other side of the main road.

Violence intensified in Bapunagar and its surrounding localities on 22 and 23 April 1985. The following descriptions are based on a documentary film shot in the area on 25–26 April, as well as on my own interviews with several people who lived there at the time.[75] After the violence, Indira Garibnagar was totally deserted, its lanes filled with ravaged *kuccha* and semi-*pucca* houses, twisted bicycles and broken carts, burnt walls, collapsed roofs and uprooted doors. Piles of torn beds, burnt kitchen utensils and pottery, rickshaws and scattered bricks of broken walls lay outside the destroyed houses. Some houses were left intact and locked, on a few the word 'Hindus' or the date '22 April 1985', was inscribed in white.

In the Aman Chowk relief camp, jute canopies were stretched over wooden bars to provide shelter for the hundreds of Muslims who had had to flee there between 22 and 23 April. Each family staked out a patch within this huge open tent. Animals roamed freely as children played in the burnt rickshaws in the surrounding area.

On 22 April there was a stone throwing incident, so we went to complain to the police. The police said there is nothing to worry about and that they will look into it. But police did nothing. It all started in the area of the huts near the Bapunagar water tank and Malek Saban stadium. A mob came from all the directions. We

---

[73] *Interview* with Chandubhai Chauhan, Estate Department, AMC, Ahmedabad, 6/1/98. Also see *National Commission on Urbanization: Interim Report*, New Delhi: Government of India, Ministry of Urban Development, January 1987, pp. 26–7, 60–1.

[74] *Interviews* with M. S. Thakkar, AMC Town Planning Officer, Ahmedabad, 6/1/98; Rajesh Patel, Assistant Town Planning Officer, AMC, Ahmedabad, 6/1/98.

[75] Manish Jani, the student leader of the 1974 NavNirman movement, recorded the documentary video film in Bapunagar. The film contains interviews that Jani conducted with Muslim refugees from Indira Garibnagar in the Aman Chowk relief camp. Manish Jani, 'The 1985 Ahmedabad Riots', private video documentary, Bapunagar, 25–26 April 1985 (henceforth 'The 1985 Ahmedabad Riots', video documentary).

were sitting outside our huts, shouting slogans to boost our morale and to let them [the Hindus] think that we were many. Twice we succeeded to send them away. However, after midnight, at about 4.00 AM in the morning, two police jeeps and one van came. The mob stood behind them. All of us block wallas, gathered and asked the police to protect us, but they started shooting at us, and organised setting on fire all our property. The police officers were Rana Patel and Yadav, from Bapunagar police. One of them had two revolvers in his hand. They gave indication for the mob to come. The Hindus came, we ran away and they set the houses on fire. The police gave the people petrol for the burning.[76]

According to some interviewees, the police jeep and the van had passed through all the surrounding Hindu localities, telling the people to be ready. 'One of them who knew me came and warned us.'[77]

The people of Anand flats started throwing burning rags on our huts. In the wake of this attack, we took our wives and children and ran through the stadium to reach Aman Chowk. When we arrived, the military was there, but apparently they received wrong information from the police who wired them that Muslims were the attackers.[78]

Amina, who lived between Morarji Chowk and Aman Chowk camp, still remembers the shouts and cries. 'The attackers came in trucks. They were outsiders. In fact, Hindus and Muslims in the area did not want violence. All were labour people who fought for their bread and butter. Their economic condition made them very sensitive.'[79] During the riots her family had had to leave their home four times and seek refuge elsewhere.

Many of the interviewees in the Aman Chowk relief camp were originally from Uttar Pradesh. They had arrived in the early 1970s, when Indira Garibnagar was set up, in quest of work, and had started working in factories in the area. For some interviewees it was not their first experience of being uprooted by riots. One of the survivors unfolded her life story as a chain of such episodes:

In 1969 we lived in Saraspur [eastern Ahmedabad]. When the riots started we had to escape. We went on a train going to Prantij. On the first stop my husband was pulled off the train and stabbed to death. I went back to our village, near Prantij. For seven years I raised by myself my four sons and two daughters. My

---

[76] Interview with Sofia (resident of Block 16), Aman Chowk relief camp, 'The 1985 Ahmedabad Riots', video documentary. The names of these police officers were also mentioned in testimonies before the *COI*. The same description was reiterated in interviews with an anonymous woman who lived under Anand Flats; Sayed, resident of Indira Garibnagar, Aman Chowk relief camp, *ibid*. I am grateful to Suchitra Seth for her help in translating the interviews.

[77] *Interviewee* (anonymous), Aman Chowk relief camp, *Ibid*.

[78] *Interviews* with Chandulal, resident of Indira Garibnagar, and another anonymous person, *ibid*.

[79] *Interview* with Amina, Morarji Chowk, Bapunagar, Ahmedabad, 27/12/97.

youngest son was a baby. For five years we managed with the compensation money I received from the government. But then, we returned to Ahmedabad in search of job. We settled in Indira Garibnagar and started working in a plastic factory. We have just started our lives again and this happened.

If the government wants to kill the Muslims they should get them together and just throw a bomb. They set fire in my daughter's house, and nothing was left.[80]

The Muslim survivors in the Aman Chowk relief camp held the government responsible for their predicament and felt deceived and betrayed by it.

The government's hand is in the whole matter.[81]

The Solanki government started this, for their chair [government position]. They have something against Muslims. Why? I have no answer. Go ask the government why they did this. They come and tell us Hindu Muslims *bhai bhai* [brothers], then they come to kill us. We trusted the police, and they betrayed us. Hindus do not want Muslims to live in Bapunagar, and riots are good excuse to evict them.[82]

Hindu organisations, however, attempted to show that Hindus were the victims of Muslims. After the violence in Bapunagar and in response to the Muslim relief camp in Aman Chowk, the VHP and the BJP set up a Hindu relief camp in the green open area at Morarji Chowk. Photos of the place, although fraudulent, even appeared in the newspapers. 'I went there with Rajni Kothari, the then president of the Peoples' Union for Civil Liberties, to visit the camps. There was not a soul in the so-called Hindu relief camp. After a while the officer who was sitting there with aid equipment confessed that since morning nobody came to ask for help.'[83] According to some evidence, in Bapunagar, as in the walled city, Hindu organisations made efforts to mobilise support from Dalits. 'Harijans were gathered by a few Bajap politicians in public meetings. They were given money and food; they brainwashed them against Muslims and even gave them weapons – lathis.'[84]

The testimonies of survivors of the violence in Bapunagar disclosed that not only did the local police take sides in the clashes, but they also helped to organise the violence. In the official account of the riots the eruption of violence on 22 April and the police misconduct were generally linked to

[80] *Interview* with an anonymous woman, resident of Indira Garibnagar near Anand Flats, Aman Chowk relief camp, 'The 1985 Ahmedabad Riots', video documentary.
[81] *Interview* with Sayed, resident of Indira Garibnagar, Aman Chowk relief camp, *ibid.*
[82] *Interview* with Bhanubibi, Aman Chowk relief camp, *ibid.*
[83] *Interview* with Achyut Yagnik, Navrangpura, Ahmedabad, 3/3/98.
[84] *Interview* with Shirin, Ahmedabad, 4/1/98. She witnessed one of these meetings. A similar description was given by Ramesh Chandraparmar, president of Dalit Panthers Ahmedabad, Gomtipur, Ahmedabad, 6/1/98.

the killing of Police Head Constable Laxman Desai in Khadia in the old city that day. Only one interviewee in the Aman Chowk relief camp knew about the incident. The residents, mainly in retrospect, when I conducted interviews in the area, argued that in Bapunagar the main problem was the growing interest in the slum dwellers' land.

Numerous residents mentioned that there was a local conflict between the residents of Anand flats and the slum dwellers of Indira Garibnagar over the dividing wall between the flats and the slum. Yet, residents in the area claimed that the real issue was that the *akhada* gymnasium people, near Indira Garibnagar, wanted the land.[85] By 1985 the cost of land and rent in the area had increased significantly. As a result of the national highway that passed nearby and made the area attractive to the new developing industries, there was an increasing demand for land, which was in short supply.[86] Many plots in the area, which initially belonged to AMC, were occupied by slum dwellers. With the growing demand for land and the price-rise there was an increasing interest in these plots. The legal status of these lands was controversial. According to high-level officers in AMC, even though people did not pay rent there was political pressure against evictions because each neighbourhood had become the stronghold of certain politicians.[87] After a slum was erected it required water and other civic amenities. In order to be eligible for the Public Distribution System (PDS), the residents needed to hold a ration card, which was issued on the basis of land or house residence and ownership. Those in possession of ration cards were also registered in the electoral roll for the municipality.[88] Politicians, therefore, pressed to allocate certain slum dwellers with ration cards and in turn secured electoral support from them. Moreover, slum dwellers who paid rent for a long period of time acquired legal rights over the land, and the slumlords were restricted from removing the residents. Riots were one means of vacating the slum lands. Residents in the area noted that during that time bootleggers had expanded their activities into land businesses. They benefited from their connections with

---

[85] *Interviews* with Manish Jani, Ahmedabad, 4/3/98; Chandraparmar, Gomtipur, Ahmedabad, 30/11/97, 6/1/98; Gaurang, Bapunagar, Ahmedabad, 6/12/97; Pankaj, Bapunagar, Ahmedabad, 7/12/97; Parmanand, Gomtipur and Bapunagar, Ahmedabad, 14/3/98; Ambalal, Bapunagar, 29/3/98.

[86] Many plots in the area were occupied by the closed textile mill, which stretched over large territories. These lands were not available since cases against the mills were pending in the courts.

[87] *Interviews* with Rajesh Patel, Assistant Town Planning Officer, AMC, Ahmedabad, 6/1/98; Chandubhai Chauhan, Estate Department, AMC, Ahmedabad, 6/1/98.

[88] *Interviews* with M. R. Kothari, Additional Residence Deputy Collector, Ahmedabad, 29/12/97; N. L. Pujara, Deputy Collector, Ahmedabad, 29/12/97; Rajesh Patel, Assistant Town Planning Officer, AMC, Ahmedabad, 6/1/98.

politicians and had access to inside information about land policies of the government and the municipality.[89]

The then Chief Minister of Gujarat, Madhavsinh Solanki, claimed that, 'in Bapunagar and the suburban areas, Patels from Saurashtra financed the events. They attacked scheduled castes and Muslim houses. They were inherently against reservation.'[90] This group, which was considered lower in status than the Patels of central Gujarat, began migrating to Bapunagar from Saurashtra from the 1970s. Members of this group prospered, for example by establishing the diamond-cutting industry, which by the mid-1980s dominated this part of the city. This group was very close to the BJP.[91] Most of them were sons of farmers who had struggled for many years with the Rajputs in the former princely states. They had been able to advance as a result of the land reforms in Saurashtra and even kept their lands when they came to Ahmedabad.[92] They set up small cooperative housing societies in Bapunagar and on the green agricultural belt, which was under the authority of the collector of Ahmedabad. Senior BJP and Congress politicians suggested that the economic growth of members of this group involved illegal construction. They also implied that members of the group took an active part in the riots.[93]

After the 1985 riots the Bapunagar area was partitioned. The local residents call one part 'Pakistan' and the other 'Hindustan' or 'diamondnagar'. SRP positions on the main road that runs between the two parts symbolically mark a border. By the end of the 1990s only Muslims lived in Morarji Chowk, which until 1985 used to be a mixed locality of both Hindus and Muslims. Small Indira Garibnagar became a lower-caste Hindu locality. All the Muslim families who had lived there had moved, most of them to Juni Chowl, near General Hospital and Bapunagar Post Office.

The partition of Bapunagar was carried out through stressed selling of houses: Muslims were evicted from Hindu-dominated localities and made to sell their property for distressed prices.[94] In an attempt to prevent these processes, the government enacted the Gujarat Prohibition Act.[95]

---

[89] *Interviews* with Amina, Morarji Chowk, Bapunagar, Ahmedabad, 27/12/97; Gaurang, Navrangpura, Ahmedabad, 7/12/97; Pankaj, Bapunagar, Ahmedabad, 7/12/97; Ramesh Chandraparmar, Gomtipur, Ahmedabad, 6/1/98.

[90] *Interview* with Madhavsinh Solanki, Delhi, 16/3/98.

[91] *Interviews* with Ashok Bhatt, BJP MLA, Khadia, Ahmedabad, 15/12/97; Anisha Mizra, Council, AMC, Raikhal, Ahmedabad, 16/12/97.

[92] *Interview* with Gordhanbhai Jhadafia, BJP MLA, Bapunagar, Ahmedabad, 16/12/97.

[93] *Interviews* with BJP and Congress politicians.

[94] *Interview* with N. L. Pujara, Deputy Collector, Ahmedabad, 29/12/97.

[95] *The Gujarat Government Gazette*, 33, 4 April 1991 (An Enactment of the Gujarat Prohibition of Transfer of Immovable Property and Provision for Protection of Tenants from Eviction from Premises in Disturbed Areas Act 1986).

The Act stipulated that Muslims and Hindus could not sell properties to each other in the riot-affected areas in order to prevent stressed sales and 'ghettoization'.[96] According to a deputy collector in Ahmedabad, 'the Act was very loosely implemented'.[97] The Act had little chance of succeeding since it sought to reverse the situation that existed on the ground after the riots, when many Hindus and Muslims were compelled to live apart. People found two principal ways of circumventing the Act. People could seek official exemption from the Act from the Collector. Bribes were sometimes paid to obtain these exemptions. Alternatively, people exploited a legal loophole, 'executing powers of attorney with consideration', whereby the transfer of property could not be revoked once the payment had passed through the attorney.[98]

The western city of Ahmedabad

In the western city of Ahmedabad the riots of 1985 started as anti-reservation agitation. The disturbances took place mainly in the upper-caste localities of Navrangpura – where most of the higher education institutions were located – and in Naranpura, Paldi and Ellisbridge. The residents of these areas were not seriously affected by the violence, which was mainly targeted against state and municipal property. The communal escalation in the riots also had no concrete effect on them as few Muslims resided in these areas. Here, it was the reservations policy that most troubled the upper-caste population. The students, who were mainly Patels and Brahmins, along with the parents and guardians organisation, violently challenged the state reservations policy in the streets. The accusations of the Akhil Gujarat Navrachna Samiti and the Akhil Gujarat Vali Maha Mandal against the government were often disseminated in pamphlets, which they distributed throughout the city:

A Challenge to Reservation[99]

The demon of reservation is waiting with open jaws to swallow up the hard work of your children and yourselves . . . This system which erodes quality achieved

[96] The Act was limited to areas in the city that the government notified as being 'disturbed'. The notification for certain areas was renewed following the recurring riots in the city from 1985.

[97] *Interview* with N. L. Pujara, Deputy Collector, Ahmedabad, 29/12/97.

[98] *Interview* with Gaurang, Navrangpura, Ahmedabad, 6/12/97. His Hindu family sold their house in Morarji Chowk to a Muslim. Also *Interviews* with Parmanand, Gomtipur, Ahmedabad, 14/3/98; Ramesh Chandraparmar, Gomtipur, Ahmedabad, 6/1/98; Amina, Bapunagar, Ahmedabad, 27/12/97; Girish Patel, Naranpura, Ahmedabad, 7/4/98; Anand Yagnik, 25/2/06.

[99] Excerpts from a pamphlet published by the Akhil Gujarat Navrachna Samiti – Akhil Gujarat Vali Maha Mandal, Ahmedabad, SETU library, 20/4/85.

by hard work, is false and is going to lose its lustre, it is definite. Be fearless in voicing your opinion, come forward and take part in all programs.

Even after 38 years of freedom, the selfish and mean show of the politicians continues in this reservation. Do you believe that the government really loves the people who are to take the benefits from this reservation? Of course not. If that was the case, they would not have kept these people so backward for so many years and they would have made some progress! Anyhow, we have to stop the government from adopting this policy. Let us stop the waste of our intellectual wealth in this manner.

In 1981, many young people have laid down their lives for this cause. Let us not make their sacrifices meaningless. Even a strong government of foreigners could not suppress the Bardoli and Kheda Satyagrahas, the Quit India Movement, the Salt Satyagraha.

THEN WHAT IS THE POWER OF THE SOLANKI GOVERNMENT?

This movement is not against any particular caste or class, but it is against the thoughtless policies of the government.

Although in private conversations some people acknowledged that the reserved seats were not filled, so that the upper castes might not have a reason to feel threatened, some upper castes from very established social strata were convinced that 'the reservation hinders the chances of our children. Their chances are cut down. When the reserved quotas for the backward castes increased, less space for competition is left for the *normal people*.'[100] Hence, upper castes felt relatively deprived since they compared their opportunities in the past with the changes they were facing.

Upper castes repeatedly argued that 'simply by reservation one can not achieve results. And to whom the reservations are going? Only to those among the scheduled castes who are already in the system – the advantaged among the disadvantaged. Educational institutions themselves are against reservation and are trying to avoid it.'[101] An accusation frequently heard was that the scheduled castes in medical colleges were always sons of government officers, and that a really disadvantaged person was unaware of the benefits available to him.

The main problem, in the upper castes' view, was that 'scheduled castes who are accepted with lower grades than those required for an open seat get scholarships, while poor Brahmins will not get anything. The question is whether you want merit or reservation. It is on the cost of efficiency.'[102] In the opinion of an academic 'the reserved seats are there anyway, but

---

[100] *Interview* with Umaben, National Institute of Design (NID), Paldi, Ahmedabad, 9/11/97 (emphasis added).
[101] *Interview* with Mina Bhatt, Director Gujarat State Archives, Gandhinagar, 8/1/98.
[102] *Ibid.*

the people who get them are not skilled. They did not get good education previous to the university because the municipal schools are very bad.'[103]

Criticism of the roster reservation system of promotion illustrated the upper castes' antagonism towards reservations:

Suppose two people were recruited on the same day. One is from scheduled caste, and was taken on the basis of reservations and the other on a general seat. The scheduled caste person will get promotion first, because of the roster system. So, today we are colleagues and tomorrow he is my boss. By roster you can not elevate the level of knowledge of a person. *Status is an important issue, and is prior to livelihood.*[104]

Thus, some forward castes ostensibly accepted the discourse on equality for the lower and backward castes, yet they repudiated the reservations policy as a means of obtaining it, claiming that the policy benefited only the top layer among the depressed. At the same time, some forward castes denied the notion of equality, realising that the reservations policy undermined the very basis of the justification of their position within the social hierarchy. Their deeper anxiety about reservations lay in the difficulty some upper castes had in accepting the notion that a Dalit could be their superior.

The upper castes' anxieties over their status and position in society were also expressed in a pamphlet by the Naranpura Patel Yuvak Mandal, which was circulated in Ahmedabad during the riots:

O BROTHER PATELS OF ALL-GUJARAT! AWAKEN, AWAKEN![105]

Now the time has come. The frequent and fatal attacks of the Muslims, Harijans and Thakors on our community are to be tolerated no longer. It is now a dire necessity that each Patel is awakened to this humiliation and a befitting reply be given. We are not going to tolerate the challenge thrown by the Kshatriyas who publicly worship the 'bow and arrow'. Now, in its reply, we too are going to unite and equip ourselves. Everyone must provide generous donations for this noble cause of a bright future of the Patel community. If the Kshatriyas can keep weapons like the sword, bow and arrow, we too should keep them ready with us. The Patel community is ready to answer them any time, and are never afraid of damage to our goods and bodies when fighting for honour, have they forgotten? Have you also forgotten that these people belong to the low community, which used to pick up the night soil from our homes? Those who used to do this work for ages are now seated in huge offices of the bank due to the Reservation policies, and have become our senior officers! We cannot tolerate this any longer. Then,

---

[103] *Interview* with Umaben, National Institute of Design (NID) Paldi, Ahmedabad, 9/11/97.

[104] *Interview* with Mina Bhatt, Director, Gujarat State Archives, Gandhinagar, 8/1/98 (emphasis added).

[105] Naranpura Patel Yuvak Mandal, Pamphlet, Ahmedabad: SETU Library, May 1985.

these non-vegetarian Muslims! We have already paid them by creating Pakistan as compensation. We must now exile them from India. The nation is now only for the Hindus. Just because the Harijans and Muslims have united in these days of riots also, they should be boycotted by us, and that is our request to the entire community of Patels.

However, the reservation policy was a direct threat to some groups among the upper castes in the city who did not own land or a business, and who relied on education for their economic advancement. For some of the Patels in the city, for example, who had established themselves since the turn of the century as professionals, 'a seat in medical school was like an asset. If someone failed to get admission for law or medicine there was a great frustration. Bachelor degree was perceived as a useless degree, not practical enough to bring mobility.'[106] Sometimes a link was made between the failure to gain admission to the desired institution and the reservations for the backward groups, particularly if the upper-caste candidate fell short of the score required for admission by only a few decimal points.[107]

The anti-reservation dispute in the western city of Ahmedabad expressed a crisis of legitimacy. At the basis of this crisis lay the upper castes' sense of uncertainty about their dominance and identity, which was related to the government policies for the benefit of lower- and backward-caste Hindus. Upper castes challenged the state, yet they adopted the state's presuppositions in their attitudes towards the residents and the violence in other parts of the city. Often, for example, residents of the western city argued that the main problem in the eastern labour area of Ahmedabad was that 'most of the people in the area are migrants from Bihar and Uttar Pradesh, which brought their violent mentality and their own conflicts from their native place'.[108] Some stated that the arrival of Patels from Saurashtra had a similar effect.

There were many riots within the riot of 1985. These were driven by disparate conflicts among the people of the three cities of Ahmedabad. Often, these small riots expressed everyday disputes over resources between citizens and state apparatuses, which intensified in the context of the violence. In the walled city, the upper-caste protagonists experienced social and economic decline and in these circumstances felt discriminated against by the state. The situation of the riots also brought to the fore local conflicts with the police. In the eastern industrial belt, rising groups violently asserted their dominance and struggled for state resources, such as

---

[106] *Interview* with Girish Patel, Naranpura, Ahmedabad, 2/1/98.   [107] *Ibid.*
[108] *Interview* with Parmanand, Ahmedabad, 14/11/97. Many people in the western side of Ahmedabad, as well as in the old city, expressed similar perceptions.

land. In western Ahmedabad, state redistribution policies and the legitimacy of these policies were challenged by the upper castes. Their struggle was driven by growing anxieties over changes in the caste order.

Although the course of the riots deviated from the initial reservation dispute, in their outcomes, both in the short and medium term, the government directly addressed only the reservation dispute. The reservations policy was not implemented and upper castes retained their political power in the state. The aftermath of the Ahmedabad riots of 1985 marked the beginnings of the political shift in Gujarat from Congress rule to the rise of the BJP, which further strengthened the upper castes' position.

In spite of an inter-Hindu caste reservation conflict and prevailing class tensions among them, an all-Hindu consolidation against Muslims emerged. The Muslim minority had no part in the reservation dispute. Their general impoverishment in the city made it difficult to explain why and how the rhetoric about their peril to the Hindu majority became persuasive. Moreover, upper-caste groups who led the anti-reservation struggle and the communal instigation started gaining support from some groups among the Dalits who did not obviously benefit from their agenda.

People's recollections of the violence and of their historical circumstances implied that, rather than resulting from a conflict between Hindus and Muslims, the communal antagonism that emerged in 1985 was related to Hindus' changing experiences of caste and the relations between caste and class in politics and in their social and economic lives. State policies and politics at the time energised these processes among them. The next chapter juxtaposes the two accounts of the riots with the context. By analysing the implications of the Ahmedabad riots for the relations between caste, class and communalism, and their relationship to the state, it seeks to explain more fully the rise of Hindu nationalism and the formation of a communal Hindu identity since the 1980s.

Part III

The making of ethnoHinduism

5   The making of ethnoHinduism: from the politics of redistribution to the politics of recognition

The ideas of a unitary 'Hindu identity' and Hindu nationalism began gaining support in Ahmedabad from the 1980s in the context of intensifying conflicts among Hindus. This chapter explores the factors that brought about this shift. The analysis shows that the rising communal antagonism against Muslims and support for Hindu nationalism was largely driven by the way in which diverse groups of Hindus experienced caste and its changing character, and in particular by deepening uncertainties within the Hindu moral order. These dynamic processes were related to state policies and politics. Caste and its relations to the state, therefore, are a critical factor in the rise of Hindu nationalism and the growth of communal antagonism since the 1980s. This chapter provides a conceptual framework for understanding the relations between communalism and caste and their interplay with the state, which came to a head in the 1985 riots. Communalism and caste should be understood as practices of ethnic politics. Hindu nationalist ideologies, ordinarily assumed to be rooted in religious difference and communal conflict, should be more accurately seen as a discourse and practice of ethnic politics, or what will be describe here as *ethnoHinduism*.

The chapter begins by providing a framework for thinking of ethnic identity formation and the practice of ethnic politics. The following three sections present an analysis of the making of ethnoHinduism in relation to caste, the state and violence.

The designation and usage of communalism have become a way of 'describing the tendency of South Asian people to divide along an Islamic–Hindu breakdown' as a 'substitute for true nationalism'.[1] The term 'communal conflicts' originated in colonial analyses of what were perceived to be religious conflicts specific to India.[2] The study

---

[1] Walker Connor, *Ethnonationalism: The Quest for Understanding*, Princeton: Princeton University Press, 1994, p. 110. The partition of the subcontinent has also been characterised in this way.

[2] See Gyanendra Pandey, *The Construction of Communalism in Colonial North India*, Delhi: Oxford University Press, 1990, pp. 6–9.

of communalism, conceptualised in this way, is problematic, because this perspective presupposes that the antagonism between Hindus and Muslims results from the very fact of being Hindu or Muslim, independent of experience.[3] It postulates two monolithic and coherent communities of Hindus and Muslims in India that are liable to be drawn into conflict with each other. Such assumptions, which, as we have seen, were also expressed in the official views of the Ahmedabad riots, may obscure a genuine understanding of communal conflicts. Examining communalism as a practice of ethnic politics avoids the kind of reasoning that proceeds from religious categorisations and their supposed effects. The principal concern in the study of communalism as an ethnoHindu phenomenon becomes the origin and consolidation of an ethnic Hindu identity in politics.

Ethnic identities have repeatedly provided a powerful means of mobilisation for defining demands and organising collectives into action. Ethnic identities are often expressed as religious nationalism or as a struggle for cultural particularism. The rhetoric and claims of ethnic or nationalist political movements, such as Hindutva – just like the terms in which they have been widely understood and analysed – have often lent fixity to these markers of identity. However, on close scrutiny, these religious and cultural identities are found to be contingent upon political rivalries, economic pressures and social contexts. At times these group identities gain political relevance and at other times they are played down. Far from constituting a foundational or ontological unit of action and analysis, social, and especially ethnic, identities should be regarded as malleable and transient.

While ethnic identity has a function, it has no fixed essence. It is impossible to pinpoint an essential characteristic of an ethnic identity without which that identity would cease to exist. As an indefinite category of difference, ethnic identity can serve, in different circumstances, as a function of other categories of social difference such as class, caste, gender and race. Precisely because ethnic identity has a function, while its properties are contingent rather than essential, ethnic identities are a particularly expedient means of negotiating leverage, and struggling over material, social and ideological resources within the context of the state. Thus, the formation processes and operation of ethnic identities are highly relevant and effective in politics.

Ethnic identities are formed and operate in the interstices of categories of social difference. The categories of difference that form the basis for

---

[3] Also see Gyanendra Pandey, *Remembering Partition: Violence, Nationalism and History in India*, Cambridge: Cambridge University Press, 2001, p. 53.

ethnic identity formation, as well as for the consolidation and action of actors, are determined by the dynamics of their interrelations with the state and among themselves. Because of the relational and contextual character of this process, ethnic identities have the potential to form and reform continuously.

In order to examine the formation processes of ethnic identities it is essential to focus on their boundaries. Exploring the boundaries illuminates why and how, under given historical circumstances, a specific feature of difference, among the various categories of social differentiation, appears to be more meaningful than any other to a significant number of people so as to provide sufficient grounds for political action. 'The cultural features that signal the boundary may change, and the cultural characteristics of the members may likewise be transformed . . . yet the fact of continuing dichotomization between members and outsiders allows us to specify the nature of continuity.'[4] The change or continuity of a group boundary, as well as the interplay between various categories of social difference in the making of this boundary, is examined here in relation to the state. Thus, the analysis of the formation processes of ethnic identities also explores boundaries between the state and social groups.

In the context of India, this study examines the making of ethnoHinduism and the formation and consolidation of Hindu identity in relation to caste, to state reservation policies and to the discourse about them. In this process, caste is understood as a practice of ethnic politics. Unlike the conventional view of caste as an identity that can be defined by essential properties,[5] this study suggests an understanding of caste identities as defined and determined in politics, in relation to other categories of social differentiation, in the context of struggles for the control of state material and ideological resources.

Caste has been most commonly perceived as the essence of Hindu identity, as the pillar of a hierarchical social structure based on Hindu religious principles. In this view, without caste there is no Hindu. State apparatuses, particularly in the context of reservation policies, sometimes entrenched this view. As mentioned in Chapter 2, the Constitution

---

[4] Fredrik Barth, 'Introduction', in F. Barth (ed.), *Ethnic Groups and Boundaries*, London: George Allen & Unwin, 1969, p. 14. Here I adopt Barth's idea of focusing on the boundaries of ethnic groups. In Barth's theory, however, there is only one boundary difference – the boundary of the ethnic group, which 'canalizes social life' – while the critical feature of an ethnic group is 'the characteristic of self-ascription and ascription by others'. *Ibid.*, pp. 13, 15. This study, by contrast, considers the diverse categories of social difference along Barth's idea of boundary, and focuses on the interrelations between them and with the state.

[5] Max Weber, 'Class, Status, Party', in H. H. Gerth and C. W. Mills (eds.), *From Max Weber: Essays in Sociology*, London: Routledge, 1991, p. 189.

(Scheduled Castes) Order of 1950 provided that 'no person professing a religion different from Hinduism shall be deemed a member of a Scheduled Caste', and the judiciary ruled that 'acceptance of a non-Hindu religion operates as a loss of caste'.[6] Yet, as we have seen in the discussion of the politics and discourse of reservations and caste, the nature of caste and its stability as a social unit depended on the definition it was given within politics, rather than on its inherent substance.

Indeed, although the reality of caste constitutes structures of social hierarchies, caste is not itself a fixed structure. Historical inquiry into the experience of castes also reveals how castes were shaped by political processes and social struggles and were not predominantly encompassed by fixed religious, moral and cultural principles. Rather, caste groups were formed and reformed within the changing historical circumstances, and particularly in the context of their struggles for leverage with the colonial state.[7] The efficacy of the social reality of caste is revealed most clearly in politics. The critical issue in the operation of caste is not the cultural features that it encompasses, but the boundary that defines the group. The boundary of caste signifies the porous membranes through which political interactions take place. In the context of redistributive reservation policies and struggles over access to various public resources, caste boundaries were defined in relation to class and religion by the state, and were also persistently renegotiated with the state.

---

[6] See Durga Das Basu, *Commentary on the Constitution of India*, 5th edn, Calcutta: S. C. Sarkar and Sons, 1965, p. 158; Marc Galanter, *Competing Equalities: Law and the Backward Classes in India*, Berkeley: University of California Press, 1984, pp. 144, 313, 315, 319. See Chapter 2 for a detailed discussion.

[7] See, for example, Nicholas Dirks, *The Hollow Crown*, Cambridge: Cambridge University Press, 1987; N. Dirks, 'The Invention of Caste: Civil Society in Colonial India', *Social Analysis*, vol. 25, September 1989, pp. 42–52; N. Dirks, *Castes of Mind: Colonialism and the Making of Modern India*, Princeton and Oxford: Princeton University Press, 2001. Bernard S. Cohn, *An Anthropologist among the Historians and Other Essays*, Oxford: Oxford University Press, 1987; David Washbrook, 'The Development of Caste Organisation in South India 1880–1925', in C. J. Baker and D. A. Washbrook (eds.), *South India: Political Institutions and Political Change 1880–1940*, Delhi: Macmillan, 1975, pp. 150–203; D. A. Washbrook, 'Caste, Class and Dominance in Tamil Nadu: Non-Brahmanism, Dravidianism and Tamil Nadu Nationalism', in Francine R. Frankel and M. S. A. Rao (eds.), *Dominance and State Power in Modern India*, Vol. I, Delhi: Oxford University Press, 1989, pp. 204–64; Rajnarayan Chandavarkar, 'Workers' Politics and the Mill District in Bombay between the Wars', *Modern Asian Studies*, vol. 15, no. 3, 1981, pp. 603–47; R. Chandavarkar, *Imperial Power and Popular Politics: Class, Resistance and the State in India, c. 1850–1950*, Cambridge: Cambridge University Press, 1998; Susan Bayly, 'The History of Caste in South Asia', *Modern Asian Studies*, vol. 17, no. 3, 1983, pp. 519–27; S. Bayly, *The New Cambridge History of India: Caste, Society and Politics in India from the Eighteenth Century to the Modern Age*, Cambridge: Cambridge University Press, 1999; Lucy Carroll, 'Colonial Perceptions of Indian Society and the Emergence of Caste(s) Associations', *Journal of Asian Studies*, vol. 38, no. 3, 1978, pp. 232–49.

Caste conflicts over state reservation policies, which evolved around the social and economic mobilisation of lower- and backward-caste Hindus, became entangled with class issues. The social, economic and political dynamics that occurred in India after independence generated transformations in caste–class relations, hierarchies and positions within the Hindu order. Class fissures occurred within castes, castes faced changes in class, and new groups emerged. The changes in the social order encompassed both class and caste categories of social difference. Groups in the society did not perceive their class and caste position in isolation from each other. In this analysis 'class dispositions' do not 'simply mirror reality. They are plausible and meaningful responses to the circumstance' that people 'find themselves in'.[8] The relational process between caste and class provided grounds for social action. The critical issue in the interrelations between caste and class was the formation process of the boundary that defined the group. The state has largely determined the boundaries of caste groups through, for example, its reservation policies in the 1980s for the benefit of the lower and backward castes. Significantly, 'backward' caste is a legal and constitutional, rather than a social category, which has been variably defined in relation to the policies of the state. In the designation of reservations, caste categories were flexible in composition. For the purpose of political alliances, the rigid distinctions purported to be embodied by castes sometimes disappeared. Caste identities were defined, redefined and attained meaning in politics, in the context of struggles for the control of political, material and social resources. Caste properties, then, were contingent rather than essential. In the 1970s and 1980s, the determination of caste boundaries for reservation policies was the subject of growing conflicts among Hindus. The state's designation of reservations intricately conflated questions of caste and class with religion and religious minority rights and therefore facilitated the rise of communal antagonism.

The following analysis seeks to unravel the complex patterns of interrelations between caste, class, communalism and the state. It therefore examines the rise of communal antagonism against Muslims and the growth of Hindu nationalism by emphasising the interdependence of political rivalries and economic pressures on the one hand, and social context and identity on the other. Like a lens for observing these dynamic processes, as well as the 'complexities and contradictions of real life',[9] the

---

[8] Ira Katznelson, 'Working-Class Formation: Constructing Cases and Comparisons', in Ira Katznelson and Aristide R. Zolberg (eds.), *Working Class Formation*, Princeton, NJ: Princeton University Press, 1986, p. 19.

[9] Bent Flyvbjerg, *Making Social Science Matter*, Cambridge: Cambridge University Press, 2001, p. 84.

analysis shifts across three levels of social operation. The first is the level of *high* politics, where political stratagems for electoral contests and for government-building are devised; the second level consists of the general patterns of social and economic change; and the third level encompasses the everyday operations of individuals and groups. These three levels capture the dynamics of interrelations between significant categories of difference and their relation to the state at major intersections, where state and society interact and impact upon each other. The second level represents the transformations that by the 1980s challenged the identity of various groups among Hindus, and particularly the meaning of their status within the Hindu moral order. At the first level of *high* politics an ongoing process of making political sense of these social dynamics is at work. At the third level, the sensitive encounters with the actors themselves uncover the workings of the state in everyday life. From these direct human experiences, it is sometimes possible to extract direct explanations for political questions. The local narratives and explanations provide a microcosm of wide-ranging social processes. Although the particular elements of their content may change, they reveal the living model of social behaviour and practices. Only by examining each level of operation as a mirror that reflects the others can a relatively coherent narrative explanation be constituted. The analysis thus exposes the underlying processes that, from the local perspective of the long period of sustained violence in Ahmedabad in 1985, would become a feature of the rise of Hindu nationalism in the coming decades.

The making of ethnoHinduism and caste

There was a time when Ahmedabad consisted only of the walled city, where the pol provided the material lived world of the people. As shown in previous chapters, the growth of the city, its expansion and development resulted in changes in the interrelations between caste and class among Hindus. Caste segmentation took the form of inter-caste and class fissures. Thus, for example, in the 1950s and 1960s, the upper-caste Patels from Vadigam, who were regarded as relatively lower in status within the Patel caste hierarchy in the city and lived adjacent to Dalits and Muslims, were considered to be the middle class. They did not themselves use the language of class but behaved as such, adopting social traits that were considered to be distinctively middle-class.[10] Although the majority of them worked in the textile mills, they perceived themselves neither in terms of *majdoor* (labour), nor in terms of class categories. Vadigam's upper castes

---

[10] For example, unlike the case in working-class families, women did not seek employment.

used the language of caste to identify themselves. At the same time, they characterised the residents of the chawls in the eastern belt around the mills as labour, as did those residents themselves. Their caste status and position as indigenous Ahmedabadis were the basis of their identification as middle class. Until the 1950s, for example, the Brahmin and Patel children of the primary schools in the walled city queued separately in the dining area and drank from different glasses, labelled by caste. These casteist practices slowly disappeared after independence. Then, from the beginning of the 1980s Vadigam's upper castes experienced downward mobility.[11]

As a result of the city's expansion and growing economic opportunities, class fissures appeared within the various caste groups. Those who were able to do so, mainly professionals, had 'crossed the river' to the developing western area of the city already before 1985. The options for those who remained were extremely limited behind the city walls. They suffered the impact of the closure of the textile mills. The demographic and residential changes across the river and 'behind the walls' contributed to the development of new class-based identifications among Hindus. The upper-caste Patels and Brahmins who remained in Vadigam gradually realised that they were living in very similar, or even worse, conditions than some of their Dalit neighbours. By the 1980s, it had become evident that the prejudiced caste differences and distance were, in fact, greater than the actual living circumstances. Instead of looking at the class fissures that had occurred among them, and at their own predicament as labour, the upper castes directed their gaze outward. The resulting social anger was, partly, an expression of deep-rooted prejudices that were being challenged. The Patels of Vadigam, and upper castes in general in the walled city, felt threatened by the mobilisation of Dalits.

After independence, caste practices in Ahmedabad became less rigid. Some groups among the Dalits were able to improve their economic situation through the jobs in the mills,[12] and by the early 1980s many Dalits had already graduated from colleges. Through reservations their numbers in governmental jobs and educational institutions increased.[13] Although the reservation quotas were never filled, there was an increasing

---

[11] All Vadigam's residents who were interviewed attested to this.

[12] See discussion in Chapter 1.

[13] See *Report of the Commission for Scheduled Castes and Scheduled Tribes April 1984–March 1985*, New Delhi: Government of India, pp. 5,7; *Report of the Commission for Scheduled Castes and Scheduled Tribes April 1985–March 1986*, New Delhi: Government of India, p. 10. Also see Ghanshyam Shah, 'Polarised Communities', *Seminar*, 470, October 1998; D. L. Sheth, 'Reservation Policy Revisited', in Gurpreet Mahajan (ed.), *Democracy, Difference and Social Justice*, New Delhi: Oxford University Press, 2000.

number of scheduled castes and scheduled tribe employees, especially in the lower-ranked positions, to which citizens were most exposed in their interaction with the state bureaucracy. 'At least one person from either of these communities is found in most government departments.'[14] Moreover, Dalits' growing participation in politics served to accelerate their mobilisation. The emergence of the Congress's KHAM strategy from the late 1970s fostered their politicisation on the basis of their caste status. Gradually, some groups among the Dalits and the backward castes in general began to consolidate themselves as politically relevant social actors.[15] Paradoxically, as the importance of caste in daily life diminished, caste gradually assumed growing political relevance and attained a new lease of life.

As a result of these political, social and economic processes, inter-caste and class segmentation also began to appear among the Dalits, overlapping with the inter-caste divisions and hierarchy that existed among them. The Vankars, who were considered to be higher in status and had established themselves first within the textile industry and the labour union, were among those able to rise in economic status. This group, as well as the Ahmedabadi Mulgami Dalits, advanced successfully through education and access to government jobs.[16] The emancipation of Dalits, partly through reservations, had created a group of 'neo-Brahmin Dalit, as a politically opportunistic strata of middle class emerged among the Dalits in the city'.[17] 'The lifestyle of the urban educated Dalits has changed. They dress, speak and behave like the middle strata of the upper castes.'[18] The mobilisation processes among the Dalits resulted in a growing sense of uncertainty within the Hindu moral order among upper castes.

The growing class fissures among upper castes resulted in the apparently sudden rise of a new middle class across the river. Members of the upper castes who had moved from the old city to the western side began differentiating themselves from their caste-fellows who remained 'behind the walls'. According to a common saying among them, the people of

---

[14] Ghanshyam Shah, 'Middle-Class Politics: A Case of Anti-Reservation Agitation in Gujarat, *Economic and Political Weekly*, Annual Number, May 1987, p. AN-163.

[15] Dalits' political awareness and assertiveness increased from 1975 also, through the growing activities of the Dalit Panther movement in the city.

[16] For benefits from reservations for Vankars, and to a lesser extent the Chamars, also see Nagindas Sanghavi, *Gujarat a Political Analysis*, Surat: Centre for Social Studies, 1996, p. 83.

[17] *Interview* with Inayat, Dalit, Kalupur, Ahmedabad, 25/2/98.

[18] Shah, 'Polarised Communities', p. 34. Also see Achyut Yagnik, 'Search for Dalit Self Identity in Gujarat', in Takashi Shinoda (ed.), *The Other Gujarat*, Mumbai: Popular Prakashan, 2002, p. 23.

the old city have their 'feet in labour, but their mind much higher. They consider themselves as intellectuals.'[19]

While castes had never been altogether homogenous in class, at that time increasingly salient class differences began emerging in many more domains of life. In the past, both rich and poor members of the same caste had resided side by side in the same pol in the old city. Class disparities had not constituted a significant marker of difference and had been contained within the caste itself, often through patronage, and at the expense of other caste groups, lower in the caste hierarchy. Gradually class became more pertinent as an emblem of social difference because, among other things, it marked more clearly the changes in castes.

The challenges to the status identity of upper castes in the walled city were exacerbated by the increasing difficulty in overcoming the deepening discrepancies between their social self-perception and their actual experiences. Previously, even as labour in the mills, upper castes in the old city had been able to maintain their middle-class self-perception. This became more complicated in the circumstances of the 1980s. The inter-caste and class fissures were inscribed upon the city's face, especially as their economically wealthier caste fellows moved 'beyond the walls' and the differences in living conditions between them and their Dalit and Muslim neighbours became less distinct. Upper-caste frustrations further intensified because, just as their caste status lost its importance, lower-caste status gained significance in politics through, for example, the KHAM caste alliance and redistribution policies such as reservations.

Reservation was a burning issue for some upper-caste groups, particularly among the new middle classes on the western side of Ahmedabad. Testimonies and pamphlets suggested that the notion of reservation challenged the upper castes' status and self-validity. Reservations enabled lower and backward castes growing access to arenas previously monopolised by upper castes. This was seen as a direct threat to the upper castes' status. Indeed, if a Dalit could be a professor, the whole idea of the 'caste system' lost its meaning.

For some groups among the upper castes, higher education or government jobs were at the time the primary path for economic advancement. This now was also the avenue for the Dalits and the backward castes. Upper-caste groups felt that reservations limited their opportunities. If there had not been reserved places in higher educational institutions, there would have been more places for their own children. The few missing decimal points that blocked an upper caste's admission into, for example, medical school, because of the limited number of general

---

[19] *Interview* with Girish Patel, Naranpura, Ahmedabad, 7/4/98.

places, would not have been an obstacle. The upper castes' sense that the reservation system was biased against them was reinforced precisely because not all the reserved places could be filled.

The rising Kadva Patel caste group in the eastern industrial belt also felt restrained in the context of the changing interrelations between caste and class among Hindus and as lower-caste status gained significance in politics. The eastern industrial belt had developed initially around textile mills surrounded by working-class neighbourhoods of chawls, slums and scattered Gujarat Housing Board flats. Gradually new entrepreneurs established more industries and businesses and settled in the area. The social group that was particularly active in the riots of 1985 were the Kadva Patels from Saurashtra. This group began migrating to this area of Ahmedabad from Saurashtra from the 1970s. They were the second generation of families that benefited from the land reforms in Saurashtra and migrated to Ahmedabad in the face of the decreasing opportunities in agriculture.[20] They were considered of lower status than the Patels from central Gujarat, but since independence they had risen economically. By 1985 one of the main barriers to their further advancement was the mounting cost of land. Many plots in the area, in which they had growing interests, were occupied by slum dwellers of which 83 per cent were lower- and backward-caste Hindu communities and 15 per cent were Muslims.[21] Some of these lands had been made available to the slum residents by the Ahmedabad Municipal Corporation.

Nevertheless, the Patels in the eastern city of Ahmedabad, as well as those Patels and Brahmins across the river, also felt politically bypassed because of the apparent success of the KHAM politics which fostered a sense of discrepancy between their social and political positions. In the view of many upper castes, the numerical strength of the members of the KHAM alliance made its groups politically more important and attractive.

While the perceptible class fissures among Hindus undermined the upper castes' status identity and its meaning, these processes also resulted in growing frustrations among some relatively prosperous Dalit groups. 'People from lower castes, like Dalits from Mehsana, rose economically and educationally, but still were not accepted socially.'[22] This was a crucial issue for the new middle class among them. These aspirations contradicted the politics at the time, like the KHAM, which was based on their low-caste status.

---

[20] *Interview* with Gordhanbhai Jhadafia, BJP MLA, Bapunagar, Ahmedabad, 16/12/97.
[21] See *Report on Census of Slums*, Ahmedabad Corporation, p. 16.
[22] *Interview* with Ashok Shrimali, Ahmedabad, 14/11/97.

The changes in the interrelations between caste and class among Hindus resulted in growing antagonism between forward and lower and backward castes. These processes drove distinct groups to act upon and place emphasis on different markers of the groups' boundary in their struggle for the control of material and ideological resources. Lower-class or descending groups among the upper castes resorted to their caste identity. Middle-class groups among the Patels and the rising middle-class Dalits emphasised their groups' class or caste boundaries in accordance with the circumstances.

These transformations in caste–class relations among Hindus began to be reflected in the modes of political mobilisation, and in particular in increasing support for the Hindu nationalist movement. Numerous testimonies from Vadigam described the help provided by various Hindu organisations during that time of economic hardship. Seeking a safe harbour in a time of insecurity, and especially in response to KHAM politics, upper castes lent support to Hindu political forces.

The construction of a 'Hindu opinion' among the Dalits was not only the outcome of the riots, but part of an ongoing process that reached a critical junction during the 1985 riots.[23] Overall, with the exception of the eastern industrial area, Dalits were not attacked during the riots. They began to be mobilised for relief work by Hindu organisations, through the informal welfare system of the VHP, which gave their youth a sense of leadership and participation. Consequently, after the 1985 riots, following the BJP's and Hindu organisations' efforts to accommodate the Dalits, the BJP gradually started to gain popularity from Dalits in the inter-mixed localities.[24] Hindu political forces used the riots and the violence to mobilise support among the Dalits, as well as among other caste groups. Thus, for example, in public meetings a few BJP politicians handed out money, food and even weapons to Dalits.[25] This marked the beginning of the political transition in Gujarat from Congress to the BJP and the dissolution of KHAM politics.

---

[23] In 1983 the RSS established the Samajik Samrasata Manch (SSM), a social assimilation platform, to attract Dalits. See Ghanshyam Shah, 'The BJP's Riddle in Gujarat: Caste, Factionalism and Hindutva', in Thomas Blom Hansen and Christophe Jaffrelot (eds.), *The BJP and the Compulsions of Politics in India*, Delhi: Oxford University Press, 1998, pp. 254–5. Also see Achyut Yagnik, 'Search for Dalit Self Identity in Gujarat', pp. 31–2; Achyut Yagnik and Suchitra Sheth, *The Shaping of Modern Gujarat: Plurality, Hindutva and Beyond*, New Delhi: Penguin Books, 2005, p. 255.

[24] *Interviews* with Inayat, Dariapur, Ahmedabad, 22/2/98, 11/3/98; Ashok Shrimali, Navrangpura, Ahmedabad, 14/11/97; Karsenbhai, Ambedkar Street, Dariapur, 29/11/97.

[25] *Interview* with Shirin, Ahmedabad, 4/1/98.

Some Dalits, who were members of the KHAM alliance, began feeling alienated from the Congress Party in the context of the crisis in the textile mills. Dalits constituted a large segment of the workforce in Ahmedabad. The Textile Labour Association (TLA), which was closely associated with the Congress Party, disappointed the workers when the mills were closed down, and its failure discredited the party as the champion of the workers. At the time the TLA did not provide aid to workers, Hindu organisations and the BJP began to support them. 'We [BJP] supplied money and relief, like we did later during the 1985 riots.'[26] Thus, the growing disparity between the Dalit workers' economic predicament and their apparent political success through the Congress's KHAM caste alliance served increasing right-wing politicisation. For the successful segments among the Dalits, for whom economic advancement and education had brought no change in their social position, affinity with an upper-caste party like the BJP created a sense of social inclusion.

The incorporation of some Dalits in the old city into the Hindu fold was also, symbolically, associated with the Hindu religious rite of the Rath Yatra. The incidents that occurred on the Rath Yatra day became deeply embedded in peoples' memories. In the old city, the event was widely recalled as a cause of the eruption of the riots even though the Yatra had taken place only towards the end of the disturbances. As noted in the previous chapter, Dalits had been allowed to participate fully in the Rath Yatra service even though they were usually excluded from taking part in religious rituals. This gesture had been very meaningful for them. Bhanu, a Dalit who participated in that Rath Yatra, testified that 'at that time we felt part of the Hindu community'.[27] This was a psychological triumph for the Dalits. Thus, Hindu organisations fulfilled both the need for a politics of redistribution and the need for pride and acceptance.

The middle- and lower-middle-class upper castes – Vadigam's and western Ahmedabad's Patels and Brahmins, and Patels in the eastern belt – as well as the rising groups among the Dalits, gradually formed the social foundation of the BJP in the city. Their motive and motif was social mobility. Some had been able to gain economic mobility by the 1980s, but had been gradually excluded from the political processes. Some groups, despite their economic advancement, had failed to attain either status or social acceptance. Others, despite their high-caste status, had experienced economic decline and political exclusion which had deprived their status of its meaning. Interestingly, even though these groups did not share

---

[26] *Interview* with Ashok Bhatt, BJP MLA, Ahmedabad, 27/11/97. This was also reiterated in *Interview* with Valgibhai Patel, Dalit Panthers, Ahmedabad, 29/11/97.

[27] *Interview* with Bhanu, Kalupur, Ahmedabad, 23/2/98.

the same frustrations, the Hindu nationalist movement was relatively successful in addressing the varying claims of distinct groups. The movement
transformed economic and social contradictions among castes, between
castes and among classes into communal ones.

The rising support for the Hindu nationalist party and communal
Hindu organisations was driven by tensions among Hindus, which were
the result of changes in the caste regime and growing uncertainties in
the Hindu moral order. These transformations among Hindus, which
were intermittently perceived according to categories of class and caste,
were ultimately linked to religion, thus serving a Hindu consolidation
against Muslims. This dynamics of the growth of Hindu nationalism was
impelled by the state and by frustrations of various Hindu groups with
it.

The state and the making of ethnoHinduism

At first sight, residents' accounts of the communal shift in the riots of 1985
indicate that people were instigated by the BJP. The official account also
emphasised the role of political manipulation in the communal turn in
the riots. However, the personal narratives of the riots reveal that people
were not simply passive pawns manoeuvred by political leaders. People
did not act as a disorderly mob, especially during the riots when they
were well organised. Indeed, many of the riots in different localities in
the walled city were not spontaneous, but planned in advance. Moreover,
even though upper castes identified themselves as agitators against their
Muslim neighbours, their anger was directed against the government,
rather than against Muslims. They argued that the government favoured
the Muslims, but were unable to specify a conflict with the latter. The rage
that was manifested in the violence was thus the result of the upper castes'
general sense of being neglected by a government that was antagonistic
to their needs during that strenuous time, and sometimes even during
normal times.

The frustrations of upper castes in the old city evolved in the light of
the class fissures that occurred within both forward and backward castes
and the narrowing avenues for advancement, which were now shared by
more groups in the society. Although the reservation issue did not affect
them directly, it amplified the sense of their own restricted opportunities. Particularly in the context of their experience of downward mobility,
reservations signalled a greater prospect for social mobility for the Dalits
and the backward castes, which were granted these preferential rights by
the state. In the view of Vadigam's upper castes, the former middle classes,
the government favoured the lower and backward castes in order to gain

their political support. After all, the government had announced its new reservation policy two months before the elections. The consolidation of the Congress's KHAM strategy further antagonised them. In their testimonies, some upper castes expressed sentiments of estrangement from the state. One resident, for example, explicitly asserted, 'I was arrested because I represented the *savarna*.'[28] Upper-caste Hindus, who began to feel politically insecure, also perceived Muslims, who were members of the KHAM alliance, as a threat to their political dominance. In the upper castes' view, Dalits and Muslims were coming together to form an alliance of classes which had a real prospect of pursuing redistribution policies. In the 1970s, policies for the benefit of the 'weaker sections' in the society had remained, on the whole, within the purview of political rhetoric or, as in the case of land and housing policies, had benefited those who were already prosperous. Residents of Vadigam argued that since Congress supported Muslims the BJP supported Hindus.[29] The notion of preferential treatment by the government towards lower- and backward-caste Hindus through the reservations policy and electoral politics easily shifted into the belief in government favouritism for Muslims.

Nonetheless, the local economic tensions at the time also worked to antagonise upper castes, as well as groups within the KHAM coalition, against Muslims. With the closure of the textile mills, many of the unemployed workers in the Dariapur area, for example, became rickshaw drivers, or started small businesses. As unskilled labour for the new developing industries, Vadigam's upper castes were suddenly competing with neighbouring unemployed Muslims and Dalit textile workers in a very limited job market, and on very similar terms. In the mills they had often held clerical and managerial jobs. A study of displaced mill workers, conducted at the end of 1984, found that among the workers who reported to have had some kind of paid work were larger percentages of Muslims and OBCs.[30] Driving a rickshaw provided at the time the highest daily earning for dismissed mill workers.[31] The rickshaw market became a significant domain of economic competition.[32] Hindu interviewees in the Dariapur area commented that because most of the rickshaw mechanics

---

[28] *Interview* with Ramesh, Vadigam, Ahmedabad, 21/3/98.   [29] *Ibid.*

[30] B. B. Patel, *Workers of Closed Textile Mills*, New Delhi: Oxford and IBH Publishing, 1988, pp. 24–5. Minorities, mainly Muslims, and the Baxi Panch castes, OBCs, constituted about 20 per cent of the workers in the study, and upper-middle castes 18 per cent. *Ibid.*, p. 17.

[31] *Ibid.*

[32] As the city expanded, transportation needs grew significantly. Between 1971 and 1985 the number of auto-rickshaws in Ahmedabad rose from 4,464 to 22,700. See *Statistical Outline of Ahmedabad City 1994–95*, Planning and Statistic Department, Ahmedabad Municipal Corporation, Ahmedabad, 1996, Table 9.15, p. 138.

and garage owners were Muslims, they were in a disadvantaged position. This local economic tension adds another layer for understanding the communal 'twist' in the Ahmedabad riots of 1985 in this particular area.

Upper castes in the western city of Ahmedabad were particularly antagonised by the government reservations policy. Even though the government insisted in its new reservation policy that caste, and not the more universal category of class, should be the defining criterion for reservation, Muslims were lumped together with the lower- and backward-caste Hindus in the intra-Hindu reservations conflict. The Naranpura Patel Yuvak Mandal argued that they were under attack by Muslims, Dalits and Thakors. They pointed out that those who 'used to pick up the night soil from our homes' were now in privileged positions as a result of reservations and sometimes even their bosses.[33]

In the context of deepening status insecurities among Hindus and growing tensions between forward and backward castes, which were related to state reservation policies and the KHAM politics, upper castes gradually came to conceive of Muslims in the same way they had perceived the position and operation of the Dalits. The two groups were regarded as being of a piece.

There are records of upper castes conflating a fear of Dalits' mobility as tantamount to a threat from Muslims. In January 1948 there was a dispute over the entry of Dalits to the Swaminarayana temple in Ahmedabad. In that context, a speaker opposed to Dalits' access to temples stated that: 'we are passing through a critical period. The internal invasion is from the untouchables and the external one is from the Muslims and Pakistan. I am not advising you to Murder Muslims, But at least show them that we are awakened and united.'[34]

Moreover, some Dalits and Muslims, especially in the old city, perceived themselves as belonging to similar groups with the same economic, political and social predicament. Some interviewees emphasised that Dalits and Muslims had shared similar dietary habits and, in contrast to the upper castes in Gujarat, were not vegetarian. Some claimed that the two communities even shared the same slaughterhouses and butchers,

---

[33] Naranpura Patel Yuvak Mandal, Pamphlet, Ahmedabad, SETU Library, 1985.

[34] Quoted in Makrand Mehta, 'The Dalit Temple Entry Movement in Maharashtra and Gujarat, 1930–1948', in Takashi Shinoda (ed.), *The Other Gujarat*, Mumbai: Popular Prakashan, 2002, p. 13. According to Sumit Sarkar, the founder of the RSS, K. B. Hedgewar, 'Located lower-caste assertion on par with the Muslim threat as the twin dangers that lay behind' the formation of the organisation. See: Sumit Sarkar, 'Indian Nationalism and the Politics of Hindutva', in David Ludden (ed.), *Making India Hindu: Religion, Community and the Politics of Democracy in India*, Delhi: Oxford University Press, 1996, p. 288.

which was also why they always resided next to each other.[35] During the 1981 anti-reservation riots, which also erupted shortly after the Congress won elections in Gujarat on the basis of the KHAM caste alliance, Muslims helped Dalits in Ahmedabad.[36] 'After 1981, efforts were taken to unite Muslims and Dalits and to create polarisation along class lines. There was a big conference and the slogan was "Dalit Muslim Bhai Bhai" (Dalit and Muslims Brothers, Brothers)'.[37] A Dalit interviewee who tried to express that these relations between Dalits and Muslims were genuine claimed that 'this was a social thing'.[38]

The dynamic whereby Dalits, as well as preferential policies for them, and Muslims were perceived en bloc was inadvertently produced by the state. As Chapter 2 elaborated, in the designation of reservations, policy makers, politicians and the judiciary conflated issues of social and economic reforms for the benefit of lower and backward Hindu groups on the basis of caste or class, with religion. In the discourse of reservations the question whether caste or class should be the criterion for determining backwardness was often posited as a choice between religiosity and secularism. Since issues of equality were addressed as if they were synonymous with the rights of religious minorities, reservations were sometimes perceived to be a compensatory act for minority groups in the society on the basis of their religion. In this way, government reservation policies enabled caste reservation conflicts to develop and generate communal antagonism against Muslims. Communalism, therefore, grew in the interstices between caste and class. The relational processes between caste, class and communalism were largely generated by state policies and practices.

Subsequently, when a minority group, such as the Muslims, obtained rights from the state on the basis of their religion – for instance the protection of the *Sharia* law for marriage and divorce – these were readily associated with the practice of reservations. All religious minorities in India were entitled to similar provisions. Thus, for example, in an anti-reservations protest in November 1992, after the Supreme Court constitutionally upheld the Mandal Commission Report for reservations for the backward castes at the national level, a student declared: 'we are going for a constitutional amendment. The government could amend the constitution to its convenience back in the Shah Bano case. Why the hell

---

[35] *Interviews* with Makbul and Pravin Rashtrapar, Dariapur, Ahmedabad, 29/11/97.
[36] *Interviews* with Karsenbhai, Ambedkar Street, Ahmedabad, 29/11/97; Makbul, Sajjan Jamadar's Moholla, Dariapur, Ahmedabad, 30/12/97. Many interviewees reiterated this claim.
[37] *Interview* with Achyut Yagnik, Navrangpura, Ahmedabad, 11/12/97.
[38] *Interview* with Parmanand, Ahmedabad, 14/11/97.

can't they do it now?'[39] Moreover, the suggestion of including backward Muslim groups was considered and in a few cases some Muslim groups were indeed included on the lists of eligible groups. From this perspective, the common saying among Muslims, that 'whenever we hear the call to abolish reservation, we realise that communal riots are about to erupt',[40] becomes more intelligible.

Already during the 1981 anti-reservation riots 'the RSS and other Hindu communal elements did try their best to turn the anti-Dalit war into a Hindu Muslim riot. But best of their efforts failed because all the oppressed and persecuted communities stood like one man.'[41] During the riots of 1985, however, communal antagonism emerged partly because Muslims and Dalits were conflated into the beneficiaries of the reservations policy. In their pamphlet against reservations the Patel Yuvak Mandal argued that Muslims and Dalits should be punished for uniting over reservations and that Muslims should be exiled to Pakistan.[42]

The reservation dispute thus became an expression of the social, economic and political dynamics that had developed in Ahmedabad since independence. These processes brought changes in caste–class relations, hierarchies and positions. After independence, the dominance of the upper castes in the city was further consolidated. The Patel caste, Shudras by Hindu law, emerged as an economic and political force, and was able to attain the *savarna*.[43] The state facilitated the strengthening of the upper castes through, for example, land reforms and the distribution of political goods. However, as the state became the source of the upper castes' domination, their dependency upon it for their well-being and legitimacy increased, and this, in turn, impaired their authority over the backward castes. In the past, their domination had functioned as a surrogate for a state. They had been able to gain command over the rest of society through various mechanisms of patronage. Now, with the growing penetration of the state, when traditional modes of mobilisation and control were changing, the upper castes began losing that form of

[39] *NewsTrack*, December 1992, 24/12/92. Shah Bano, an elderly Muslim divorcee, appealed in 1986 to the court in a matter of long-term alimony, which Muslim religious law does not allow for. The Supreme Court decided that the provisions of the Indian penal code on maintenance take precedence over the *Sharia* and allowed her maintenance payments. However, Rajiv Gandhi's government at the time yielded to the pressure mounted by the conservative orthodox members of the Muslim community and overturned the court's decision through legislation. Subsequently, this gesture was 'balanced' by opening the Babri mosque in Ayodhya for Hindu worship.
[40] *Interview* with Inayat, Dariapur, Ahmedabad, 22/2/98.
[41] V. T. Rajshekar Shetty, File 220.9/4, SETU Archive Files, 1981, p. 2.
[42] Excerpt from Naranpura Patel Yuvak, pamphlet.
[43] Ashish Nandy et al., *Creating a Nationality: The Ramjanmabhumi Movement and Fear of the Self*, Delhi: Oxford University Press, 1997, pp. 100–1.

domination. The crisis evolved as political parties began to recognise the electoral importance of backward groups.

From an upper-caste viewpoint, segments of the lower and backward castes were mobilising. 'Caste politics', whereby caste alliances were politically instituted in order to obtain majorities, did not necessarily improve the lower groups' economic situation, but their growing politicisation gradually generated social achievements. State reservations policy, for example, enabled backward castes to negotiate political leverage on the basis of their formal low-caste status.

With the growing class fissures among and between castes it gradually became apparent that the widely perceived harmony between the 'cosmological' Hindu order and everyday reality was breaking down. If, for example, the relatively low-status upper castes in the walled city had previously been able to justify their self-representation as middle-class, this was no longer negotiable in the context of the mid-1980s. Although at that time some upper-caste groups, especially in the old city, shared similar objective circumstances to those of the Dalits and Muslims, their actions were guided by their caste identification. Rather than addressing the 'cultural' clash among Hindus, upper castes transferred it to a conflict with the Muslims. In their aspiration to restore their position, as well as the Dalits', within the Hindu order to its former state, upper castes substituted Muslims for Dalits. In the circumstances of the 1980s, the fault-lines in society were thus redefined along the lines of religion.

The construction of an all-Hindu front against Muslims in the mid-1980s emerged in the context of political attempts to unite Dalits and Muslims, along with intensifying economic pressures, on the one hand, and the growing identity concerns and social frustrations among Hindus, on the other. Some upper-caste groups among Hindus felt that the new opportunities for social mobility over the past two or three decades did not benefit them sufficiently. At the same time other people of lesser status were able to exploit these opportunities equally or even more fully. Upper castes identified the reason for their own 'limited' mobility in the preference government policies appeared to give to minorities, including Muslims.

Some of the incidents during the riots that appeared to be communal violence were in fact related to everyday disputes between groups in the society and representatives of the state.[44] An examination of the workings

---

[44] Similar findings on how violence tends to be related to local and private conflicts rather than to the war's 'master cleavage' is found in Stathis N. Kalyvas, 'The Ontology of "Political Violence": Action and Identity in Civil War', *Perspectives on Politics*, vol. 1, no. 3, September 2003, pp. 475–94.

of the state in citizens' daily lives reveals the dynamics by which the communalistion of the state and the society that appeared to overwhelm the various local tensions developed.

Communal violence and the state

The official account of the Ahmedabad riots of 1985 primarily presented a picture of anti-reservation and communal agitations in a city suffering from the total collapse of law and order. The second account unveiled three cities, in which the violence took different shapes and expressed disparate tensions. The personal recollections of the riots suggested that beneath the apparent anarchy, below the horizon of the state, some social order, as well as qualitative social interactions, prevailed. The emerging tensions were driven by diverse struggles over political, economic and social resources. A great deal of these tensions resulted from contests over the regulation of relations between groups in the society and the state apparatuses. Some of the state's mechanisms for the maintenance of everyday law and order exhibited a vested interest in the perpetuation of lawlessness that in fact worked to undermine the state. For example, the competition within the police over posts in 'profitable areas' in the old city resulted in a growing sense among the residents that they were being exploited by the state. They expressed frustrations over the state's lack of accountability and its failure to provide them with social and economic security and consequently held the government and politicians responsible for the events.

The state apparatuses' malpractices drove people away from the state. Residents in the old city commonly kept in stock basic commodities that could last for as long as a year, along with a supply of home-made weapons. By possessing their own means of violence, they compromised the basic monopoly power of the state. At the locality level many people experienced non-state support through collective organisation, mainly in the form of civic defence and relief for riot victims. Precisely during the times of violence, in response to what appeared to be a collapse of the social order, people organised collectively at the local levels for their protection and subsistence. These efforts gave them a sense of belonging to a community, as well as social meaning to their existence as individuals, beyond the state. This was perhaps why residents, although describing the difficulties of that period, also expressed nostalgia for the good community life and even social harmony that had prevailed in their localities at that time. These sentiments, and the particular events that were associated with them, informed people's memories of the riots, which therefore may not always have reflected the accurate chronology of events. The ability to obtain subsistence at the time independently of the state was associated with the efforts of Hindu organisations towards people.

The residents' informal regulating mechanisms in their localities personified the concept of authority and marked a space in their life that they could control almost physically. The residential community within the localities was largely cohesive and attained its authority through an informal information system by means of blackboards and, often false, rumours. The combination of the spatial organisation of the living place and its caste social composition created unity among people, which especially at times of crisis reinforced the community and obedience to its rules. Thus, the residents of the pols in particular, but also the dwellers of a housing society and even a slum, behaved like citizens of their own *polis*.

At the same time, at the micro-locality level people appeared to adopt flexible and improvised methods for negotiating with formal authority. Corruption became, to some extent, a means of mediating between the formal and informal governing orders. At that level politicians were perceived to be social workers; the police 'helped us because we were Hindus'.[45] People who were designated by the state as anti-social elements were able to address needs that the state failed to provide. The state law established, for example, dowry as an illegal practice, yet the law was not strictly enforced and the custom prevailed. For some social groups dowry remained a serious economic constraint. Latif, the underworld don, provided the necessary help. The so-called anti-social elements, rather than the state, sustained the people during the riots and to many they became a symbol of resistance. These social dynamics appear to indicate the functional aspect of corruption and anti-social activity. It is likely, however, that they reflected symptoms of social anomie, but not the root of the problems. Through corrupt practices disadvantaged groups within the state and the society created their leverage and a firm hold on the state. But at the same time these dynamics perpetuated the dependence of disadvantaged groups on local patronage, thus eroding the standing of the state.

The recollections of residents of the old city demonstrated that, in effect, the state apparatuses that were intended to maintain impartial law and order actually functioned on the basis of a very loose and skewed set of rules. These informal standards, as well as the relationships between residents and the state representatives for the maintenance of law and order, were contingent upon the local personal relations and everyday working conditions of the police and politicians. Thus, a resident of the

---

[45] *Interview* with Ramesh, Vadigam, Ahmedabad, 21/3/98.

old city explained that the State Reserve Police near his locality were able to secure the availability of basic goods during the curfew because the people in his neighbourhood had good relations with them.[46] Another resident argued that if the police had wanted they could have stopped the violence. On the contrary, in his locality they instigated violence to extort protection money from bootleggers and shopkeepers.[47] Therefore, the fragmentation and incoherence of the state during the riots, which emerged from the official account of the event, were revealed to be characteristic of the state in everyday life. During the period of violence this face of the state simply became more visible.

The political fault-lines of communalism reflected those that emerged in the disputes over reservations. Both were mainly driven by Hindus' recent experiences of caste and the changing patterns of the interrelations between caste and class, which engendered growing uncertainties in the social, political and Hindu moral order. The political discourse of Hindutva, based on a sentiment of a unitary Hindu identity, provided an alternative to that reality. This discourse offered a persuasive ground for political mobilisation because it assuaged the social uncertainties and contradictions that had arisen out of the changes in the caste regime in the 1980s. It provided a shift from the politics of redistribution to the politics of recognition.

An understanding of the communal 'twist' that occurred in the 1985 anti-reservation riots cannot be limited to the narrow facts of the riots themselves. It needs to be examined within the wider processes of transformations in caste and class among Hindus and their relation to the state. The growth of communalism and militant Hinduism after 1985 had its seeds in these concrete social transformations and was driven by their effect.

The next chapter examines this analysis of the making of ethnoHinduism in relation to the communal riots that occurred in Ahmedabad in 1969 and the pogrom against Muslims in the city in 2002. The chapter examines the role of violence in ethnic politics. It offers an understanding of the role and effects of large-scale violence in the construction of ethnoHinduism by examining its relations to the nature and formation processes of ethnic identities that were developed in this chapter.

---

[46] *Interview* with Makbul, Sajjan Jamadar's Moholla, Dariapur, Ahmedabad, 29/11/97.
[47] *Interview* with Saurabh, Vadigam, Ahmedabad, 26/3/98.

The previous chapter showed how an all-Hindu consolidation against
Muslims emerged in the mid-1980s and argued that communalism is
related to caste and that both are better understood as practices of ethnic
politics. The making of an ethnoHindu identity in the context of the
mid-1980s was driven by the relational processes between caste and class
and the ways in which the state policies and politics had bearings upon
these interrelations. Despite the circumstantial and relational character
of the formation process of caste, communal and ethnic identities, and
the instability of these identities, violence kept recurring in Ahmedabad
from the mid-1980s along what were widely viewed as communal lines.

This chapter explicates the relations between the unstable character
of caste and communal identities and the recurrence and intensification
of communal violence from the mid-1980s.[1] The first part develops an
argument about the links between the effects of large-scale violence and
the formation process of ethnic identities. The second part of the chapter
analyses the role of violence in ethnic politics and the rise of communalism
from the mid-1980s in relation to Ahmedabad's history of violence since
independence.

The first large-scale post-independence communal conflagration in
India occurred in Ahmedabad in 1969. This violence did not, however,
immediately lead to an all-Hindu consolidation and a growth in Hindu
nationalism, even though on several occasions over previous months tensions between Hindus and Muslims had been interpreted as caused by
religious offences experienced by the respective groups. The rhetoric
about the Muslim peril to the Hindu majority could have been persuasive in 1969, and yet a communal Hindu identity did not emerge in its
wake. On the contrary, Hindu–Muslim tensions in the 1970s and early

---

[1] The question of the social construction of ethnic identities and how this process leads
to ethnic violence is also discussed in James D. Fearon and David D. Laitin, 'Violence and the Social Construction of Ethnic Identity', *International Organization*, vol. 54,
no. 4, 2000, pp. 845–77.

1980s were insignificant. The ethnic conflicts of the early 1980s were primarily between forward- and backward-caste Hindus about reservations policy and the status of the backward castes. It is unclear, then, why the riots of 1969 were not an immediate precursor to the rise of Hindu nationalism.

From the mid-1980s, in spite of the changing significance of caste and communal identities, Hindu nationalism grew and communal violence persisted. Sporadic communal violence occurred in Ahmedabad thereafter. In 1990 and 1992 major riots again broke out in the city, coinciding with communal riots throughout the subcontinent. In February 2002 there was a pogrom against Muslims in Ahmedabad and throughout large parts of Gujarat. Government officials openly aided in the attacks on the Muslim minority by members of militant Hindu organisations and the government did not act to stop the carnage.[2]

Taking the riots of 1985 as the basis for a comparison, this chapter explores why the riots of 1969 did not immediately lead to the growth of a communal Hindu identity; and how the widespread communalisation of the state that was manifested in 2002 emerged.

As the previous chapter suggested, ethnic identities are formed in the effect of the interrelations between various categories of social differentiation. These dynamics of interrelations are most clearly revealed in the context of struggles over a range of state resources. The markers of social differentiation, which become most relevant for a large number of people as a basis for social and political action, under certain circumstances, are determined by the interrelations among these categories of difference and between them and the state. Because of the relational and contextual character of this formation process, ethnic identities have the potential to change in composition.

Three main characteristics can be discerned from this formation process of ethnic identities. First, ethnic identity formation is a practice and politics of social differentiation, which occurs along the boundaries of markers of difference. Second, at the basis of this formation process lie the relations between various social groups and the state. Third, ethnic identities and their boundaries are impermanent and temporal.

---

[2] See Siddharth Varadarajan (ed.), *Gujarat: The Making of a Tragedy*, New Delhi: Penguin Books, 2002; Aakar Patel, Dileep Padgaonkar and B. G. Verghese, *Rights and Wrongs: Ordeal by Fire in the Killing Fields of Gujarat*, New Delhi: Editors Guild Fact Finding Mission Report, May 2002; John Dayal (ed.), *Gujarat 2002: Untold and Retold Stories of the Hindutva Lab*, Delhi: Media House, 2002; Chaitanya Krishna (ed.), *Fascism in India: Faces, Fangs and Facts*, Delhi: Manak, 2003; report by People's Union for Democratic Rights, *'Maaro! Kaapo! Baalo!' State, Society, and Communalism in Gujarat*, Delhi: PUDR, 2002; Achyut Yagnik and Suchitra Sheth, *The Shaping of Modern Gujarat: Plurality, Hindutva and Beyond*, New Delhi: Penguin Books, 2005, pp. 278–84.

Violence entails three principal effects in relation to the formation process of ethnic politics. First, violence serves as a means of radically demarcating boundaries between categories of difference. Communal riots mark boundaries along the Hindu–Muslim divide.[3] As we have seen, Hindu, as well as Muslim identities, like ethnic identities, have no fixed composition. An act of large-scale violence that is widely labelled or perceived to be taking place along a Hindu–Muslim divide clearly defines the boundaries between two such groups. Violence that seemed to be communal is often revealed to be, on closer examination, a manifestation of disparate social conflicts and the settling of various scores between social groups, and between them and the state. Yet the general representation of violence as communal, in official and popular discourses, simplified this complexity and hardened its communal characterisation. Second, riots and violence serve as a means of gaining leverage on the state. Ethnic identities are determined by the dynamics of interrelations between them and with the state. Through violence groups seek to harness the power and resources of the state to their benefit, while the conduct of state apparatuses during riots signals the communal proclivities of the state. Third, large-scale communal violence produces an enduring effect, becoming inscribed in the collective memory of the people and in the localities in which it occurred.[4] Large-scale violence in ethnic politics, therefore, has the effect of ossifying the lines of difference between groups, as well as the demarcation of relations between the state and certain groups. Thus, violence has a particular constitutive effect in the formation process of ethnic identities. It counteracts the changeable dimensions of ethnic identities, both the relational and the contextual.

The following analysis examines the effects of violence in the making of ethnoHinduism in relation to the Ahmedabad riots of 1969 and the

---

[3] This point is suggestive of Stanley Tambiah's argument that riots involve processes of 'focalization and transvaluation', which 'contribute to a progressive polarization and dichotomization of issues and partisans, such that the climatic acts of violence by groups and mobs become in a short time self-fulfilling manifestations, incarnations and re-incarnations of allegedly irresolvable communal splits'. Stanley Tambiah, 'Presidential Address: Reflections on Communal Violence in South Asia', *Journal of Asian Studies*, vol. 49, no. 4, 1990, p. 750. Also see Charles King, 'The Micropolitics of Social Violence', *World Politics*, vol. 56, no. 3, April 2004, p. 452; Fearon and Laitin, 'Violence and the Social Construction of Ethnic Identity', p. 846; Chaim Kaufmann, 'Possible and Impossible Solutions to Ethnic Wars', *International Security*, vol. 20, no. 4, 1996, p. 137.

[4] Paul Brass's study of the production of Hindu–Muslim riots analyses the issue of persistence of Hindu–Muslim riots in India. One of the three arguments that he develops in relation to this question, and which has similarities with the argument suggested here, is that 'there exists in India a discourse of Hindu–Muslim communalism that has corrupted history, penetrated memory, and contributes in the present to the perpetuation of communal violence'. See Paul R. Brass, *The Production of Hindu–Muslim Violence in Contemporary India*, London: University of Washington Press, p. 34; see also pp. 382–4.

pogrom of 2002. The argument developed in this study is used in the analysis to illuminate the recurring communal riots from the mid-1980s, and particularly the pogrom of 2002, as well as to explain why the riots of 1969 did not in the short term bring about a rise in communalism. It starts by examining the relations between large-scale violence and the formation process of a communal Hindu identity in relation to the riots of 1985.

1985

The Ahmedabad riots of 1985 began as an intra-Hindu caste conflict over the Gujarat government reservations policy and turned into violence between Hindus and Muslims. A range of conflicts evolved within the riots, which brought diverse social identities into play. The violence of the rioters, particularly at the beginning, was mainly directed against state property, and only later against Muslims and their properties. During the riots, the communal violence defined the boundaries of difference along the sectarian divide more forcefully than government policies demarcated the boundaries of differences between castes. Through the means of the riots and violence, the Bharatiya Janata Party (BJP) and Hindu organisations were able actively to integrate some lower castes, particularly Dalits, within the Hindu nationalist agenda and thereby bring about an all-Hindu consolidation. The recruitment of Dalits into the Hindu fold was part of a shift in strategy of the Hindu nationalist forces. As we have seen in Chapter 4, Dalits testified, for example, that some BJP Members of the Legislative Assembly (MLAs) who had persecuted them during the anti-reservation caste riots of 1981 provided aid in the riots of 1985. In the old city upper castes did not attack Dalits, as they had done in previous agitations.[5] During the riots of 1985 the BJP and other Hindu organisations provided Dalits with money, food, legal aid and even weapons.[6] The violence during the Rath Yatra procession, in which Dalits were allowed to participate, also became an opportunity to mobilise lower castes in the name of all Hindus on the basis of religion.

The conduct of state apparatuses during communal clashes was also an indicator and a means for agitators, as well as the victims, to mark their position in relation to the state: 'police gave us support. They came

---

[5] Overall, during the violence of 1985 there were a few incidents whereby upper castes attacked Dalits. Violence against Dalits occurred mainly on the eastern side of the city.

[6] *Interviews* with Revaben, Kalupur, Ahmedabad, 25/2/98; Karsenbhai, Ambedkar Street, Ahmedabad, 28/11/97, 29/11/97; Inayat, Dariapur, Ahmedabad, 22/2/98, 11/3/98; Ashok Shrimali, Navrangpura, Ahmedabad, 14/11/97; Shirin, Ahmedabad, 4/1/98.

on our terraces and helped us because we were Hindus.'[7] A resident of
the old city explained that in contrast to the riots of 1985 and 1969,
'in [the riots of] 1941 we were not able to fight the Muslims, we could
not dare. Muslims were superior, and it was due to British politics.'[8]
In the experiences of Muslim victims, for example in the industrial area
of Ahmedabad, police had aided the Hindu rioters and participated in
the violence. Some people believed that 'the government want to kill the
Muslims'.[9] The official Commission of Inquiry Report into the riots of
1985 concluded that on many occasions the police had been inactive and
negligent in the face of violence against Muslims.[10] The state apparatuses'
bias towards Hindus during communal violence deepened the division
along sectarian lines. It also served to exacerbate Hindus' anxiety about
Muslims even though the violence was not a result of a real Muslim threat
to the Hindu majority. For this reason, even when the violence was in fact
linked to various tensions between the police and different groups among
the city's residents, it was easily represented by state authorities as having
been communal. Thus, for example, although it was a dispute between
some Hindus and the police that underlay the initial mayhem on the
day of the Rath Yatra religious procession, most interviewees recalled the
event solely as a sectarian clash between Hindus and Muslims.

In Ahmedabad in 1985, various groups struggled over access to public
resources such as government jobs and places in educational institutions.
There were also local contests over the regulation of relations between
groups in the society and the state. In this context, episodes of communal
violence, wherein state authorities systematically took one side, whether
actively or passively, highlighted the difference in power between groups.
By effectively harnessing the state to their side in the context of communal violence, upper-caste Hindus, who were the social force behind
the initial struggle with the state over reservations, were able to derive
benefits from the state. The government withdrew the new reservations
policy and upper castes retained power in the cabinet. The demarcation

[7] *Interview* with Ramesh, Vadigam, Ahmedabad, 21/3/98.
[8] *Interview* with Saurabh, Vadigam, Ahmedabad, 26/3/98. On this point also see Girish
Patel, 'Narendra Modi's One-Day Cricket', *Economic and Political Weekly*, 30 November
2002, p. 4830; Ghanshyam Shah, 'Caste, Hindutva and the Making of Mob Culture',
in Siddharth Varadarajan (ed.), *Gujarat: The Making of a Tragedy*, New Delhi: Penguin
Books India, 2002, p. 417.
[9] Interview with an anonymous woman, in Manish Jani, 'The 1985 Ahmedabad Riots', private video documentary, Bapunagar, 25–26 April 1985 (henceforth 'The 1985 Ahmedabad Riots', video documentary).
[10] See, for example, Judge V. S. Dave's, *Report of the Commission of Inquiry: Into the Incidents
of Violence and Disturbances which Took Place at Various Places in the State of Gujarat since
February, 1985 to 18th July, 1985*, Ahmedabad: Government of Gujarat, April 1990,
Vol. I, pp. 269–70, Vol. II, p. 16.

of boundaries along a Hindu–Muslim divide brought about by the violence also facilitated the pre-emption of a consolidation of workers at a time of crisis in the textile industry.

The large-scale communal violence of 1985 wrought a profound change in the life of the city, as there was extensive segregation along communal lines in residential neighbourhoods. Even though the riots began as anti-reservation agitations, and even though there were many riots within the riot of 1985, in the collective memory of people who experienced the riots they were remembered as communal. In the old city of Ahmedabad, most interviewees recalled the Rath Yatra as having been the cause of the eruption of the riots of 1985, even though the procession took place four months after the agitation started. Moreover, when remembering the riots of 1985, people often linked them to the 1969 communal riots and their effects. Some interviewees described the processes of residential segregation along religious lines as having started in the wake of the 1969 riots.[11] Some residents in the old city mentioned that after the riots of 1969 'even Hindus and Muslims who were friends lost trust'.[12] For some people the experience of the communal violence in 1985 was like a replay of the violence in 1969.[13]

1969

The large-scale communal riots of 1969 in Ahmedabad were sparked by an accidental clash on the afternoon of 18 September between Sadhus of the Jagannath temple in the Jamalpur area of the old city and Muslims who were celebrating the local Urs festival at the tomb of a Muslim saint near the temple. While the Sadhus were bringing the Jagannath temple's cows back to their compound through the crowd, several Muslim women were injured. In the ensuing turmoil some of the Sadhus were attacked and were injured by Muslim youths and the temple windows were damaged.[14]

---

[11] *Interviews* with Viral, Navrangpura, Ahmedabad, 11/1/98; also in Kalupur (Panchbhai), 14/1/98.

[12] *Interview* with Saurabh, Vadigam, Ahmedabad, 26/3/98. Some other residents of the locality expressed a similar opinion.

[13] See, for example, *Interview* with Rasul, Naginapol, Ahmedabad, 30/12/97; *Interview* with an anonymous woman who resided in Indira Garibnagar, *The 1985 Ahmedabad Riots*, video documentary.

[14] Judge J. Reddy, *Report of the Commission of Inquiry: Ahmedabad Communal Disturbances (1969)*, Ahmedabad: Government of Gujarat, 1970 (henceforth *Reddy Commission Report*), pp. 22, 212. Also see *The Hindu*, 23 September 1969; Ghanshyam Shah, 'Communal Riots in Gujarat: Report of a Preliminary Investigation', *Economic and Political Weekly*, Annual Number, January 1970, pp. 189–91; Sampradayikta Virodhi Committee, *Ahmedabad Riots X-Rayed*, New Delhi: Sampradayikta Virodhi Committee, 1970,

Violence erupted in Ahmedabad on the following afternoon, after a protest gathering of Muslims against the damage of a *dargah* (tomb) near the temple. The Hindu Hullad Pidit Sahayata Samiti stated that 'even not satisfied by the first attack, the Muslims gathered in the number of about 2,500 to 3,000 had with menacing and militant mood again come to the Jagannath temple on September 19 1969 in the afternoon at about 2.30 PM with a view to attack the temple over again [*sic*]'.[15] Throughout the night of 19 September the incidents of arson, murders, attacks on Muslims and on places of worship escalated. By the morning, Muslim families, particularly in the suburban eastern areas, had begun leaving their homes to safe areas and 'the stream in the morning became almost a flood within 24 hours'.[16] Several trains carrying fleeing Muslims were stopped and attacked. Muslim refugees gathered in the railway station and in camps established by Muslim organisations. 'This orgy of violence – massacre, arson and looting – continued for three days.'[17]

The violence was selective and well organised. On the basis of evidence it examined regarding the situation on 20 September, the Reddy Commission of Inquiry into the 1969 riots suggested that 'crowds were being directed by persons who were leading them and they had lists of Muslim houses in their hands.'[18] Curfew was imposed that evening. The next day the army was called into the city, and thereafter the situation began to improve. Within a week, between the afternoon of 19 September and the morning of 24 September, 514 people were killed and 6,123 houses, huts and shops were damaged, looted and set on fire, mainly by Hindus.[19]

The Reddy Commission concluded that 'it was Hindu crowds which started on a career of violence', and that 'Hindu communal elements were on the aggressive and the Muslim violence was a reaction'.[20] In the Commission's view, evidence indicated that 'organized attacks were being made on Muslim properties and Muslims, lorries [*sic*] being used to carry rioter and weapons, the crowds being led and directed'.[21]

---

pp. 4, 12–15; Ashutosh Varshney, *Ethnic Conflict and Civic Life: Hindus and Muslims in India*, New Haven: Yale University Press, 2002, pp. 264–5.

[15] *Reddy Commission Report*, p. 143.   [16] *Ibid.*, p. 157.

[17] Shah, 'Communal Riots in Gujarat', p. 195. Also see *Frontier*, 4 October 1969.

[18] *Reddy Commission Report*, p. 162. The witness suggested that the lists were carried by a member of the Hindu Jan Sangh. He could not confirm that these were necessarily the electoral lists, but was certain about the use of lists. As already mentioned, the Jan Sangh Party was the predecessor of the BJP. Also see Shah, 'Communal Riots in Gujarat', p. 193.

[19] *Reddy Commission Report*, pp. 145, 151, 155, 159, 160, 163. *The Hindu* declared that 'Till the army intervened the law of jungle prevailed': *The Hindu*, 1/10/69.

[20] *Reddy Commission Report*, pp. 149, 151.

[21] *Ibid.*, p. 217. For the advance planning in the riots also see *The Hindu*, 23/9/69; Shah, 'Communal Riots in Gujarat', p. 195.

Other incidents which occurred a few months earlier may also have contributed to tensions between Hindus and Muslims in Ahmedabad. For example, in March 1969, when a police superintendent in Ahmedabad moved a hand cart that was apparently obstructing traffic, a Koran that was on the cart fell to the ground. In the subsequent Muslim protest twelve policemen were injured. On 31 August a massive demonstration was held in Ahmedabad to protest the burning of the Al Aqsa mosque in Jerusalem. On 4 September a Muslim police officer was said to have insulted the Ramayana, which led to the formation of the Hindu Dharma Raksha Samiti organisation. After its protests the police officer was suspended.[22] In late December 1968 at a big RSS rally in Ahmedabad, one of its key ideologues who was also one of the founders of the VHP, Golwalkar, pleaded for a 'Hindu *Rashtra*' (nation).[23] Yet, the communal riots of 1969 did not immediately lead to an all-Hindu consolidation.

Hindu organisations defined their dispute during and prior to the riots in terms of religious categories and violently targeted Muslims. But rather than identifying a profound conflict with the Muslims, the Hindu organisations' main accusation during the riots of 1969 was that the government was appeasing the Muslims. In a pamphlet that was circulated in Ahmedabad on 26 September 1969 a Hindu organisation, Sangram Samiti, claimed that 'it had been attempted to encourage abolition of Hindu religion under the name of secularism. They [government] have always been flattering Muslims and Muslim religious heads.'[24] Hindu organisations asserted that the government had been quick to appease the Muslims in the Koran incident, in which the police officer had to apologise twice to the local Muslims, 'whereas it took days for taking any steps when the Hindus were similarly insulted' during the Ramayan incident.[25]

On closer scrutiny, the driving forces behind the violence of 1969 appear to have been related to disparate discontents of various groups with the government, both at the centre and in the states. From the mid-1960s there were widespread frustrations with the inability of governments to resolve social and economic problems and crises. In their struggles over public resources at the time, group attempts to define demands from the state and organise into collective action intermittently were made along caste, class and religious lines of difference. During the mid- and

---

[22] *Reddy Commission Report*, pp. 21–2. Also see Shah, 'Communal Riots in Gujarat', p. 189; Sampradayikta Virodhi Committee, *Ahmedabad Riots X-Rayed*, p. 7; Varshney, *Ethnic Conflict and Civic Life*, p. 265.

[23] Shah, 'Communal Riots in Gujarat', p. 189.

[24] *Reddy Commission Report*, p. 109. Also see Patel, 'Narendra Modi's One-Day Cricket', pp. 4831–2.

[25] Shah, 'Communal Riots in Gujarat', pp. 190–1.

late 1960s recurring general strikes took place, in, among others, Bihar, Orissa, Delhi, Punjab, West Bengal, Maharashtra and Uttar Pradesh (UP). There were rising agrarian discontents and widespread student protests over the outdated curricula and spiralling fees. As was shown in Chapter 1, in Ahmedabad, as in other fast-growing urban centres, social pressures emerged in the 1960s as a result of persistent housing shortages. This was a combination of labour migrating from the dire conditions in the rural areas and the local and state government's inadequate housing and licensing policies. Between 1961 and 1971, the city's territory did not expand, but its population grew by almost 38 per cent and the proportion of dwellings increased by only 20 per cent.[26] This period saw rapid growth of slums on the eastern side of Ahmedabad.

The 1960s also marked the beginnings of the transformations in Ahmedabad's economy and its urban landscape. Already from the 1960s there was a significant growth in state-supported small-scale industries in the city, in contrast to the large-scale integrated production systems of the composite mills, which had dominated its economy. During the late 1960s seven mills in Ahmedabad were closed down and about 17,000 workers lost their jobs. At the time it was estimated that 'Harijan workers are faced with greater degree of insecurity than the Muslim workers, who were more skilled in weaving.'[27] Much of the violence in 1969 took place in the growing industrial and slums area of Ahmedabad, on the eastern side of the walled city.[28] In numerous incidents, textile workers, who were mainly Dalits and Muslims, clashed with each other.

The political impact of the growing social and economic discontents in the 1960s, both at the centre and the state, as well as in Ahmedabad, was first manifested in the 1967 general elections when the Congress Party lost its power in eight states. The growing political fragmentation reached its apex just before the Ahmedabad riots of 1969 as the Congress Party split. The 1969 riots took place against the background of intensifying conflict between Indira Gandhi and what was popularly known as the party's syndicate, which was composed of the state bosses. The party bosses ascribed the failure of Congress to sustain its power to Indira Gandhi's leftist policies. In July 1969 Indira Gandhi declared the nationalisation of banks,[29] a policy that the Gujarati Congress leader,

---

[26] *Statistical Outline of Ahmedabad City 1994–95*, Ahmedabad: Planning and Statistic Department, Ahmedabad Municipal Corporation, 1996, Table 3.1, p. 8 and Table 3.2, p. 9; *Ahmedabad Municipal Corporation Revised Development Plan 1975–1985*, Vol. I, p. 70.

[27] B. K. Roy Burman, 'Social Profile', *Seminar*, 125, 1969, p. 36; Shah, 'Communal Riots in Gujarat', p. 197.

[28] *The Hindu*, 26/9/69; 1/10/69.

[29] In August the Lok Sabha passed the Bank Nationalisation Bill: *The Hindu*, 5/8/69.

Morarji Desai, strongly opposed. After Indira Gandhi deprived him of the finance portfolio that he held in the cabinet, Desai stepped down from the Union Government ministry. His resignation 'came as a shock to Gujarat Congress'[30] and was perceived to have 'plunged the Congress in the worst crisis it has known for many years'.[31] In August the crisis between Indira Gandhi and the syndicate over economic policies was exacerbated as the Indian presidential elections took place and Indira Gandhi rigged the Congress's primary elections. The executive committee of the Congress nominated Sanjiva Reddy as the party's official candidate for the presidential elections against Indira Gandhi's wishes and decided that there should not be a free vote. Reddy lost the elections to V. V. Giri, whose victory 'was hailed by Mrs Gandhi'.[32] Indira Gandhi had bypassed the party's executive committee. Mrs Gandhi feared that members of the syndicate would dismiss her from office with Reddy's support.[33] The power struggles within the Congress resulted in the party's split in September 1969 into Indira Gandhi's Congress(I) faction and Congress(O), which represented the party's organisational wing. The political situation remained unresolved until November, when the split was formalised.

In Ahmedabad, a week before the outbreak of the riots, Balraj Madhok, a leader of the Hindu Jan Sangh, predecessor party to the BJP, called attention in this context to the position of Muslims in India. In a speech in the city he said that 'banks have been unnecessarily nationalised. What should be nationalised are Muslims in India. Their Bharatiyakaran (Indianisation) not done so far must be done now!'[34] The Hindu Jan Sangh's frustration was related to the wider political changes that began to take shape at the time and which heralded the rise of the backward castes to the centre of politics. Already in the 1967 elections the BKD party, which directly appealed to the common economic interests of the peasantry among the backward castes, surpassed the Jan Sangh and emerged as the second largest party in UP. In 1969 the reserved seats in the parliament for the SCs and STs were renewed for another ten years for the first time. Indeed, shortly afterwards Indira Gandhi's Congress(I) had begun promoting the lower and backward castes and later consolidated political alliances between them and Muslims.

The violence of the 1969 riots was systematically targeted against Muslims, with much of it being instigated and well organised by Hindu

---

[30] 'Editorial', *Economic and Political Weekly*, 16 August 1969, p. 1324.

[31] *Times of India* (henceforth *TOI*), 17 July 1969.   [32] *TOI*, 21 August 1969.

[33] For a detailed account of the political dynamics that finally led to the Congress's split see Zaidi A. Moin, *The Great Upheaval 1969–1972*, India: Orientalia, 1972; *TOI* between 13 August and 30 August 1969.

[34] Quoted in Sampradayikta Virodhi Committee, *Ahmedabad Riots X-Rayed*, p. 8.

organisations and members of the Jan Sangh.[35] The RSS and VHP began promoting the notion of a Hindu *Rashtra*. But the riots of 1969 did not lead to an all-Hindu consolidation and a growth in Hindu nationalism. The demarcation of boundary difference along a Hindu–Muslim divide remained partial. Hindu organisations, which were led by upper-caste Hindus, did not make premeditated efforts in 1969 to mobilise the lower- or the backward-caste Hindus prior to or during the riots. Their agenda was limited to a minority among Hindus. Indeed, the social boundary difference, which became politically relevant after 1969, consolidated along caste and class divisions among Hindus and not along a Hindu–Muslim divide. It was only from the mid-1980s that Hindu organisations as well as the BJP consciously sought in their rhetoric and welfare programmes to include the lower castes in the unitary Hindu fold.[36]

India experienced widespread social conflicts, in both cities and the rural areas during the late 1960s. The state governments for a variety of reasons, including internal factional conflicts, did not engage with the roots of the social problems that these discontents expressed. Demonstrations, strikes, student protests and local riots were systematically addressed and defined as problems of law and order. The responsibility for dealing with these social problems was delegated to the police.[37] The state used violence to address struggles over its distribution of resources. Its methods were then adopted by groups that were trying to gain leverage over it.

In the case it presented before the Reddy Commission of Inquiry, the government claimed that the riots of 1969 broke out on the evening of 19 September because of the attack on the Jagannath temple on 18 September and because of 'the assembly of the aggressive Muslim crowd in attacking mood at the Jagannath temple on 19th afternoon'.[38] In his testimony before the Commission, the Chief Minister stated that 'the Inspector General of Police received the message from the D.C.Ps . . . that a menacing crowd had collected at the Jagannath temple'.[39] According to evidence of the police in the temple's area, this was a crowd of about 500 who had come to protest about the *dargah* that had been damaged opposite the temple. The local police stated that no offence had

---

[35] See, for example, *Reddy Commission Report*, pp. 212, 218.

[36] By the end of the 1990s Hindu organisations and the BJP had also extended their efforts towards the mobilisation of the scheduled tribes. See Patel, 'Narendra Modi's One-Day Cricket'; *Interview* with Girish Patel, Ahmedabad, 3/3/02.

[37] Francine R. Frankel, *India's Political Economy 1947–1977*, Princeton: Princeton University Press, p. 381; A. R. Desai, 'The Gujarat Struggle and its Vilifiers', *Economic and Political Weekly*, 20 April 1974, p. 626.

[38] *Reddy Commission Report*, p. 143.   [39] *Ibid.*, p. 144.

been committed by the Muslims and that they had persuaded them to withdraw. Significantly, the area of the Jagannath temple was not affected on 19 September, when violence erupted.[40]

The Reddy Commission resolved that 'the assemblage of Muslims was not for the purpose of attacking the Jagannath temple as is sought to be made out but because the *dargah* had been damaged'.[41] The Commission rejected the government's view on the 19 September incident and determined that police officers and the Chief Minister were speaking 'not from personal knowledge but on the basis of information conveyed to them ... The Chief Minister when he was informed of this incident by the Inspector General of Police was neither told that the grave [*dargah*] was damaged or that the crowd which had collected there was complaining about the grave being damaged.'[42] The Commission claimed that the government and senior police officers had attempted 'to persuade the Commission that this was a threatened attack on the Jagannath temple and it was this attempt to attack the temple again that started the riotous incidents which took place in the afternoon of the 19th. We reject this suggestion.'[43]

In the riots of 1969 there were attempts to mobilise state apparatuses against Muslims, but the state was only partially harnessed to Hindu organisations. Many testimonies that were presented before the Commission claimed that the authorities had been negligent, apathetic and unable to provide protection for Muslims during the violence.[44] With regard to some incidents, like the destruction of a Muslim hostel for university students, the Shabeburani mosque and *dargah*, the Commission was 'left with the impression that the rioting crowd were allowed, notwithstanding the intimation of the police, to proceed unhindered in the systematic destruction'.[45] The Commission, however, entirely rejected the claims that 'all this was permitted to be done either by the government or by the police deliberately to enable the decimation or genocide of Muslims ... The police, in our opinion, were caught napping and became confused and had misappreciated [*sic*] and mis-judged the seriousness of the situation.'[46]

The Reddy Commission mentioned that in the written submission of the government 'an attempt has been made to minimize the part played by the army in bringing the situation back to normalcy'.[47] It was only after the army took over that law and order was enforced. The Commission

---

[40] *Ibid.* Also see Shah, 'Communal Riots in Gujarat', p. 193.
[41] *Reddy Commission Report*, p. 144.   [42] *Ibid.*   [43] *Ibid.*   [44] *Ibid.*, pp. 22–7.
[45] *Ibid.*, p. 153. Also see Shah, 'Communal Riots in Gujarat', p. 195.
[46] *Reddy Commission Report*, p. 214.   [47] *Ibid.*, p. 164.

also disclosed the indecisiveness of some state authorities during the violence, as well as their later attempt to hush up their misconduct. The Commissioner of Police claimed initially that the Hindu Dharma Raksha Samiti and the Jan Sangh, which was behind its formation, had stirred up communal trouble in the city. Later he denied that the Hindu Dharma Raksha Samiti was formed with the participation of the Jan Sangh. The Commission claimed that 'the police had reason to believe that some local Jan Sangh leaders and workers were actively participating in the riots though officers . . . plead ignorance of such participation'.[48]

The Reddy Commission also exposed the attitudes of government officials towards people who testified about police negligence. The government, in its official submission, argued that the witnesses, in their attempts to get aid from the police, 'pestered the police officers'.[49] The Commission criticised the government and commented that 'it is unfortunate that the citizens' approach to the police officers for protection which is the duty of the police officers to give and not the obligation of the citizens to seek is considered pestering'.[50]

The violence of 1969 did not lead to an all-Hindu consolidation in its immediate aftermath. The demarcation of difference along a Hindu–Muslim divide in the society, as well as the harnessing of the state to Hindu organisations, was limited. The lower castes were not included in the Hindu agenda. The complicity of the state in the violence was a result of oversight, incompetence and fragmentation within its apparatuses.

But the Ahmedabad riots of 1969 had a long-term impact. They were frequently referred to by the residents of Ahmedabad in relation to the riots of 1985. Some people suggested that as a result of the 1969 riots, residential neighbourhoods in the city gradually began to be divided along sectarian lines. The riots of 1969 and 1985 became living memories, which turned into a source that foretold the patterns and chronicle of violence of the next riots.

2002

On the morning of 3 March 2002, when the curfew was lifted from the old city of Ahmedabad after the first week of violence against Muslims, my informant explained to me confidently over the phone that, 'at around 10.30 stabbing will start in the city, so why don't you call again after 14.00 to check if it is possible to come?'[51] He was right. The attacks on

---

[48] *Ibid.*, p. 218.   [49] *Ibid.*, p. 215.   [50] *Ibid.*
[51] *Telephone Interview* with Karsenbhai, Dariapur, Ahmedabad, 5/3/02. The following discussion on the 2002 pogrom is mainly based on the author's visit to

Muslims started in Ahmedabad on 27 February and spread throughout the state of Gujarat after 58 Hindus, mainly women and children, died when the S-6 cabin of the Sabarmati Express was stoned and set on fire outside Godhra railway station. The train, on its way to Ahmedabad, was carrying Hindu *karsevaks* (religious volunteers) returning from Ayodhya, where they were gathering in preparation for the foundation of a Hindu Ram temple that was scheduled for 15 March. Before any formal investigation had even been initiated, and despite the fact that there were conflicting accounts about the incident, state officials, among them the Chief Minister Narendra Modi, as well as militant Hindu organisations, promptly declared it an organised Islamic terrorist attack. Some officials even suggested that the Pakistani secret service, the ISI, was involved.[52] The VHP promptly called for a Gujarat *bandh* for the following day. On the next morning an organised and systematic persecution of the Muslim minority began in Ahmedabad and through large parts of the state. Within a week, about one thousand people were killed, of whom the overwhelming majority were Muslims. Muslim families were burnt alive in their homes; they were stabbed and stoned, their houses were damaged, and shops and businesses owned by Muslims were looted and set on fire. Mosques and Islamic monuments were destroyed. The tomb of the Urdu poet Wali Gujarati was paved over. A Gujarat High Court Judge and several former judges – all Muslims – had to move with their families from their homes to safer places.[53] The violence was selective and well-planned, drawing on information, protection and direct help from public authorities.[54]

Ahmedabad during that time. For other [non-official] reports and documentation of the violence of 2002 see Editors Guild Fact Finding Mission Report, *Rights and Wrongs: Ordeal by Fire in the Killing Fields of Gujarat*; Fact-finding by a Women's Panel, *The Survivors Speak: How Has the Gujarat Massacre Affected Minority Women?* http://203.199.93.7/today/TheSurvivorsSpeakX.html.htm, 21/4/02; *Gujarat Carnage 2002: A Report to the Nation*, By an Independent Fact Finding Mission; Human Rights Watch Report, *'We Have No Orders to Save You': State Participation and Complicity in Communal Violence in Gujarat*, Vol. 14, No. 3(C), April 2002; *Citizens for Justice and Peace*, Concerned Citizens Tribunal Gujarat 2002, http://www.sabrang.com/tribunal/volI/index.html, 18/11/04; National Human Rights Commission, *Order on Gujarat*, New Delhi, May 2002; People's Democratic Union, *Maaro! Kaapo! Baalo!*; Report by the International Initiative for Justice (IIJ), *Threatened Existence: A Feminist Analysis of the Genocide in Gujarat*, December 2003; Siddharth Varadarajan (ed.), *Gujarat: The Making of a Tragedy*.

[52] Also see Siddharth Varadarajan, 'Chronicle of a Tragedy Foretold', in Varadarajan (ed.), *Gujarat: The Making of a Tragedy*, pp. 5–8.

[53] The house of the retired justice of the Gujarat High Court, A. N. Divecha, was set on fire in Ahmedabad. *TOI*, 5 March 2002.

[54] Also see Varadarajan, 'Chronicle of a Tragedy Foretold', p. 9.

Four years later, the Gujarat government has yet to provide evidence to support its claim that the Godhra incident was a premeditated terrorist attack. A forensic science laboratory report showed that the fire on the Sabarmati Express could only have been caused from inside the cabin.[55] The case was carelessly probed by the state investigative authorities. 'It is almost as if the political authorities – having committed themselves to the theory of a well organised "Islamic" terrorist plot – did not want investigative and criminal forensics to come in the way.'[56] In their discourse and conduct during the brutal communal violence, members of the BJP government, both in Gujarat and at the centre, categorically warned of an all-Muslim threat to the nation. The state apparatuses revealed themselves to be totally mobilised to the benefit of Hindu militant forces.

In many instances the police led Hindu rioters in their onslaught. A resident of Dariapur in the old city testified that as violence intensified on the *bandh* day, Muslims called the police control-room in Ahmedabad and begged for help. The police promised to come, but did not turn up. When policemen finally arrived, towards the afternoon, they positioned themselves at the head of a large crowd of Hindu rioters and started firing tear-gas shells towards the Muslims. The first blast was accompanied by loud chanting of the Hindu crowd of 'Bharat Mata Ki Jai!' (Victory to Mother India).[57] A Muslim resident of the Johapura area recalled: 'We went out of our houses to protect ourselves, but policemen that were present in the area demanded that we go back inside. When we asked the police to send away the Hindu attackers, the policemen aimed their guns at us.'[58] On the evening of the *bandh* day forty people were burnt alive in the Muslim Gulbarg Society. A former Congress Member of Parliament, Ahsan Jaffrey, was among them. He repeatedly called the police for help, but his efforts were in vain. A Dalit resident of Gomtipur in the industrial area of the city attested that on the evening when the Indian government decided to call the army into Ahmedabad, police arrived in his Hindu locality and told the people to 'finish everything tonight because tomorrow the army is coming. Policemen also suggested that the Hindus burn the Muslims' shops, rob, attack and stone their houses and then, when Muslims would try to retaliate they would fire at them so as to control their mob.'[59]

[55] Jyoti Punwani, 'The Carnage at Godhra', in Varadarajan (ed.), *Gujarat: The Making of a Tragedy*, p. 45.
[56] Varadarajan, 'Chronicle of a Tragedy Foretold', p. 7.
[57] *Interview* with Karsenbhai, Navrangpura, Ahmedabad, 6/3/02.
[58] *Interview* with Hanif, Ahmedabad, 6/3/02 and 7/3/02.
[59] *Interview* with Pragnesh of Gomtipur, Ahmedabad, 1/3/02 and 7/3/02.

The violence was entirely selective in the destruction of property. The Hindu rioters systematically picked off shops and businesses owned by Muslims, leaving the adjacent Hindu shops virtually untouched. In one case, a manned police jeep was parked on the CG Road in front of a shop that was looted and then burnt. Rather than preventing the plunder the police appeared to be protecting the looters.[60] The authorities' selective sanctioning of violence was starkly illustrated when the office of the Muslim Wakf board was burnt within the compound of the Gujarat government high security zone, just 500 meters from the Chief Minister's office.

The impending course of events and the patterns of violence could have readily been foreseen after the incident in Godhra, and particularly after the VHP's declaration of a state-wide *bandh*, both by the city's residents and government authorities. It had become common knowledge in India that *bandh* days brought riots in their wake. On this occasion, the violence started on the evening of the Godhra event, making it evident that it would continue the next day. Despite the Indian Supreme Court's 1998 ruling that the call for a *bandh* is 'unconstitutional and illegal' and 'violative of fundamental rights',[61] no action was taken by the government to prevent the *bandh* or to curb the violence. On the contrary, while the persecution of Muslims was taking place, government officials and political leaders in the state legitimised the violence. The Chief Minister himself stated in media interviews that the violence was a 'natural response to the incident in Godhra'. At the end of the massacre of Muslims in the city throughout the *bandh* day he extolled the people of Gujarat for 'observing restraint in the wake of great provocation'. In a gathering at the Gujarat Chamber of Commerce on 5 March, Modi claimed that it was a 'natural *bandh*'.[62]

Moreover, some state authorities and government officials seemed to have helped to perpetuate the violence and even to have impeded efforts to quell it. Army columns began to arrive in the city at midnight after the first day of the violence and they were due to be deployed early the next morning. Yet the army did not take up positions until the afternoon of that day, mainly because the Gujarat government did not provide the instructions and support it needed. When the army finally was deployed, in the most affected areas of the old city it 'flag marched' for an hour before retreating, allowing the mayhem to continue. When the cable TV station, Star News, showed footage of police inactivity in the face of

---

[60] Witnessed by the author, Navrangpura, Ahmedabad, 28/2/02.
[61] Durga Das Basu, *Shorter Constitution of India*, 13th edn, Nagpur: Madhwa and Company Law Publishers, 2001, p. 222.
[62] *TOI*, 6 March 2002.

violence against the Muslims, the state authorities blacked out the cable channel in large areas of Ahmedabad. The police later said this had been done in order to stop the media from airing provocative reports.[63] There is evidence to suggest that the police received instructions from members of the BJP to turn a blind eye to the killing of Muslims. Some people witnessed a BJP MLA instruct police not to take action. Furthermore, as the violence started, two members of the BJP and the Gujarat government cabinet took over the supervision of the police control-room in Ahmedabad, as well as the state police control-room in Gandhinagar. Police officials complained that 'they are finding it awkward to take orders from ministers not connected to the Home department'.[64] The decision to deploy cabinet ministers in the police control-room was taken by the Chief Minister 'as he felt that he would have direct control over police operation'.[65]

The state authorities, in their total bias against Muslims during the violence, created the sense of an all-Muslim threat to the well-being of the nation, and thus kindled a notional fear of Muslims. The state conduct clearly demarcated boundaries between Hindus and Muslims. The official view was that the Godhra incident, which had provoked the violence, was an act of Islamic terrorism. In April, while violence was still taking place, the then Prime Minister of India, Atal Bihari Vajpayee, stated that 'if there had been no Godhra, the tragedy in Gujarat would not have occurred'.[66] He added that 'Wherever there are Muslims they do not want to live with others. Instead of living peacefully, they want to preach and propagate their religion by creating fear and terror in the minds of others.'[67] Thus, this notion of an all-Muslim threat also provided the government with grounds for explaining and justifying its actions, as though Muslims provoked the violence against them by their very existence as Muslims.

In response to the Godhra incident, and against the background of the revival of the campaign for the construction of a Hindu Ram temple in Ayodhya, the BJP government swiftly re-rallied around the Hindu nationalist movement's claim that the Muslim minority in India threatened Hindus. This position was adopted despite almost a decade of relatively peaceful inter-communal relations since the BJP's rise to power. Moreover, the politics of India's Muslims had never been primarily driven by their religious faith. They refrained from religious politics even after the destruction of the Babri mosque in Ayodhya in 1992, nor did they rally around the dispute over Kashmir. Rather, the BJP government's

---

[63] *The Indian Express*, 3 March 2002.   [64] *The Sunday Times*, 3 March 2002.
[65] *Ibid.*   [66] *The Hindu*, 13 April 2002.   [67] *Ibid.*

position should be seen within the context of rising tensions within the all-Hindu fold that the Hindu nationalist movement had fostered since the 1980s and upon whose basis it had come to power. Once the Hindu–Muslim divide that rested upon intangible hostilities became less acute, the underlying tensions among Hindus surfaced.

The following analysis examines the dynamics between caste, communalism and the state in the 1990s and the effects of violence on the interrelations between them in order to understand better the trajectory that led to the pogrom of 2002.

Violence and ethnoHinduism in the 1990s

In the 1980s, communal antagonism was driven by growing caste conflicts among Hindus, particularly those between forward and backward castes over reservation policies. As noted above, after the riots of 1985 the BJP and Hindu organisations continued with their effort to integrate the lower castes into the Hindutva movement. In 1986, when communal violence again broke out in Ahmedabad on the occasion of the annual Rath Yatra, the BJP and the VHP invited Dalits 'to join the holy war to protect Hinduism'.[68] The stated aim of the Ram-Janaki Dharma Yatra, which the VHP organised in Gujarat in 1987, was 'to transcend caste and sect differences in the worship of Lord Ramachandra and to affirm the unity of Hindus'.[69] By 1990, the position of Dalit leaders in Ahmedabad was being challenged by the BJP. The party established a welfare network for Dalits, providing them with health support and legal aid, which Dalit leaders were not able to offer.[70] In the 1990 assembly elections in Gujarat the BJP increased its seats from 11 in 1985 to 67, and joined the coalition government of the Janata Dal, headed by Chimanbhai Patel.

In August 1990, large-scale anti-reservation riots erupted throughout India over the V. P. Singh government's decision to implement the Mandal Commission's recommendations on reservation for the Other Backward Castes (OBCs) at the national level. The 1989 election manifesto of

---

[68] Ashish Nandy et al., *Creating a Nationality: The Ramjanmabhumi Movement and Fear of the Self*, Delhi: Oxford University Press, 1997, p. 106.

[69] *Ibid.*, p. 108. For similar efforts of Hindu organisations in Maharashtra, see Thomas B. Hansen, 'BJP and Politics of Hindutva in Maharashtra', in Hansen and Christophe Jaffrelot (eds.), *The BJP and the Compulsions of Politics in India*, Delhi: Oxford University Press, pp. 139–40. In UP, particularly in the 1990s, see Amrita Basu, 'Mass Movement of Elite Conspiracy? The Puzzle of Hindu Nationalism', in David Ludden (ed.), *Making India Hindu: Religion, Community and the Politics of Democracy in India*, Delhi: Oxford University Press, 1996, pp. 69–70; Christophe Jaffrelot, *India's Silent Revolution: The Rise of the Lower Castes in North India*, London: Hursh & Company, pp. 454–62.

[70] *Interview* with Achyut Yagnik, Ahmedabad, 1/12/97.

Singh's Janata Dal, which by and large represented the backward-caste groups, emphasised the party's commitment to reservation policies as part of its programme for social justice.[71] Already in July 1989 Janata Dal Chief Minister of UP, Mulayam Singh Yadav, had promulgated an ordinance providing the OBCs with a quota of 15 per cent in the state administration.[72] In September 1990, the BJP, which at that time backed Singh's National Front coalition, withdrew its support from the government and announced the demolition of the Babri Masjid mosque in Ayodhya as its major priority. The then BJP party leader, L. K. Advani, launched a Rath Yatra religious procession from Sommnath to Ayodhya with the intention of liberating God Ram's birthplace.[73] The Yatra sparked communal violence throughout the subcontinent. The inauguration of a Yatra to Ayodhya at this juncture 'rapidly changed the political discourse from reservation to Hindu nationalism and Hindu unity'.[74] The *Aaj* newspaper declared that 'Due to the aura of Ram, the demon of Reservation ran away.'[75]

In Gujarat, the anti-reservation riots that followed V. P. Singh's decision to implement reservations for the OBCs at the national level were relatively subdued. On the one hand, the Chief Minister expressed his government's disagreement with the proposed policy and announced that it would tackle promptly any public conflict, and on the other hand, the social groups that had won the reservation dispute in the mid-1980s were now dominating positions of power in the state.[76] Violence escalated in Ahmedabad on 23 October following Advani's arrest during the Rath Yatra and Chimanbhai Patel's request that his BJP cabinet

[71] Christophe Jaffrelot, 'The Rise of the Other Backward Classes in the Hindi Belt', *Journal of Asian Studies*, vol. 59, no.1, February 2000, p. 96.

[72] Zoya Hasan, 'Community and Caste in Post-Congress Politics in Uttar Pradesh', in Amrita Basu and Atul Kohli (eds.), *Community Conflicts and the State in India*, Oxford: Oxford University Press, p. 149. This was two years before he founded the Samajvadi Party (SP).

[73] See Sunita Parikh, 'Religion, Reservations and Riots: The Politics of Ethnic Violence in India', in Basu and Kohli (eds.), *Community Conflicts*, pp. 43–8; Ghanshyam Shah, 'The BJP's Riddle in Gujarat: Caste, Factionalism and Hindutva', in Hansen and Jaffrelot (eds.), *The BJP and the Compulsions of Politics in India*, pp. 243–9; Nandy *et al.*, *Creating a Nationality*, pp. 72–3. The VHP announced plans to launch a few Ram Yatras before Advani announced his Yatra procession. See Nandy *et al.*, *Creating a Nationality*, p. 108.

[74] Hasan, 'Community and Caste in Post-Congress Politics in Uttar Pradesh', p. 104.

[75] *Aaj* (newspaper published in Banares), 9 December 1990. Quoted in Arvind Rajagopal, *Politics after Television: Hindu Nationalism and the Reshaping of the Public in India*, Cambridge: Cambridge University Press, 2001, p. 167. I thank William Gould for bringing this quotation to my attention.

[76] See Sunita Parikh, *The Politics of Preference: Democratic Institutions and Affirmative Action in the United States and India*, Ann Arbor: University of Michigan Press, 2000, p. 184.

members resign after the party withdrew its support from the coalition.[77] The BJP and VHP called for a general strike and organised systematic attacks on government property and upper-class Muslim homes. In the industrial area Dalits and Muslims clashed as the BJP and VHP tried to close down Muslim shops to enforce a complete strike. The BJP's mayor and deputy mayor of Ahmedabad helped organise road blocks in the city to assist the VHP and BJP in their call for a second general strike on 30 October. People were stopped at the blockades and were forced to say 'Jai Shri Ram' (Victory to Lord Ram). While the 'Chief Minister was busy trying to save his ministry', there was no state authority to deal with the law and order.[78] Thus, through systematic violence, in the name of defending Hinduism, between Dalits and Muslims in the working-class neighbourhoods and attacks on the few upper-class Muslim localities in the city, Hindu organisations with the help of BJP politicians intensified the Hindu–Muslim divide. 'By the end of 1990, the residents of almost all Dalit *chawls* [near Muslim chawls] in the industrial areas had erected high walls around them, interrupted by iron gates.'[79]

By the time communal violence engulfed Ahmedabad, as well as the rest of the country, following the destruction of the mosque in Ayodhya in December 1992, no association at all was made between the communal fury and the question of caste reservation. Nonetheless, in the preceding month, after the Supreme Court upheld the Mandal Commission Report for reservations for the backward castes at the national level, the reservation issue had indeed occupied the public agenda, and student protests had been held.[80] The Mandal Commission Report declared over 80 Muslim groups to be backward. It estimated that non-Hindu OBCs formed 8.4 per cent of the population, a figure that included about half of the Muslim population in India.[81] The inclusion of Muslim groups

---

[77] Nandy *et al.*, *Creating a Nationality*, pp. 114–15.
[78] *Ibid.*, p. 115 n.14 and pp. 114–18.   [79] *Ibid.*, p. 121.
[80] The Court endorsed the basic recommendations of the Mandal Commission Report in November 1992, including its principle that caste and not class should be the criterion for identifying backwardness. However, the Court added a few qualifications: first, that neither the advanced sections among the backward castes nor the poor among the forward castes should receive reservation benefits; and second, that the list of the backward communities should be divided into 'Backward' and 'More Backward' categories. See John Wood, 'On the Periphery but in the Thick of it: Some Current Indian Political Crises Viewed from Gujarat', paper presented at the International Seminar on Gujarat Society: Development and Deprivation, 6–9 December 1994, Centre for Social Studies, Surat, p. 14. Also see *NewsTrack*, 24/12/92. In 1993, the Narasima Rao Congress government identified the 'creamy layers' among the backward castes. It specified for that purpose the children of top constitutional office holders, top civil servants and military officers.
[81] *Report of the Backward Classes Commission*, New Delhi: Government of India, 1980, Vol. I, pp. 55–6.

also contributed to the shift from the upper castes' sense of narrowing opportunities because of reservations to their sense of restricted prospects for mobility, as a result of the preferential treatment government policies appeared to offer Muslims.[82]

From 1990 the confusion of reservations with religious minority rights was openly made. A BJP leader from an OBC background in Maharashtra explained during the Mandal crisis in 1990 that the BJP's main problem with reservations was the inclusion of Muslims as OBCs: 'those who embrace these religions believe that they are totally free of social discrimination, why should now seek [*sic*] the benefits of these recommendations?'[83]

This shift in the way upper castes perceived the threat to their status was intensified in the mid-1990s by the tendency of political parties and various state governments to overtly conflate the issue of reservations for the backward castes with the rights of religious minorities. In November 1994 the Congress Union Welfare Minister, Sitaram Kesari, proposed that Muslims be included *en masse* in the OBC category for reservations in the civil service and education. Most Muslims were indifferent to the proposal, which was perceived as a Congress bid to win the Muslim vote after Ayodhya.[84] In Andhra Pradesh and Karnataka, a month before the 1994 elections, the Congress chief ministers announced up to 27 per cent reservations for Muslims. Bihar's Chief Minister, Laloo Prasad Yadav, promised 10 per cent reservations for Muslims and in Assam, where Muslims were being killed in Bodoland, Muslims were promised 24 per cent reservations.[85] L. K. Advani, now the BJP president, warned that this 'shameless espousal of vote-bank politics and pursuing of minority vote . . . will sow the seeds of another partition'.[86] There were also efforts by some Muslims and Christians to be included in the backward caste lists.[87] In Bihar, the Bihar Backward Muslims Morcha and the Muslim Reservation Front were formed to that end. At the same time, the central

---

[82] It was in this context that the Shah Bano case was brought up by protesting students who related the Mandal issue to government favouritism towards Muslims. See discussion in Chapter 5.

[83] Quoted in Hansen, 'BJP and Politics of Hindutva in Maharashtra', p. 135 n. 18. For the expressions of growing anxiety over the Hindu moral order among Hindu organisations in the context of Mandal see, for example, Christophe Jaffrelot, 'The Sangh Parivar between Sanskritization and Social Engineering', in Hansen and Jaffrelot (eds.), *The BJP and the Compulsions of Politics in India*, pp. 25–6.

[84] *India Today*, 30 November 1994, p. 83.

[85] *Ibid.* Also see Theodore Wright, 'A New Demand for Muslim Reservations in India', *Asian Survey*, vol. 37, no. 9, 1997, p. 853.

[86] *India Today*, 30 November 1994, p. 83.

[87] Laura Dudley Jenkins, 'Becoming Backward: Preferential Policies and Religious Minorities in India', *Commonwealth and Comparative Politics*, vol. 39, no. 1, July 2001, pp. 33–4.

government, as well as various state governments, took steps to advance the Mandal agenda for the backward castes and also expanded the lists of SCs and STs. In 1994 Tamil Nadu doubled the number of groups on the OBC list from 150 in 1970 to 310.[88] In May 1995, a year before the 1996 general elections, Madhya Pradesh, Orissa and Haryana declared new reservations for the OBCs. The government at the centre contemplated amending the constitution in order to circumvent the 50 per cent ceiling for reservations that was set by the Supreme Court.[89]

The efforts by political parties to extend reservations and also to include Muslims in the OBC category strengthened the link between caste reservations and communalism. But from the 1990s, the state's official recognition of groups as backward castes for the purpose of preferential treatment had become less pertinent in the struggle over material, social and ideological resources. In the context of the liberal economic reforms, which India fully embarked on from 1991, government jobs gradually became less attractive for upper castes as a path for mobility, particularly with the growing opportunities in the private sector, to which reservations did not apply. Reservations then, to a greater extent than before, offered fewer genuine opportunities for social and economic advancement. Even some BJP governments in the late 1990s offered reservations. In the context of economic liberalisation, there was an increasing discrepancy between the rhetoric of reservations and policy directions that turned away from preferential economic policies for social justice. Hence, in the 1990s, the liberalisation and deregulation of the economy gave a new impetus to the dynamics of interrelations between caste and class. These economic reforms promoted tensions and emphasised divisions among Hindus, thus undermining the all-Hindu unity and communal platform promoted by the BJP and Hindu organisations.

As one of India's fastest growing states, Gujarat underwent extensive liberalisation and attracted the highest rates of industrial investment in large and medium-sized industries during 1991–97.[90] The trend in employment between 1980 and 1998 in the state public sector slowly declined, while it grew in the private sector.[91] The decline in public sector employment resulted from the ban on recruitment of new employees

[88] *India Today*, 30 November 1994, p. 91.   [89] *India Today*, September and June 1995.
[90] Indira Hirway, 'Dynamics of Development in Gujarat: Some Issues', in Indira Hirway, S. P. Kashyap and Amita Shah (eds.), *Dynamics of Development in Gujarat*, Ahmedabad: Centre for Development Alternatives, 2002, p. 12.
[91] *Socio-Economic Review: Gujarat State 1999–2000*, Directorate of Economics and Statistics, Government of Gujarat, Gandhinagar, February 2000, p. s-107; N. Lalitha, and Arti Oza, 'Employment Trends in the Manufacturing Sector of Gujarat', in Hirway, Kashyap and Shah (eds.), *Dynamics of Development in Gujarat*, p. 323.

as part of the restructuring programme, as well as the state government's liquidation of selected state-owned enterprises.[92] However, the rapid economic growth that Gujarat achieved was not favourable to 'human development' in the state. Gujarat's UNDP Human Development Index (HDI) for 1996–97 was 0.566, 'which was way behind Kerala (0.775), Punjab (0.744), Maharashtra (0.655) and Haryana (0.624)'.[93] Although the state ranked fourth in literacy, there had been a deceleration in literacy improvement in Gujarat, particularly in the performance of women. Improvement in health indicators such as life expectancy at birth and infant mortality rates also slowed.[94] Moreover, 'the share of educated unemployed in the total unemployed had increased from 57 per cent in 1980 to 75 per cent in 1994, which is indicative of the low and declining employability of the educated labourpower [sic] in the state'.[95] Between 1995 and 1999 the number of graduate job-seekers rose from 76,483 to 109,905 and the number of post-graduates from 12,184 to 16,715.[96]

Liberalisation produced increasing tensions among various Hindu social groups. While the middle-class stratum grew with liberalisation, the value changes generated by this process produced growing frustrations among this group. The middle classes were heterogeneous in caste. The transformations in their lifestyle and standard of living, mainly the growing consumerism, made it difficult for some groups among them to sustain their middle-class status. 'The need to take part in the life of the community may induce demands for modern equipment (televisions, automobiles and so on).'[97] The average monthly Consumer Price Index for Urban Non-manual Employees for the urban centres of Gujarat for the year 1999/2000 was highest in Ahmedabad, which experienced a 7.1 per cent increase compared with the same period in the previous year.[98] Under increasing liberalisation '[M]ore income is needed to buy enough commodities to achieve the *same social functioning*.'[99] Groups that could not easily maintain a middle-class way of life experienced a growing sense of relative deprivation. For members of the middle classes with a lower- or backward-caste status the frustrations were more acute, since the difficulty of keeping up with the economic demands of their new class status was inextricably linked to their persistent struggle for social acceptance.

[92] *Ibid.*   [93] Hirway, 'Dynamics of Development in Gujarat: Some Issues', p. 38.
[94] *Ibid.*, pp. 38–43.
[95] Between 1980 and 1995, the number of educated unemployed had increased in Gujarat from 2.70 lakhs to 6.82 lakhs: *ibid.*, p. 21.
[96] *Socio-Economic Review: Gujarat State 1999–2000*, p. s-111.
[97] Amartya Sen, *Development as Freedom*, New York: Anchor Books, 1999, p. 89.
[98] *Socio-Economic Review: Gujarat State 1999–2000*, p. 63. The corresponding increase for all India over this period was 4.8 per cent.
[99] Sen, *Development as Freedom*, p. 89.

Some rising upper-caste groups had had similar frustrations with regard to reservations in the 1980s.

Liberalisation processes also produced growing uncertainties among Dalits. Although many Dalits acquired higher education, partly through reservations, their access to the private sector remained limited. At the same time, the economic reforms reduced the prospect and availability of government jobs, which in the 1970 and 1980s had been the key to their social and economic security and advancement. 'There is no job opportunity for scheduled castes from reservations because privatisation takes place; so all government services become private. Education become [sic] private; a lot become private, where scheduled castes are not allowed.'[100] A gap emerged between the conditions of life and the aspirations of young Dalits. Many Dalit university graduates could only find jobs as 'liftboys, deliver-boys or behind shop counters with low income'.[101] These experiences among both Dalits and segments of the middle class highlighted divisions and growing discontents among Hindus.

These processes found their political expression in the persistent losses of the BJP between 2000 and 2002 in the panchayat, municipal and assembly elections in Gujarat, as well as elsewhere in India. In February 2002, before the outbreak of violence against Muslims, the BJP lost two assembly by-elections in the state. The party's only victory was of the Chief Minister Narendra Modi. While the Gujarat pogrom was taking place, the party lost the Delhi municipal election. The BJP also performed poorly and lost the State assembly elections in Manipur, Punjab, UP and Uttaranchal that same month.[102] The election results indicated the further growth in the aspirations and political power of the lower and backward castes, which caused anxiety among the upper-caste propagators of Hindu nationalism. In particular, the success of the Bahujan Samaj Party (BSP) in UP, on the basis of lower castes' support, reflected the tensions and deep divisions among Hindus, which the Hindu nationalist movement strove to overcome. While the BJP's seats in UP halved from 174 in 1996 to 88, the BSP, led by Mayawati, showed a remarkable growth from 67 seats in 1996 to 99 seats in the 2002 elections.[103] The BJP was rejected in favour of parties that recognised frustrations and fissures in the unitary Hindu front.

In Gujarat, the BJP's defeat in the February 2002 assembly by-elections came a year after its ruling government lost gram panchayat elections,

---

[100] *Interviews* with Karsenbhai, Ahmedabad, 6/3/02.

[101] *Ibid.*, also *Interview* with Pragnesh, Ahmedabad, 28/2/02.

[102] *India Election Commission*, http://www.eci.gov.in/ElectionResults_ElectionResults_fs. htm, 18/12/04.

[103] *Ibid.*

which the government had delayed for one-and-a-half years out of fear of the 'prevailing public mood'.[104] When these elections finally took place, Narendra Modi offered a new scheme whereby up to Rs 1 lakh (100,000) would be granted to panchayats with uncontested elections. 'The people of Gujarat realized that it was the BJP way of muzzling the voice of the weak – Dalits, Adivasis, backward castes and women in the name of social harmony and manufactured consensus.'[105] Since the BJP's rise to power in Gujarat in 1995 the party had devoted considerable efforts to containing the backward castes. Before the elections the party had selected numerous candidates from what is known in Gujarat as the Baxi communities for the electoral list: fifty-two from backward Kshatriya, twenty-nine Adivasis, fourteen Dalits and one Muslim. In the 1995 Gujarat state elections, the first after the Ayodhya riots, the BJP focused its campaign on the Hindutva agenda. The party secured 122 out of the 182 assembly seats and formed a government headed by Keshubhai Patel. A crisis soon emerged within the party in the state and brought about the fall of the government in 1996. The crisis disclosed the fragility of the party's politics of appropriation of the lower and backward castes. The rivalries within the BJP centred on competition over the patronage of these groups. Sankersinh Vaghela, who claimed to be the patron of the backward communities within the party, was marginalised from the leadership and the decision-making process. He reacted by defecting, taking forty-seven MLAs with him. The BJP's national leaders hastened to intervene and the compromise they reached resulted in the nomination of Suresh Mehta as a Chief Minister. In August 1996, after a month of presidential rule, Vaghela formed the Rashtriya Janata Party (RJP) in Ahmedabad. In the subsequent power struggle the state governor dismissed Mehta's government. Vaghela's RJP formed a new ministry. In the 1998 Gujarat Assembly elections the BJP, again led by Keshubhai Patel, re-emerged as the dominant political force in the state and won the elections in Gujarat.[106] Yet, Keshubhai's government was viewed to be a 'non-performing government, doing nothing except declaring big schemes under sanskritised names. His government failed miserably to deal with successive crises and disasters, the last one was the earthquake

---

[104] *The Hindustan Times*, 8 November 2000.

[105] George Mathew, 'A Dismal Record of Grassroots Democracy', *PULC Bulletin*, September 2002, http://www.pucl.org/Topics/Religion-communalism/2002/grassroots.htm, 23/12/04.

[106] For the political dynamics in Gujarat behind the 1998 elections see: *Times of India*, 11/1/98–31/3/98. For the 1999 elections see Priyavadan Patel, 'Sectarian Mobilisation, Factionalism and Voting in Gujarat', *Economic and Political Weekly*, 21–28 August 1999, pp. 2423–33.

on January 26, 2001.'[107] The central leadership of the BJP intervened in October 2001 and brought in Narendra Modi as Chief Minister 'as "a defender of the Hindu Faith"'.[108]

Once the tensions along the boundaries of difference among Hindus had come to the fore, the ill-defined sectarian boundaries, which upper-caste propagators of Hindu nationalism exploited to mitigate the rising aspirations of the lower and backward castes, regained political relevance. This shift from caste to communalism had a receptive constituency in the circumstances of 2002 for several reasons. As noted above, the state apparatuses' complicity in the violence against Muslims after the Godhra incident solidified the Hindu–Muslim divide. The government's role in the violence was driven by political leaders and cabinet ministers who were stalwarts of militant Hindu organisations such as the VHP and the RSS (the Chief Minister wore his RSS *pracharak* badge of a full-time cadre on his sleeve). The collaboration between the state authorities and militant Hindu activists had begun earlier with the renewed campaign for the building of a Ram temple in Ayodhya. BJP MLAs in Gujarat reserved train compartments for the *karsevaks* who went to Ayodhya, and three days before the Godhra incident the Western Railways had made half a train available for them for free. When the VHP called for a *bandh*, Gujarat BJP president, Rajendrasinh Rana, announced that the state BJP would support it in spite of the illegal nature of the action.[109] The government's immediate assessment that Godhra was an Islamic attack fomented a sense of threat from the Muslims.

The Gujarat government, as well as senior members of militant Hindu organisations, made their hasty public declarations about Godhra in conducive circumstances. In the post-September 11 world order and the discourse of global Islamic terrorism, Hindu nationalists could more readily recast the Muslims in India as a threat to Hindus. Exploiting the Gujarat violence, the BJP president, for example, announced an 'anti-internal terrorism day' for 9 March.[110] The media also adopted this discourse: while the controversies surrounding the construction of a Ram temple continued unabated, the news from Ayodhya was presented as 'reports from Ground Zero'.[111]

By appropriating the language of the global Islamic threat, the state government replaced almost imperceptibly the discourse concerning the threat of liberalisation and globalisation. In the 1990s, liberalisation and its effects had posed a greater challenge to certain groups in society and to

---

[107] Patel, 'Narendra Modi's One-Day Cricket', p. 4833.   [108] *Ibid.*
[109] *The Sunday Times*, 3 March 2002.   [110] *The Indian Express*, 4 March 2002.
[111] *The Sunday Times*, 3 March 2002. Other newspapers used the term as well.

human development in the state than the abstract dangers of Islamic terrorism. Just before the pogrom in Gujarat, during the election campaign in UP, the BSP leader Mayawati reminded her lower-caste Hindu voters that 'terrorism by the administration is worse than the global threat of terrorism'. The BSP, which defeated the BJP in the February 2002 Assembly elections in UP, framed its ideology in terms of caste conflict, aiming to 'break upper caste oppression and by using state power to uplift the downtrodden'.[112] The BSP grew out of the Backward and Minority Communities Employees Federation (BAMCEF), an organisation of government employees founded in 1978 by Kanshi Ram. Its initial base had been formed by Dalits who continued to experience social discrimination despite their advancement through reservations.[113] In Gujarat, backward-caste politics originating in unions, such as those that developed in UP, Punjab and Bihar, did not succeed. Numerous Dalits were well educated in Ahmedabad. Yet, the structure and environment of industrial relations that emerged in the city between the 1920s and 1940s, the gradual shift in the economy and structure of employment from the mid-1980s and the extensive economic reforms from the 1990s were significant impediments to the emergence of political formations by backward castes and Dalits. A leader of the Dalit Panther in Ahmedabad, Valjibhai Patel, said that the new generation of Dalits 'have forgotten resistance against injustice and atrocities . . . Careerist approach, selfishness and mindset for compromise and adjustment have destroyed the Dalit movement.'[114]

From the mid-1980s, the brotherhood of 'Dalit-Muslim Bhai Bhai' in Ahmedabad was undermined by the Hindu organisations' continuous efforts to mobilise Dalits through communal violence and the invitation to join the Hindutva agenda. Moreover, in the circumstances of the early 2000s when, despite the significant advances of some Dalits, there was a growing gap between their education and employment, on the one hand, and their social expectations, on the other hand, some Dalits felt relatively deprived by comparison with Muslims. Dalits perceived their class and caste status in relation to the position of those whom they, as well as other groups, regarded as their co-equals. In their view, since Muslims did not enjoy the benefit of reservations, and education was less likely

[112] http://www.bahujansamajparty.com/, 24/12/04.
[113] See Kanchan Chandra, 'The Transformation of Ethnic Politics in India: The Decline of Congress and the Rise of the Bahujan Samaj Party in Hoshiarpur', *Journal of Asian Studies*, vol. 59, no. 1, February 2000, p. 35 and pp. 28, 43.
[114] Valjibhai Patel, *Karmashil ni Kalame*, Valgibhai Patel Sanman Samiti, Vallabha Vidhyanagar. Quoted in Shah, 'Caste, Hindutva and the Making of Mob Culture', pp. 424–5.

to expand their opportunities, many Muslims had preferred to acquire technical skills and develop small businesses. During the violence of 2002, an educated Dalit complained that 'with their technical skills, any Muslim youth would make his Rs.40 daily earning by even standing on the pavement for the whole day'.[115] Some Dalits, mainly the young, increasingly felt marginalised in comparison to their Muslim contemporaries. In this shift from caste and class issues to communalism, Dalits, as well as the status-frustrated groups among the middle classes, were attracted to the upper-caste agenda partly as a means of assuaging their status insecurity. A Dalit leader testified that between 2000 and 2002 the VHP had organised public meetings for Dalits in Ahmedabad, which propagated the notion that 'their [Dalits'] life is not safe as long as the Muslims are here. In the meetings they also distributed small metal trishuls, like Shivaji's weapon, for free.'[116] The facts that the Dalits were spared from the violence in 2002 and that the state manifested a clear bias against Muslims reinforced their sense of having the state on their side.

The shift from caste and class to communalism manifested in the pogrom of 2002 was fed by the enduring effects and memories of the large-scale communal violence of 1969 and from the mid-1980s through the early 1990s. On the *bandh* day in 2002, a resident of the city said, 'I remembered the 1969 riots, when the government gave three days for free fight and no police was around.'[117] The long-lasting effects of the large-scale violence from the mid-1980s through the early 1990s might also better explain why by 2002 the course of violence in Ahmedabad could easily be foretold. The violence along a Hindu–Muslim divide over this period not only remained in people's memories, but also left its mark on the city's landscape, which was already by 2002 divided along religious lines.

The long-term effects of violence and the dynamics of state society relations and the changes they brought upon each other unravel the communalisation of the state that was manifested in 2002. The role of the state in the pogrom of 2002 had its roots in the conduct of official authorities during the violence of 1969 as well as 1985. The deepening communal conflict in Gujarat, the communalisation of its democratic government and the collapse of law and order which were revealed in 2002 are therefore impossible to understand without reference to the history of the role of state authorities in the violence.

---

[115] *Interview* with Pragnesh, Ahmedabad, 28/2/02. Also *Interview* with Valgibhai Patel, Navrangpura, Ahmedabad, 6/3/02.
[116] *Interview* with Valgibhai Patel, Navrangpura, Ahmedabad, 6/3/02.
[117] *Interviews* with Karsenbhai, Ahmedabad, 1/3/02.

Rather than a real breakdown of law and order during the massacre of 2002, there was a selective abuse of power by the state authorities against the Muslims. This state conduct had begun developing much earlier. The Commission of Inquiry into the Ahmedabad riots of 1985 presented evidence of the complicity of the police in the violence and also accused the police of perpetrating their own atrocities. It even referred to the police as a 'mob'. Similar evidence had been exposed in reports on the 1984 Delhi riots against the Sikhs, which claimed that the violence had been executed with 'open assistance from the police and the government machinery'.[118] The report of the Srikrishna Commission into the December 1992 and January 1993 Bombay riots stated that the bias of policemen against Muslims 'was seen in the active connivance of police constables with Hindu mobs on occasions'. The report suggested that the police attitude towards appeals from desperate Muslim victims was that 'one Muslim killed, was one Muslim less'.[119] There was, therefore, little new about the apparent incapacity of the police to maintain law and order, or indeed, their role in perpetuating the disorder. But the critical difference was that in previous riots, such as the riots of 1969, the police was complicit through negligence and incompetence. In 1985, the involvement of the police in the violence was a result of policemen's illegal and intricate activities within specific localities. In the violence of 2002 the blatant anti-Muslim bias of the police was directed from the top and was backed by high-ranking public officials.[120] During the violence politicians bypassed the line of command, and the police became a political instrument in the hands of the government.

Insights from the Ahmedabad violence of 1985, as well as recognition of the continuum of violence in 1969, 1985 and 2002, help to explain the lawlessness of the state that emerged in 2002. The way some of the communal violence in 1985 was related to disputes between state apparatuses and groups in society during ordinary times is particularly revealing. In Ahmedabad, there were systematic violations of the law in various areas of life. Thus, for example, although alcohol is prohibited in Gujarat, the

---

[118] *The Hindu*, 20 April 2002.

[119] Hon. Justice B. N. Srikrishna, *Report of the Srikrishna Commission Appointed for Inquiry into the Riots at Mumbay During December 1992 and January 1993*, High Court Mumbay, Published by Jyoti Punwani Vrijendra, 1998, p. 33.

[120] The development in police conduct between 1969 and 1985 is reminiscent of Walter Benjamin's insightful comment on the police that 'their spirit is less devastating where they represent, in absolute monarchy, the power of a ruler in which legislative and executive supremacy are united, than in democracies where their existence, elevated by no such relations, bears witness to the greatest conceivable degeneration of violence'. Walter Benjamin, 'Critique of Violence', in *Reflections*, New York: Schocken Books, 1978, p. 287.

Miyanbhai Commission Report on prohibition in the state suggested that the police played a central role in violating this policy. The police were hand in glove with the illicit liquor traders. By enabling the bootlegging of liquor, corrupt police officers secured a sizable illegal income.[121] By 2002 the law was so blatantly breached that a placard with the slogan 'Don't Drive While Being Drunk' was displayed on one of Ahmedabad's main intersections.

Since the mid-1980s, when de-industrialisation processes started in the city's textile industry, there had been a continuing infringement of labour laws. Violations of the law also prevailed in the construction industry. Land and housing policies were bypassed through manipulation of building schemes and zoning regulations.[122] Land, as in Bapunagar during the 1985 riots, was sometimes vacated and acquired through violence. Following the collapse of 'some 80 buildings and death of 700 people' in the earthquake that struck Ahmedabad in January 2001, the extent to which building regulations had been systematically violated was unravelled. Building codes had not been enforced, 'inadequate quantities of steel . . . short cuts in cement, lack of plinths and building in soft soil were common problems discovered in the collapsed structures'.[123]

This lawlessness, which the state authorities were part of, gradually became ingrained in everyday life. It often reflected the means by which individuals and groups, as well as state representatives, struggled to obtain state resources. The patterns of everyday law and order demarcated the framework of public norms, perceptions and attitudes with regard to the law. Consequently, there was a thin line between the lawlessness of everyday life of both the state and the public, and the lawlessness that prevailed during times of violence. During riots, various local disputes assumed the overtones of communal violence, while communal violence became an opportunity for both state apparatuses and social groups to gain a firmer hold on each other. Thus, a day after the Godhra incident the state revenue department demolished some 150 dwellings in the Muslim locality near Godhra railway station. The official explanation was that these hutments encroached on government land. Similarly, in Ahmedabad, AMC bulldozers flattened houses that had been burnt during the violence, leaving the citizens no time to respond. These houses were defined by the AMC as 'encroaching dwellings', whose location

---

[121] Also see Julio Ribeiro, *Bullet for Bullet: My Life as a Police Officer*, Delhi: Penguin Books, 1998, p. 256; Howard Spodek, 'Crises and Response: Ahmedabad 2000', *Economic and Political Weekly*, 12 May 2001, p. 1631.

[122] See the discussion in Chapter 1. Also see Spodek, 'Crises and Response: Ahmedabad 2000', p. 1632.

[123] Spodek, 'Crises and Response: Ahmedabad 2000', pp. 1631–2.

obstructed AMC 1992 town planning.[124] In another incident during the 2002 violence in Ahmedabad, the police were called to the middle-class locality of Naranpura, where a gas cylinder shop had been broken into and looted. The thieves ran away as the police appeared, but the latter did not leave before loading six cylinders on the jeep for themselves.[125] When asked to address the breakdown of law and order, the Ahmedabad Police Commissioner explained that, 'policemen are not insulated from the general social milieu and there should be some contagious element'.[126]

During the riots of 1969 some people who sought aid from the police were viewed by government officials as 'pesters'. The riots of 1985 showed how in response to the public authorities' malpractice people withdrew from the state and created informal regulating mechanisms for their subsistence and safety. In 2002 it appeared that, on the basis of their experiences of the state's lack of responsiveness, people developed similar practices to the enforcement of justice.

On the sixth day of the 2002 pogrom, at a big junction on the outskirts of the city, a car hit a rickshaw, overturned it and sped away. A driver who witnessed the event pursued the offender until he was able to force him off the road to a standstill. The pursuer stepped out of his car and confronted the hit-and-run driver brandishing a hockey stick, shouting loudly and fiercely at the driver and the woman at his side to get out of the car. Within minutes dozens of people had gathered around. They forced the culprits to return to the junction and to settle matters with the rickshaw driver. One person even joined them in their car to make sure that they went back, and many others followed in their own vehicles. The runaway driver paid the rickshaw owner on the spot for all the expenses for repairing his vehicle.[127] Through an ad hoc arrangement people had applied instant justice on behalf of an anonymous victim. The police were not called, or even mentioned in this sequence of events. This particular incident, which was unrelated to the ongoing violence against Muslims at the time, seemed to represent peoples' efforts to maintain law and order. Specifically, they tried to safeguard the right to protection of an anonymous citizen and to ensure that justice would be done. In that pursuit, people allowed themselves to take the law into their own hands because they knew that the police and the judiciary would be unlikely to do so. On this occasion, the offenders were terrorised by fellow citizens in order to bring justice for a rickshaw driver they had injured. In other areas of the city state apparatuses and people would act similarly, based

[124] *TOI*, 5 March 2002.   [125] *Interview* with Hemang, Naranpura, Ahmedabad, 3/3/02.
[126] Police Commissioner, C. Pande in an interview with Star News TV, 28 February 2002.
[127] Incident witnessed by the author in Ahmedabad, Drive-in road, 3 March 2002.

on the same informal principle and rationale, in pursuit of a summary notion of 'collective justice' in which Hindus saw themselves as victims and Muslims as the perpetrators.

These developing social practices were also driven by the state apparatuses' tendency to lay the responsibility for the violence on the people. Even during the state-sanctioned violence in 2002, the Police Commissioner repeatedly suggested in TV interviews that, 'this is all happening due to mob fury and if one wants to understand it one should ask the mobs'. If, as the state officials suggested, the violence was a result of a 'natural' retaliation for what had happened in Godhra, then the application of justice by ordinary citizens, as well as state complicity in the violence, was to be expected, and perhaps even justified.

The gradual harnessing of the state against Muslims through communal violence also served these developments in state and society because it contributed to perpetuating the tendency among the state apparatuses to lay the blame hastily on Muslims. In the riots of 1969 this was a result of incompetence and fragmentation among the authorities. In 1985 the Police Commissioner elaborated before the Commission on the tendency of over-religious people to 'drift to be communalised', and in 2002 the state officials determined forthwith that Godhra was an Islamic attack. Precisely these terminologies, like the global discourse of 'Islamic terrorism' or 'clash of civilisations' that re-emerged after September 11 and was readily assimilated in Gujarat, provided a convenient means for legitimising, for example, a pogrom such as the one that took place in Gujarat against Muslims in 2002. At best, such perceptions, which were sometimes taken as given, particularly by the state, can only obscure our understanding of communalism in India since the 1980s.

The pattern of events in the Ahmedabad riots of 1985 revealed the dynamics of the interrelations between caste and class and their relation to the state, which underlay the growth of communalism since the 1980s. The recurring large-scale violence served to ossify the fault-lines in the society along a Hindu–Muslim divide. These processes took place in the context of struggles over state resources, wherein state representatives and society interacted with each other and wrought changes in each other. The complicity of some state officials in communal violence and their exploitations of these events served as a means of perpetuating divisions along sectarian lines, as well as prejudices about groups in the society. During communal violence people frequently took upon themselves functions of the state, particularly with regard to law and order. The efforts by social groups to find informal ways to access state resources, as well as the role of the state officials in exacerbating communal tensions, appeared to have been accelerated with the growing economic liberalisation, involving, among other things, a retreat of the state from some economic sectors, particularly those that provided employment for the poor. The communal violence of 1969 took place prior to the rise of Hindu nationalism and the consolidation of all-Hindu identity. It was only later that these riots were assimilated to an apparent continuum of communal tension over three decades. Viewing the period from 1969 to 2002 as a continuum helps to understand better the dynamics by which the state's communalised practices developed and the communalisation of the society deepened.

Bibliography

OFFICIAL PUBLICATIONS

GOVERNMENT OF INDIA

Census of India 1981, Series-5 Part IV – A, Social and Cultural Tables, Ahmed-abad: Government of India.

Census of India 1981, Series-5 Part V – A & B, Migration Tables, Ahmedabad: Government of India.

Census of India 1991, Series-7 Part XII – A & B, District Census Handbook, Ahmedabad: Government of India.

Debates (India Costituent Assembly), Manager of Publications, Delhi, 1946–1947 New Delhi: Government of India Press.

Election Commission of India, *Order on Holding of General Elections to the Gujarat Legislative Assembly*, No. ECI/PN/35/2002/MCPS Dated: 16 August 2002.

Gazetteer of the Bombay Presidency, Vol. IV, Bombay: Ahmedabad, Government Central Press, 1879.

National Commission on Urbanization: Interim Report, New Delhi: Government of India, Ministry of Urban Development, January 1987.

Report of the Commissioner for Scheduled Castes and Scheduled Tribes 1966–67, Delhi: Government of India, Manager of Publications, 1968.

Report of the Commissioner for Scheduled Castes and Scheduled Tribes 1968–69, Delhi: Government of India, Manager of Publications, 1969.

Report of the Commissioner for Scheduled Castes and Scheduled Tribes 1978–79, New Delhi: Government of India (through the Minister of Home Affairs).

Report of the Backward Classes Commission [Mandal Commission], New Delhi: Government of India, 1980, 7 vols.

Report of the Commission for Scheduled Castes and Scheduled Tribes April 1984–March 1985, New Delhi: Government of India.

Report of the Commission for Scheduled Castes and Scheduled Tribes April 1985–March 1986, New Delhi: Government of India.

Statistical Report on General Election, 1972 to the Legislative Assembly of Gujarat, New Delhi: Election Commission of India, http://eci.gov.in/infieci/key_stat/keystat_fshtm (2 October 2004).

Statistical Report on General Election, 1975 to the Legislative Assembly of Gujarat, New Delhi: Election Commission of India, http://eci.gov.in/infieci/key_stat/keystat_fshtm.

Statistical Report on General Election, 1980 to the Legislative Assembly of Gujarat,
New Delhi: Election Commission of India, http://eci.gov.in/infieci/key_stat/
keystat_fshtm.

GOVERNMENT OF GUJARAT

Ahmedabad District Gazetteer, Ahmedabad: Government of Gujarat, 1984.

*Gujarat Prohibition of Transfer of Immovable Property and Provision for Protection
of Tenants from Premises in Disturbed Areas Act* (Repeal of the 1986 Gujarat
Prohibition of Transfer of Immovable Property and Provision for Protection
of Tenants from Premises in Disturbed Areas Act, Section 17)', *Gujarat
Government Gazette,* vol. 33, 4 April, Ahmedabad, 1991.

Report of the Socially and Educationally Backward Classes [second] Commission [Rane
Commission], Gujarat State, 1983.

Socio-Economic Review: Gujarat State 1965–66, Ahmedabad: Bureau of Economic
and Statistics, Government of Gujarat, 11 vols.

Socio-Economic Review: Gujarat State 1999–2000, Directorate of Economics and
Statistics, Government of Gujarat, Gandhinagar, February 2000.

COMMISSIONS OF INQUIRY

Judge V. S. Dave, *Report of the Commission of Inquiry: Into the Incidents of Violence
and Disturbances which Took Place at Various Places in the State of Gujarat since
February, 1985 to 18th July, 1985,* Ahmedabad: Government of Gujarat, April
1990.

Judge N. M. Miyanbhai, *Report of the Commission of Inquiry into the Prohibition
Policy in Gujarat,* Ahmedabad: Government of Gujarat, 1983 (excerpts translated from Gujarati).

Judge J. Reddy, *Report of the Commission of Inquiry: Ahmedabad Communal Disturbances (1969),* Ahmedabad: Government of Gujarat, 1970.

AHMEDABAD MUNICIPAL CORPORATION

Ahmedabad Municipal Corporation Revised Development Plan 1975–1985, Vols. I
and II, Ahmedabad: Town Development Department, Ahmedabad Municipal Corporation, 1975.

Amdavad, Ahmedabad: Ahmedabad Municipal Corporation, Sahitya Mudra-
nalaya, 1992.

City Election Wards (Population Area & Density) [map], Ahmedabad: Ahmedabad
Municipal Corporation, 1991.

Dariapur, Ahmedabad City Survey [map], Sheet No. 18 & 19. Ahmedabad: Estate
Department, Ahmedabad Municipal Corporation.

Growth of the City (1857–1986) [map], Ahmedabad: Ahmedabad Municipal Corporation.

Growth of the City Ahmedabad, Ahmedabad: Estate Department Ahmedabad
Municipal Corporation, 1991.

Report on the Census of Slums Ahmedabad City 1976, Ahmedabad: Ahmedabad
Municipal Corporation, 1976.

Statistical Outline of Ahmedabad City 1984–85, Ahmedabad: Ahmedabad Municipal Corporation, 1986.

Statistical Outline of Ahmedabad City 1994–95, Ahmedabad: Planning and Statistics Department, Ahmedabad Municipal Corporation, 1996.

Statistical Outline of Ahmedabad City, Ahmedabad: Ahmedabad Municipal Corporation, 1976.

Walled City Revitalization Plan, Ahmedabad: Ahmedabad Municipal Corporation, 1997.

COURT PROCEEDINGS

Shri Rasiklal N. Shah and Others v. *State of Gujarat and Others*, in the High Court of Gujarat, Ahmedabad, Special Criminal Application No. 284, 29/4/1985.

PAPERS AND NON-OFFICIAL PUBLICATIONS

Committee for the Protection of Democratic Rights, *A Report of the CPDR Fact Finding Team: The Gujarat Reservation Agitation*, Bombay, 1981.

Desai, Khandubhai. K, *Textile Labour Association Ahmedabad: An Indigenous Experiment in Trade Union Movement*, Ahmedabad: Textile Labour Association, 1976.

Is Ahmedabad Dying?, seminar and publication, coordinated by Jayendra N. Bhatt, Ahmedabad: CEPT Ahmedabad and Gujarat Institute of Civil Engineering and Architects, 1987.

Jani, Manish, *Textile Worker: Jobless and Miserable* (a report based on interviews with workers of textile mills closed in Ahmedabad), Ahmedabad, SETU, 1984.

Jhabvala, Renana, *Closing Doors: A Study on the Decline in Women Workers in the Textile Mills of Ahmedabad*, Ahmedabad: SETU, 1985.

Lobo, Lancy, 'Social Stratification and Mobility among the Kolis of North Gujarat', *International Seminar on 'Gujarat Society'*, Surat: Centre for Social Studies, 17–20 December 1986.

Mehta, Sanat, *Plight of Textile Workers*, Baroda: Gujarat Foundation for Development Alternatives, 1997.

Mujahid (anonymous), 'An Inquiry Report on 1985 Communal Riots in Ahmedabad City, 18th March and After: Real Facts', Unpublished Pamphlet, SETU Archive Files (translated from Gujarati).

Patel, Girish, in *Is Ahmedabad Dying?*, Seminar and Publication coordinated by Jayendra N. Bhatt, Ahmedabad: CEPT Ahmedabad and Gujarat Institute of Civil Engineering and Architects, 1987.

Patel, Sujata, 'The Ahmedabad Riots, 1985: An Analysis', *Reports-Papers*, Surat: Centre for Social Studies, 1985.

Patel, Sujata, *Contract Labour in Textile Industry of Ahmedabad*, Ahmedabad: SEWA, 1984.

Raval, Kirit. N, 'Law and Order in Ahmedabad', *Is Ahmedabad Dying?*, Seminar and Publication coordinated by Jayendra N. Bhatt, CEPT Ahmedabad: Ahmedabad and Gujarat Institute of Civil Engineering and Architects, 1987.

Request for Assistance from the National Renewal Funds for Ahmedabad Textile Mills, Ahmedabad: Textile Labour Association (TLA), 1993.

Shah, Ganshyam, A Lecture delivered in the 'Western Region Jesuits' Meeting', SETU Archive paper 234.5/2.

Shah, Kirtee, Ahmedabad Study Action Group, in *Is Ahmedabad Dying?*, Seminar and Publication coordinated by Jayendra N. Bhatt, Ahmedabad: CEPT Ahmedabad and Gujarat Institute of Civil Engineering and Architects, 1987.

Shetty, V. T. Rajshekar, File 220.9/4 SETU Archive Files, 1981.

Sing, Ravindra. G., *Traditional Urban Indian Neighbourhoods: A Case Study of 'Pols' in Ahmedabad*, Ahmedabad: School of Planning, 1981.

The Shattering of Gujarat, a background paper for private circulation, Series 1985, No.2, Bombay: BUILD Documentation Centre, 1985.

Textile Labour Association, Ahmedabad, Annual Report 1974 & 1975, Ahmedabad: Gandhi Majoor Sevalaya, Bhadra, 1977.

The Textile Labour Association, Ahmedabad: Constitution, Ahmedabad: Textile Labour Association, 1993.

Wood, John R., 'On the Periphery but in the Thick of it: Some Current Indian Political Crises Viewed from Gujarat', Paper presented at International Seminar on Gujarat Society: Development and Deprivation, 6–9 December 1994, Surat: Centre for Social Studies, 1994.

Yagnik, Indulal, *Aatmakathaa* [Autobiography], Vol. VI, Dhanwant Oza (ed.), Ahmedabad: Maha Gujarat Seva Trust, 1973 (unpublished transl. English, Devaurat Pathak, Howard Spodek and John Wood).

BACKGROUND READING

Mehta, Barjor. E, *Urban Rejuvenation Through Property Redevelopment: Reusing Lands of the Textile Mills under Liquidation in Ahmedabad City*, Ahmedabad: School of Planning, 1992.

Mehta, M. J., 'Business Environment and Urbanization: Ahmedabad in the 19th Century', *Studies in Urban History*, Amritsar: University of Amritsar, 1981.

Society for Participatory Research in Asia, *The Land Acquisition Act (A Guide for Activists)*, Delhi: PRA, October 1989.

PAMPHLETS CIRCULATED IN AHMEDABAD DURING THE 1985 RIOTS

'A Challenge to Reservation', Akhil Gujarat Nav Rachana Samiti, Akhil Gujarat Vali Maha Mandal, Ahmedabad, 20 April 1985.

'O Brother Patels of all-Gujarat! Awaken, Awaken!', Naranpura Patel Yuvak Mandal, Ahmedabad, May 1985.

'The Cow of the Temple Decapitated: Its Head Thrown in the Temple at Dariapur', Hindu Yuvak Mandal near Sarkhej Roja', Ahmedabad, May 1985, SETU Archive.

NON-OFFICIAL REPORTS

Citizens for Justice and Peace, Concerned Citizens Tribunal Gujarat 2002, http://www.sabrang.com/tribunal/volI/index.html, 18/11/04.

Editors Guild Fact Finding Mission Report (Aakar Patel, Dileep Padgaonkar, B. G. Verghese), *Rights and Wrongs: Ordeal by Fire in the Killing Fields of Gujarat*, New Delhi: Editors Guild, May 2002.

Fact-finding by a Women's Panel, *The Survivors Speak: How Has the Gujarat Massacre Affected Minority Women?*, http://203.199.93.7/today/TheSurvivorsSpeakX.html.htm, 21/4/02.

Gujarat Carnage 2002: A Report to the Nation, By an Independent Fact Finding Mission.

Human Rights Watch Report, *'We Have No Orders to Save You' State Participation and Complicity in Communal Violence in Gujarat*, Vol. 14, No. 3(C), April 2002.

Indian Research Society for Welfare of Backward Classes, *Research Project on Atrocities on Harijans for 102 Days in Gujarat*, Research Project No. 10, IRS, Ahmedabad, [year of publication unknown].

Jani, Manish, 'The 1985 Ahmedabad Riots', private video documentary including interviews with survivors from Amen Chowk Relief Camp, Bapunagar, 25–26 April, 1985.

National Human Rights Commission, *Order on Gujarat*, New Delhi, May 2002.

Patel, Girish, *Lok Adhikar Sangh Fact Finding Committee Report Ahmedabad Riots*, Ahmedabad: SETU Archive Files, 1985.

People's Union for Democratic Rights, *'Maaro! Kaapo! Baalo!' State, Society, and Communalism in Gujarat* Delhi: PUDR, 2002.

Report by the International Initiative for Justice (IIJ), *Threatened Existence: A Feminist Analysis of the Genocide in Gujarat*, December 2003.

Sampradayikta Virodhi Committee, *Ahmedabad Riots X-Rayed*, New Delhi: Sampradayikta Virodhi Committee, 1970.

Srikrishna, Hon. Justice B. N., *Report of the Srikrishna Commission Appointed for Inquiry into the Riots at Mumbai During December 1992 and January 1993*, High Court Mumbai, Published by Jyoti Punwani Vrijendra, 1998.

NEWSPAPERS

Economic and Political Weekly
Frontier
Frontline
The Hindu
The Hindustan Times
Illustrated Weekly
India Today
Indian Express
Janata Weekly
Manushi (Delhi), March–June 1991, pp. 6–30.
NewsTrack, December 1992 (videotape), 24/12/02
Outlook
Patriot
Surya India, July 1981
Times of India (*TOI*)

BOOKS AND ARTICLES

Ahmed, Imtiaz, 'Introduction' in Imtiaz Ahmed (ed.), *Caste and Social Stratification among the Muslims*, Delhi: Manohar, 1973, pp. xx–xxxiii.

Alavi, Hamza, 'Politics of Ethnicity in India and Pakistan', in H. Alvi and H. John (eds.), *Sociology of Developing Societies*, London: Macmillan, 1989, pp. 222–46.

Bagchi, Amiya, 'Predatory Commercialisation and Communalism in India', in Sarvepalli Gopal (ed.), *Anatomy of a Confrontation: Ayodhya and the Rise of Communal Politics in India*, London: Zed Books, 1991, pp. 193–218.

Banu, Zenab, *Politics of Communalism: A Politico-Historical Analysis of Communal Riots in Post-Independence India with Special Reference to the Gujarat and Rajasthan Riots*, London: Sangam Books, 1989.

Barth, Fredrik (ed.), *Ethnic Groups and Boundaries*, London: George Allen & Unwin, 1969.

Basu, Amrita, 'Mass Movement or Elite Conspiracy? The Puzzle of Hindu Nationalism', in David Ludden (ed.), *Making India Hindu: Religion, Community and the Politics of Democracy in India*, Delhi: Oxford University Press, 1996, pp. 55–80.

Basu, Amrita, and Atul Kohli (eds.), *Community Conflicts and the State in India*, Delhi: Oxford University Press, 1998.

Basu, Durga Das, *Commentary on the Constitution of India*, 5th edn, Calcutta: S. C. Sarkar and Sons, 1965 (also 4th edn 1964).

Basu, Durga Das, *Shorter Constitution of India*, 13th edn, Nagpur: Madhwa and Company Law Publishers, 2001.

Basu, Tapan *et al.*, *Khaki Shorts and Saffron Flags*, Delhi: Orient Longman, 1993.

Baxi, Upendra, 'Reflections on the Reservations Crisis in Gujarat', in Veena Das (ed.), *Mirrors of Violence*, New Delhi: Oxford University Press, 1990, pp. 215–39.

Bayly, Susan, 'The History of Caste in South Asia', *Modern Asian Studies*, vol. 17, no. 3, 1983, pp. 519–27.

Bayly, Susan, *The New Cambridge History of India: Caste, Society and Politics in India from the Eighteenth Century to the Modern Age*, Cambridge: Cambridge University Press, 1999.

Benjamin, Walter, 'Critique of Violence', in *Reflections*, New York: Schocken Books, 1986, pp. 277–300.

Bhabha, Homi K., *The Location of Culture*, London: Routledge, 1994.

Bhargava, Rajeev (ed.), *Secularism and Its Critics*, New Delhi: Oxford University Press, 1998.

Bhatt, Manesh, 'Housing Problem of a Growing Metropolis', *Economic and Political Weekly*, 22 April 1972, pp. 849–51.

Bhatt, Manesh and Chawda, V. K, 'Housing the Poor in Ahmedabad', *Economic and Political Weekly*, 8 May 1976.

Blair, Harry, D., 'Rising Kulaks and Backward Classes in Bihar', *Economic and Political Weekly*, 12 January 1980, pp. 64–74.

Bose, Pradip Kumar, 'Social Mobility and Caste Violence: A Study of the Gujarat Riots', *Economic and Political Weekly*, 18 April 1981, pp. 713–16.

Bose, Pradip Kumar, 'Mobility and Conflict: Social Roots of Caste Violence in Bihar', in Dipanikar Gupta (ed.), *Social Stratification*, Delhi: Oxford University Press, 1991, pp. 369–86.

Bose, Sumantra, '"Hindu Nationalism" and the Crisis of the Indian State: A Theoretical Perspective', in Sugata Bose and Ayesha Jalal (eds.), *Nationalism, Democracy and Development*, Oxford: Oxford University Press, 1997, pp. 104–64.

Brass, Paul, 'Elite Groups, Symbol Manipulation and Ethnic Identity among the Muslims of South Asia' in David Taylor and Malcolm Yapp (eds.), *Political Identity in South Asia*, London: Curzon Press, 1979.

Brass, Paul, 'Ethnic Groups and the State' in Brass (ed.), *Ethnic Groups and the State*, Totowa, NJ: Barnes & Noble Books, 1985, pp. 1–56.

Brass, Paul, *Theft of an Idol*, Princeton, NJ: Princeton University Press, 1997.

Brass, Paul, 'The Strong State and the Fear of Disorder', in Francine R. Frankel, Zoya Hasan, Rajeev Bhagava and Balveer Arora (eds.), *Transforming India: Social and Political Dynamics of Democracy*, Oxford: Oxford University Press, 2000, pp. 59–88.

Brass, Paul, *The Production of Hindu–Muslim Violence in Contemporary India*, London: University of Washington Press, 2003.

Breman, Jan, *Footloose Labour: Working in India's Informal Economy*, Cambridge: Cambridge University Press, 1996.

Breman, Jan, *The Making and Unmaking of an Industrial Working Class: Sliding down the Labour Hierarchy in Ahmedabad, India*, New Delhi: Oxford University Press, 2004.

Burman, B. K. Roy, 'Social Profile', *Seminar*, vol. 125, 1969, pp. 33–8.

Burman, B. K. Roy, 'The Two Banks of the River', *Economic and Political Weekly*, 18 September 1976.

Carroll, Lucy, 'Colonial Perceptions of Indian Society and the Emergence of Caste(s) Associations', *Journal of Asian Studies*, vol. 38, no. 3, 1978, pp. 232–49.

Chandavarkar, Rajnarayan, 'Workers' Politics and the Mill District in Bombay between the Wars', *Modern Asian Studies*, vol. 15, no. 3, 1981, pp. 603–47.

Chandavarkar, Rajnarayan, *Imperial Power and Popular Politics: Class, Resistance and the State in India, c. 1850–1950*, Cambridge: Cambridge University Press, 1998.

Chandra, Kanchan, 'The Transformation of Ethnic Politics in India: The Decline of Congress and the Rise of the Bahujan Samaj Party in Hoshiarpur', *Journal of Asian Studies*, vol. 59, no. 1, February 2000, pp. 26–61.

Chatterjee, Partha, 'Secularism and Tolerance', *Economic and Political Weekly*, 9 July 1994, pp. 1768–77.

Chatterji, Joya, *Bengal Divided*, Delhi: Cambridge University Press, 1994.

Cohn, Bernard S., *An Anthropologist among the Historians and Other Essays*, Oxford: Oxford University Press, 1987.

Connor, Walker, *Ethnonationalism: The Quest for Understanding*, Princeton, NJ: Princeton University Press, 1994.

Corbridge, Stuart, 'Competing Inequalities: The Scheduled Tribes and the Reservation System in India's Jharkhand', *Journal of Asian Studies*, vol. 59, no. 1, February 2000, pp. 62–85.

Das, Bhagwan, 'The Reservation Policy and the Mandal Judgment', *Social Action*, vol. 43, October–December 1993, pp. 427–38.

Das, Veena, 'The Spatialization of Violence: Case Study of a "Communal Riot"', in Kaushik Basu and Sanjay Subrahmanyam (eds.), *Unravelling the Nation: Sectarian Conflict and India's Secular Identity*, Delhi: Penguin, 1996, pp. 157–203.

David, Esther, *The Walled City*, Madras: Manas, 1997.

Dayal, John (ed.), *Gujarat 2002: Untold and Retold Stories of the Hindutva Lab*, Delhi: Media House, 2002.

De, D. J., *Interpretation and Enforcement of Fundamental Rights*, New Delhi: Eastern Law House, 2000.

Desai, A. R., 'The Gujarat Struggle and its Vilifiers', *Economic and Political Weekly*, 20 April 1974, pp. 625–6.

Desai, Anjana, *Environmental Perception: The Human Factor in Urban Planning*, Delhi: Ashish Publishing House, 1985.

Desai, I. P., 'Anti-Reservation Agitation and Structure of Gujarat Society', *Economic and Political Weekly*, 2 May 1981, pp. 819–23.

Desai, I. P., 'Should "Caste" Be the Basis for Recognising the Backwardness?', *Economic and Political Weekly*, 14 July 1984, pp. 1106–16.

Desai, I. P. *et al.*, *Caste, Caste Conflicts and Reservations*, Surat (Ajanta, Delhi): Centre for Social Studies, 1985.

Dirks, Nicholas, *The Hollow Crown*, Cambridge: Cambridge University Press, 1987.

Dirks, Nicholas, 'The Invention of Caste: Civil Society in Colonial India', *Social Analysis*, vol. 25, September 1989, pp. 42–52.

Dirks, Nicholas B., *Castes of Mind: Colonialism and the Making of Modern India*, Princeton and Oxford: Princeton University Press, 2001.

Dudley Jenkins, Laura, 'Becoming Backward: Preferential Policies and Religious Minorities in India', *Commonwealth and Comparative Politics*, vol. 39, no. 1, July 2001, pp. 32–50.

Dumont, Louis, *Homo Hierarchicus*, Chicago: University of Chicago Press, 1980.

Eapen, Mridul, 'The New Textile Policy', *Economic and Political Weekly*, 22–29 June 1985, pp. 1072–3.

Engineer, Asghar Ali, 'From Caste to Communal Violence', *Economic and Political Weekly*, 13 April 1985, pp. 628–9.

Engineer, Asghar Ali, *The Muslim Communities of Gujarat*, Delhi: Ajanta Publications, 1989.

Fearon, James D. and David D. Laitin, 'Violence and the Social Construction of Ethnic Identity', *International Organization*, vol. 54, no. 4, 2000, pp. 845–77.

Flyvbjerg, Bent, *Making Social Science Matter*, Cambridge: Cambridge University Press, 2001.

Frankel, Francine R., *India's Political Economy, 1947–1977: The Gradual Revolution*, Princeton: Princeton University Press, 1978.

Frykenberg, Robert Eric, 'Hindu Fundamentalism and the Structural Stability of India', in Martin Marty and R. Scott Appleby (eds.), *Fundamentalism and the State: Remaking Politics, Economies and Militance*, Chicago: University of Chicago Press, 1993, pp. 233–55.

Galanter, Marc, 'Who Are the Other Backward Classes?', *Economic and Political Weekly*, 28 October 1978, pp. 1812–28.

Galanter, Marc, *Competing Equalities: Law and the Backward Classes in India*, Berkeley: University of California Press, 1984.

Galanter, Marc, 'The India Constitution and Provisions for Special Treatment', in Gurpreet Mahajan (ed.), *Democracy, Difference and Social Justice*, New Delhi: Oxford University Press, 2000, pp. 570–9.

Gandhi, M. K., *Collected Works of Mahatma Gandhi*, Vol. LXXX, www.gandhiserve.org/cwmg/cwmg.html.

Geertz, Clifford, *The Interpretation of Culture*, London: Fontana, 1995.

Gillion, Kenneth L., *Ahmedabad: A Study in Indian Urban History*, Berkeley and Los Angeles: University of California Press, 1968.

Gold, Daniel, 'Organised Hinduism: From Vedic Truth to Hindu Nation', in Martin Marty and R. Scott Appleby (eds.), *Fundamentalism Observed*, Chicago: University of Chicago Press, 1991, pp. 531–93.

Goyal, Santosh, 'Social Background of Officers in the Indian Administrative Service', in Francine R. Frankel and M. S. A. Rao (eds.), *Dominance and State Power in Modern India*, Vol. I, Delhi: Oxford University Press, 1989, Appendix II, pp. 425–32.

Gupta, Akhil, 'Blurred Boundaries: The Discourse on Corruption, the Culture of Politics, and the Imagined State', *American Ethnologist*, vol. 22, no. 2, 1995, pp. 375–402.

Hansen, Thomas B., 'BJP and Politics of Hindutva in Maharashtra', in Thomas B. Hansen and Christophe Jaffrelot (eds.), *The BJP and the Compulsions of Politics in India*, Delhi: Oxford University Press, 1998, pp.121–62.

Hansen, Thomas B., *Wages of Violence*, Princeton and Oxford: Princeton University Press, 2001.

Hardiman, David, *Peasant Nationalists of Gujarat: Kheda District 1917–1934*, Delhi: Oxford University Press, 1981.

Harvey, David, *Justice, Nature and the Geography of Difference*, Oxford: Blackwell, 1996.

Hasan, Mushirul, 'Indian Muslims since Independence: In Search of Integration and Identity', *Third World Quarterly*, vol. 10, no. 2, April 1988, pp. 818–42.

Hasan, Mushirul, *Legacy of a Divided Nation: India's Muslims since Independence*, Delhi: Oxford University Press, 1997.

Hasan, Zoya, *Quest for Power: Oppositional Movements and Post-Congress Politics in Uttar Pradesh*, Delhi: Oxford University Press, 1998.

Hasan, Zoya, 'Community and Caste in Post-Congress Politics in Uttar Pradesh', in Amrita Basu and Atul Kohli (eds.), *Community Conflict and the State in India*, Delhi: Oxford University Press, 1998, pp. 93–107.

Hirway, Indira, 'Dynamics of Development in Gujarat: Some Issues', in Indira Hirway, S. P. Kashyap and Amita Shah (eds.), *Dynamics of Development in Gujarat*, Ahmedabad: Centre for Development Alternatives, 2002, pp. 1–47.

Hooda, Sagar Preet, *Contesting Reservation*, New Delhi: Rawat Publications, 2001.

Jaffrelot, Christophe, *The Hindu Nationalist Movement in India, and Indian Politics 1925 to the 1990s*, Delhi: Viking, 1996.

Jaffrelot, Christophe, 'The Sangh Parivar between Sanskritization and Social Engineering', in Thomas B. Hansen, and Christophe Jaffrelot (eds.), *The BJP and the Compulsions of Politics in India*, Delhi: Oxford University Press, 1998, pp. 22–71.

Jaffrelot, Christophe, 'The Rise of the Other Backward Classes in the Hindi Belt', *Journal of Asian Studies*, vol. 59, no. 1, February 2000, pp. 86–108.

Jaffrelot, Christophe, *India's Silent Revolution: The Rise of the Lower Castes in North India*, London: Hursh & Company, 2003.

Jalal, Ayesha, *The Sole Spokesman*, Cambridge: Cambridge University Press, 1985.

Jhawala, Renana and Usha Jumeni, 'Ahmedabad 2001: Planning for the Poor: A Focus on Self-Employed Women', *Nagarlok*, vol. 20, no. 4, October–December 1988.

Jones, Dawn E., and Rodney W. Jones, 'Urban Upheaval in India: The 1974 Nav Nirman Riots in Gujarat', *Asian Survey*, 16 November 1976, pp. 1012–33.

Kakar, Sudhir, 'Some Unconscious Aspects of Ethnic Violence in India', in Veena Das (ed.), *Mirrors of Violence*, Delhi: Oxford University Press, 1990, pp. 135–45.

Kakar, Sudhir, *The Colors of Violence: Cultural Identities, Religion, Conflict*, Chicago: Chicago University Press, 1996.

Kalelkar, Kaka, 'Backwardness, Caste and the Question of Reservations', (excerpted from the *Report of the Backward Classes Commission* headed by Kaka Kalelkar, Government of India Publication, 30 March 1955), in Gurpreet Mahajan (ed.), *Democracy, Difference and Social Justice*, New Delhi: Oxford University Press, 2000, pp. 451–62.

Kalyvas, Stathis, N., 'The Ontology of "Political Violence": Action and Identity in Civil War', *Perspectives on Politics*, vol. 1, no. 3, September 2003, 475–94.

Katznelson, Ira, 'Working-Class Formation: Constructing Cases and Comparisons', in Ira Katznelson and Aristide R. Zolberg (eds.), *Working Class Formation*, Princeton, NJ: Princeton University Press, 1986, pp. 3–41.

Katznelson, Ira, *Marxism and the City*, Oxford: Clarendon, 1993.

Kaufmann, Chaim, 'Possible and Impossible Solutions to Ethnic Wars', *International Security*, vol. 20, no. 4, 1996, pp. 136–75.

Kaviraj, Sudipta, 'Religion, Politics and Modernity', in U. Baxi and B. Parekh (eds.), *Crisis and Change in Contemporary India*, Delhi: Sage Publications 1995, pp. 295–316.

Khare, Harish, 'An Unending Struggle for Gujarat's Political Soul', *Seminar*, vol. 470, October 1998.

King, Charles, 'The Micropolitics of Social Violence', *World Politics*, vol. 56, no. 3, April 2004, pp. 431–55.

Kohli, Atul, *Democracy and Discontent*, Cambridge: Cambridge University Press, 1990.

Kothari, Rajni, *Politics and the People*, Vol. II, Delhi: Ajanta, 1990.

Krishna, Chaitanya (ed.), *Fascism in India: Faces, Fangs and Facts*, Delhi: Manak, 2003.

Kumar, Dharma, 'The Affirmative Action Debate in India', *Asian Survey*, vol. 32, no. 3, March 1992, pp. 290–302.

Kundu, Amitabh, 'Urbanisation, Employment Generation and Poverty under the Shadow of Globalisation', in Indira Hirway, S. P. Kashyap and Amita Shah (eds.), *Dynamics of Development in Gujarat*, Ahmedabad: Centre for Development Alternatives, 2002, pp. 99–130.

Lal, Vinay, 'Hindu "Fundamentalism" Revisited', *Contention*, vol. 4, no. 2, Winter 1995, pp. 65–73.

Lalitha, N., and Arti Oza, 'Employment Trends in the Manufacturing Sector of Gujarat', in Indira Hirway, S. P. Kashyap and Amita Shah (eds.), *Dynamics of Development in Gujarat*, Ahmedabad: Centre for Development Alternatives, 2002, pp. 321–39.

Ludden, David (ed.), *Making India Hindu: Religion, Community and the Politics of Democracy in India*, Delhi: Oxford University Press, 1996.

Madan, T. N., 'Whither Indian Secularism?', *Modern Asian Studies*, vol. 27, no. 3, 1993, pp. 667–97.

Mahadevia, Darshini, *Globalisation, Urban Reforms and Metropolitan Response: India*, Delhi: School of Planning, Centre for Environmental Planning and Technology, Ahmedabad in association with Manak, 2003.

Masselos, J. C., 'The Khojas of Bombay: The Defining of Formal Membership Criteria during the Nineteenth Century', in Imtiaz Ahmed (ed.), *Caste and Social Stratification among the Muslims*, Delhi: Manohar, 1973, pp. 1–19.

Mathew, George, 'A Dismal Record of Grassroots Democracy', *PUCL Bulletin*, September 2002, http://www.pucl.org/Topics/Religion-communalism/2002/grassroots.htm, 23/12/04.

Mehta, Makrand, 'The Dalit Temple Entry Movement in Maharashtra and Gujarat, 1930–1948', in Takashi Shinoda (ed.), *The Other Gujarat*, Mumbai: Popular Prakashan, 2002, pp. 1–21.

Mehta, Meera, 'Urban Housing Processes and the Poor: A Case Study of Ahmedabad', *Nagarlok*, vol. 14, no. 2, April–June 1982, pp. 106–28.

Michell, George and Shelal Shah (eds.), *Ahmedabad*, Bombay: Marg Publications, 1988.

Migdal, Joel, S., 'The State in Society: An Approach to Struggles for Domination', in Joel S. Migdal, Atul Kohli and Vivienne Shue (eds.), *State Power and Social Forces: Domination and Transformation in the Third World*, Cambridge: Cambridge University Press, 1994.

Migdal, Joel, 'Studying the State', in Mark Irving Lichbach and Alan S. Zuckerman (eds.), *Comparative Politics: Rationality, Culture and Structure*, Cambridge: Cambridge University Press, 1997, pp. 208–35.

Migdal, Joel, S., *State in Society: Studying how States and Societies Transform and Constitute One Another*, Cambridge: Cambridge University Press, 2001.

Misra, Satish, C., *Muslim Communities in Gujarat*, London: Asia Publishing House, 1964.

Mitchell, Timothy, 'The Limits of the State: Beyond Statist Approaches and their Critics', *American Political Science Review*, vol. 85, no. 1, 1991, pp. 77–96.

Mitra, Subrata, 'The Perils of Promoting Equality: The Latent Significance of the Anti-Reservation Movement in India', *Journal of Commonwealth and Comparative Politics*, vol. 25, no. 3, 1987, pp. 292–312.

Moin, Zaidi A., *The Great Upheaval 1969–1972*, India: Orientalia, 1972.

Mukherjee, Aditya, 'Colonialism and Communalism', in Sarvepalli Gopal (ed.), *Anatomy of a Confrontation: Ayodhya and the Rise of Communal Politics in India*, London: Zed Books, 1991, pp. 164–78.

Nandy, Ashish, 'The Politics of Secularism and the Recovery of Religious Tolerance', in Veena Das (ed.), *Mirrors of Violence*, Delhi: Oxford University Press, 1990, pp. 69–93.

Nandy, Ashish, *The Intimate Enemy Loss and Recovery of Self under Colonialism*, Delhi: Oxford University Press, 1993.

Nandy, Ashish et al., *Creating a Nationality: The Ramjanmabhumi Movement and Fear of the Self*, Delhi: Oxford University Press, 1997.

Narayanan, Harini, 'In Search of Shelter: The Politics of the Implementation of the Urban Land (Ceiling and Regulation) Act 1976 in Greater Mumbai', in Sujata Patel and Jim Masselos (eds.), *Bombay and Mumbai: The City in Transition*, New Delhi: Oxford University Press, 2003, pp. 183–206.

Oza, Ajay, 'Majur Mahajan Asserts its Identity', *Economic and Political Weekly*, 13 November 1971, pp. 2303–4.

Pande, Rohini, 'Can Mandated Political Representation Increase Policy Influence for Disadvantaged Minorities? Theory and Evidence from India', *The American Economic Review*, vol. 93, no. 4, September 2003, pp. 1132–51.

Pandey, Gyanendra, *The Construction of Communalism in Colonial North India*, Delhi: Oxford University Press, 1990.

Pandey, Gyanendra, 'The Colonial Construction of "Communalism"', in Veena Das (ed.), *Mirrors of Violence*, Delhi: Oxford University Press, 1990, pp. 94–132.

Pandey, Gyanendra, 'Which of Us Are Hindus?', in G. Pandey (ed.), *Hindu and Others*, Delhi: Viking, 1993, pp. 232–72.

Pandey, Gyanendra, *Remembering Partition: Violence, Nationalism and History in India*, Cambridge: Cambridge University Press, 2001.

Papola, T. S. and K. K. Subrahmanian, 'Structure of a Local Labour Market: A Study in Ahmedabad', *Economic and Political Weekly*, Annual No., February 1973, p. 291.

Papola, T. S. and K. K. Subrahmanian, *Wage Structure and Labour Mobility in a Social Labour Market: A Study in Ahmedabad*, Ahmedabad: Sardar Patel Institute of Economic and Social Research, 1975.

Parikh, Sunita, *The Politics of Preference: Democratic Institutions and Affirmative Action in the United States and India*, Ann Arbor: The University of Michigan Press (1997), 2000.

Parikh, Sunita, 'Religion, Reservations and Riots: The Politics of Ethnic Violence in India', in Amrita Basu and Atul Kohli (eds.), *Community Conflicts and the State in India*, Oxford: Oxford University Press, 1998, pp. 33–57.

Parikh, Sunita, 'Affirmative Action, Caste, and Party Politics in Contemporary India', in John David Skrentny (ed.), *Color Lines: Affirmative Action,*

Immigration, and Civil Rights Options for America, Chicago and London: University of Chicago Press, 2001.

Parry, Jonathan P., 'Two Cheers for Reservation: The Satnamis and the Steel Plant', in Ramachandra Guha and Parry (eds.), *Institutions and Inequalities*, Oxford: Oxford University Press.

Patel, B. B., 'Price Spread and Farmer's Share: Oil and Groundnut in Gujarat', *Economic and Political Weekly*, 17 July 1971, p. 1435.

Patel, B. B., *Workers of Closed Textile Mills*, New Delhi: Oxford and IBH Publishing, 1988.

Patel, Girish, 'Narendra Modi's One-Day Cricket', *Economic and Political Weekly*, 30 November 2002, pp. 4826–37.

Patel, Sujata, 'Contract Labour and Public Interest Litigation', *Economic and Political Weekly*, 17 December 1983, pp. 2152–3.

Patel, Sujata, 'Debacle of Populist Politics', *Economic and Political Weekly*, 20 April 1985, pp. 681–2.

Patel, Sujata, 'Collapse of Government', *Economic and Political Weekly*, 27 April 1985, pp. 749–50.

Patel, Sujata, 'Nationalisation, TLA and Textile Workers', *Economic and Political Weekly*, 7 December 1985, pp. 2154–5.

Patel, Sujata, *The Making of Industrial Relations: The Ahmedabad Textile Industry 1918–1939*, Delhi: Oxford University Press, 1987.

Patel, Sujata, 'Urbanization, Development and Communalisation of Society in Gujarat', in Takashi Shinoda (ed.), *The Other Gujarat*, Mumbai: Popular Prakashan, 2002, pp. 204–20.

Pocock, D. F., *Kanbi and Patidar: A Study of the Patidar Community of Gujarat*, Oxford: Clarendon, 1972.

'Politics of Groundnut Oil' ('From our correspondence'), *Economic and Political Weekly*, 17 July 1971, p. 1435.

Punwani, Jyoti, 'The Carnage at Godhra', in Siddharth Varadarajan (ed.), *Gujarat: The Making of a Tragedy*, New Delhi: Penguin Books India, 2002, pp. 45–74.

Rajagopal, Arvind, *Politics after Television: Hindu Nationalism and the Reshaping of the Public in India*, Cambridge: Cambridge University Press, 2001.

Rayachaudhri, Tapan, 'Shadows of the Swastika: Historical Reflection on the Politics of Hindu Communalism', *Contention*, vol. 4, no. 2, 1995, pp. 141–62.

Ribeiro, Julio, *Bullet for Bullet: My Life as a Police Officer*, Delhi: Penguin Books, 1998.

Roy, C. N., *Liberalisation and Urban Social Sources: Health and Education*, Jaipur and Delhi: Rawat, 2003.

Roy, Tirthankar, 'Development or Distortion? "Powerlooms" in India 1950–1997', *Economic and Political Weekly*, 18 April 1998, pp. 897–911.

Roy, Tirthankar, 'Economic Reforms and Textile Industry', *Economic and Political Weekly*, 8 August 1998, pp. 2173–6.

Said, Edward W., *Orientalism*, New York: Vintage Books, 1979.

Sanghavi, Nagindas, *Gujarat a Political Analysis*, Surat: Centre for Social Studies, 1996.

Sarkar, Sumit, 'Indian Nationalism and the Politics of Hindutva', in David Ludden (ed.), *Making India Hindu: Religion, Community and the Politics of Democracy in India*, Delhi: Oxford University Press, pp. 270–93.

Savarkar, V. D., *Hindutva, Who is a Hindu?*, Bombay: Veer Savarkar Prakashan, 1969.

'A Second Sardar Patel' ('From our correspondence'), *Economic and Political Weekly*, 21 July 1973, p. 1273.

Sen, Amartya, 'The Threats to Secular India', *New York Review of Books*, 8 April 1993, pp. 26–32.

Sen, Amartya, *Development as Freedom*, New York: Anchor Books, 1999.

Shah, Ghanshyam, 'Communal Riots in Gujarat: Report of a Preliminary Investigation', *Economic and Political Weekly*, Annual Number, January 1970, pp. 187–200.

Shah, Ghanshyam, *Caste Association and Political Process in Gujarat: A Study of Gujarat Kshatriya Sabha*, Bombay: Popular Prakashan, 1975.

Shah, Ghanshyam, 'Anatomy of Urban Riots: Ahmedabad 1973', *Economic and Political Weekly*, Annual No., February 1974, pp. 233–40.

Shah, Ghanshyam, 'The Upsurge in Gujarat', *Economic and Political Weekly*, August 1974, Special No., pp. 1429–54.

Shah, Ghanshyam, 'Special Report on Reservation', *The Herald Review*, vol. 1, no. 28, 17–23 March 1985, pp. 38–9.

Shah, Ghanshyam, 'Middle-Class Politics: A Case of Anti-Reservation Agitation in Gujarat', *Economic and Political Weekly*, Annual Number, May 1987, pp. 155–72.

Shah, Ghanshyam, 'Caste Sentiments, Class Formation and Dominance in Gujarat', in Francine R. Frankel and M. S. A. Rao (eds.), *Dominance and State Power in Modern India*, Vol. II, Delhi: Oxford University Press, 1990, pp. 59–114.

Shah, Ghanshyam, 'Strategies of Social Engineering: Reservation and Mobility of Backward Communities in Gujarat', in Ramashray Roy and Richard Sisson (eds.), *Diversity and Dominance in Indian Politics*, Vol. II, New Delhi: Sage Publications, 1990, pp. 111–45.

Shah, Ghanshyam, 'Agitations in Gujarat', *Seminar*, vol. 375, November 1990.

Shah, Ghanshyam, 'The BJP's Riddle in Gujarat: Caste, Factionalism and Hindutva', in Thomas B. Hansen, and Christophe Jaffrelot (eds.), *The BJP and the Compulsions of Politics in India*, Delhi: Oxford University Press, 1998, pp. 243–66.

Shah, Ghanshyam, 'Polarised Communities', *Seminar*, vol. 470, October 1998.

Shah, Ghanshyam, 'Caste, Hindutva and the Making of Mob Culture', in Siddharth Varadarajan (ed.), *Gujarat: The Making of a Tragedy*, New Delhi: Penguin Books India, 2002, pp. 416–25.

Shani, Ornit, 'The Resurgence of *EthnoHinduism* – a Theoretical Perspective', in Shlomo Ben-Ami, Yoav Peled and Alberto Spektrovski (eds.), *Ethnic Challenges to the Modern Nation State*, London: Macmillan, 2000, pp. 267–93.

Sheth, D. L., 'Reservation Policy Revisited', in Gurpreet Mahajan (ed.), *Democracy, Difference and Social Justice*, New Delhi: Oxford University Press, 2000, pp. 489–508.

Sheth, Pravin, *Political Development in Gujarat*, Ahmedabad: Karnavati Publications, 1998.

Shinoda, Takashi, *The Other Gujarat*, Mumbai: Popular Prakashan, 2002.

Spodek, Howard, 'From Gandhi to Violence: Ahmedabad's 1985 Riots in Historical Perspective', *Modern Asian Studies*, vol. 23, no. 4, 1989, pp. 765–95.

Spodek, Howard, 'Crises and Response: Ahmedabad 2000', *Economic and Political Weekly*, 12 May 2001, pp. 1627–38.

Stern, Robert W., *Changing India*, Cambridge: Cambridge University Press, 1993.

Tambiah, Stanely, 'Presidential Address: Reflections on Communal Violence in South Asia', *Journal of Asian Studies*, vol. 49, no. 4, 1990, pp. 741–60.

Tambiah, Stanley, *Levelling Crowds: Ethnonationalist Conflicts and Collective Violence in South Asia*, Berkeley: University of California Press, 1996.

Thapar, Romila, 'Imagined Religious Communities? Ancient History and the Modern Search for a Hindu Identity', in Romila Thapar (ed.), *Interpreting Early India*, Delhi: Oxford University Press, 1992, pp. 60–88.

Vadhva, Kiran, 'Private Sector and Urban Housing: A Case Study of Ahmedabad', *Nagarlok*, vol. 18, no. 3, July–September 1986, pp. 61–83.

Van der Veer, Peter, 'The Foreign Hand: Orientalist Discourse in Sociology and Communalism', in Carol A. Breckenbridge and Peter van der Veer (eds.), *Orientalism and the Post-Colonial Predicament*, Philadelphia: University of Pennsylvania Press, 1993, pp. 23–44.

Van der Veer, Peter, *Religious Nationalism*, London: University of California Press, 1994.

Van der Veer, Peter, 'Writing Violence', in David Ludden (ed.), *Making India Hindu: Religion, Community and the Politics of Democracy in India*, Delhi: Oxford University Press, 1996, pp. 250–69.

Vanaik, Achin, *The Furies of Indian Communalism*, London: Verso, 1998.

Varadarajan, Siddharth, 'Chronicle of a Tragedy Foretold', in S. Varadarajan (ed.), *Gujarat: The Making of a Tragedy*, New Delhi: Penguin Books India, 2002, pp. 3–41.

Varshney, Ashutosh, *Ethnic Conflict and Civic Life: Hindus and Muslims in India*, New Haven and London: Yale University Press, 2002.

Visaria, Pravin, and Sudershan Iyengar, 'Economic Prospects', *Seminar*, vol. 470, October 1998.

Washbrook, David, 'The Development of Caste Organisation in South India 1880–1925', in C. J. Baker and D. A. Washbrook (eds.), *South India: Political Institutions and Political Change 1880–1940*, Delhi: Macmillan, 1975, pp. 150–203.

Washbrook, David, 'Caste Class and Dominance in Tamil Nadu: Non-Brahmanism, Dravidianism and Tamil Nadu Nationalism', in Francine R. Frankel and M. S. A. Rao (eds.), *Dominance and State Power in Modern India*, Vol. I, Delhi: Oxford University Press, 1989, pp. 204–64.

Weber, Max, 'Class, Status, Party', in H. H. Gerth and C. W. Mills (eds.), *From Max Weber: Essays in Sociology*, London: Routledge, 1991.

Wilkinson, Steven, I., *Votes and Violence: Electoral Competition and Ethnic Riots in India*, Cambridge: Cambridge University Press, 2004.

Wolpert, Stanley, 'Resurgent Hindu Fundamentalism', *Contention*, vol. 2, no. 3, Spring 1995, pp. 9–18.

Wood, John R., 'Extra-Parliamentary Opposition in India: An Analysis of Populist Agitations in Gujarat and Bihar', *Pacific Affairs*, vol. 48, no. 3, 1975, pp. 313–34.

Wood, John R., 'Congress Restored? The "Kham" Strategy and Congress(I) Recruitment in Gujarat', in John R. Wood (ed.), *State Politics in Contemporary India: Crisis or Continuity?*, Boulder and London: Westview, 1984, pp. 197–227.

Wood, John R., 'Reservations in Doubt: The Backlash against Affirmative Action in Gujarat', in Ramashray Roy and Richard Sisson (eds.), *Diversity and Dominance in Indian Politics*, Vol. II, London: Sage, 1990, pp. 146–69.

Wright, Theodore, 'A New Demand for Muslim Reservations in India', *Asian Survey*, vol. 37, no. 9, 1997, pp. 852–8.

Yadav, Yogendra, 'Understanding the Second Democratic Upsurge: Trends of Bahujan Participation in Electoral Politics in the 1990s', in Francine Frankel, Zoya Hasan, Rajeev Bhargava and Balveer Arora (eds.), *Transforming India: Social and Political Dynamics of Democracy*, New Delhi: Oxford University Press, 2000, pp. 120–45.

Yagnik, Achyut, 'Spectre of Caste War', *Economic and Political Weekly*, 13, 28 March 1981, pp. 553–5.

Yagnik, Achyut, 'Paradoxes of Populism', *Economic and Political Weekly*, 27 August 1983, pp. 1505–7.

Yagnik, Achyut and Anil Bhatt, 'The Anti-Dalit Agitation in Gujarat', *South Asia Bulletin*, vol. 4, no. 1, Spring 1984, pp. 45–60.

Yagnik, Achyut, 'Search for Dalit Self Identity in Gujarat', in Takashi Shinoda (ed.), *The Other Gujarat*, Mumbai: Popular Prakashan, 2002, pp. 22–37.

Yagnik, Achyut and Suchitra Sheth, *The Shaping of Modern Gujarat: Plurality, Hindutva and Beyond*, New Delhi: Penguin Books, 2005.

Young, Robert J. C., *Colonial Desire*, London: Routledge, 1995.

Zizek, Slavoj, 'Eastern Europe's Republic of Gilead', in Chantal Mouffe (ed.), *Dimensions of Radical Democracy: Pluralism, Citizenship, Community*, London: Verso, 1993.

UNPUBLISHED DISSERTATIONS

Deo, Vinayak Narhar, 'Urban Land Policy: Evaluation of Urban Land (Ceiling and Regulation) Act 1976', Ph.D. thesis, School of Planning, Ahmedabad, May 1982.

Mehta, Barjor, 'Urban Housing Objective Realities for the Poor', unpublished Ph.D. thesis, School of Planning, Ahmedabad, 1980.

Parikh, Manju, 'Labour–Capital Relations in the Indian Textile Industry: A Comparative Study of Ahmedabad and Combators', unpublished Ph.D. thesis, University of Chicago, 1988.

Raychaudhuri, Siddhartha, 'Indian Elites, Urban Space and the Restructuring of Ahmedabad City 1890–1947', unpublished Ph.D. thesis, Cambridge University, 1997.

BACKGROUND READING

Abusalen, Shariff, 'Socio-Economic and Demographic Differentials between Hindus and Muslims in India', *Economic and Political Weekly*, 18 November 1995, pp. 2947–54.

Ahmed, Imtiaz, 'Indian Muslims and Electoral Politics', *Economic and Political Weekly*, 11 March 1967, pp. 521–3.

Ahmad, Aijaz, 'Culture, Community, Nation: On the Ruins of Ayodhya', *Social Scientist*, vol. 21, no. 7–8, 1993, pp. 17–48.

Andersen, Walter K. and Shridhar D. Damle, *The Brotherhood in Saffron: The Rashtriya Swayamsevak Sangh and Hindu Revivalism*, Delhi: Vistaar Publications, 1987.

Apter, David E. (ed.), *The Legitimation of Violence*, New York: New York University Press, 1997.

Basu, Kaushik, and Sanjay Subrahmanyam (eds.), *Unravelling the Nation: Sectarian Conflict and India's Secular Identity*, Delhi: Penguin, 1996.

Baxi, Upendra, 'Caste, Class and Reservation', *Economic and Political Weekly*, 19 January 1985, pp. 462–65.

Bayly, C. A., 'The Pre-History of "Communalism"? Religious Conflict in India, 1700–1860', *Modern Asian Studies*, vol. 19, 1985, pp. 177–203.

Bayly, Susan, 'Caste and "Race" in Colonial Ethnography', in Peter Robb (ed.), *Concept of Race in South Asia*, Oxford: Oxford University Press, 1995, pp. 165–218.

Berenson, Frances, 'Understanding Art and Understanding Persons', in S. C. Browns (ed.), *Objectivity and Cultural Divergence*, Royal Institute of Philosophy Lecture Series, 17, Cambridge: Cambridge University Press, 1984, pp. 43–60.

Béteille, André, "Distributive Justice and Institutional Well-Being", in Gurpreet Mahajan (ed.), *Democracy, Difference and Social Justice*, New Delhi: Oxford University Press, 2000, pp. 463–88.

Bhargava, Rajeev, 'Democratic Vision of a New Republic: India, 1950', in Francine Frankel *et al.* (eds.), *Transforming India: Social and Political Dynamics of Democracy*, New Delhi: Oxford University Press, 2000, pp. 26–59.

Bidwai, Praful, Harbans Mukhia and Vanail Achin (eds.), *Religion, Religiosity and Communalism*, Delhi: Manohar, 1996.

Bougle, C., *Essays on the Caste System*, Cambridge: Cambridge University Press, 1971.

Brass, R. Paul, *Language, Religion and Politics in North India*, Cambridge: Cambridge University Press, 1974.

Brass, R. Paul, *The Politics of India Since Independence*, Delhi: Cambridge University Press, 1992.

Brass, R. Paul (ed.), *Riots and Pogroms*, London: Macmillan, 1996.

Breman, Jan, 'A Dualistic Labour System? A Critique of the "Informal Sector" Concept. I: The Informal Sector', *Economic and Political Weekly*, 27 November 1976, pp. 1870–6.

Breman, Jan, 'A Dualistic Labour System? A Critique of the "Informal Sector" Concept. II: A Fragmented Labour Market', *Economic and Political Weekly*, 4 December 1976, pp. 1905–8.

Breman, Jan, 'A Dualistic Labour System? A Critique of the "Informal Sector" Concept. III: Labour Force and Class Formation', *Economic and Political Weekly*, 11 December 1976, pp. 1939–44.

Buch, M. N., 'The Law and Order Machinery of the State', *Social Action*, vol. 43, no. 2, April–June 1993, pp. 165–74.

Chakrabarty, Dipesh, 'Modernity and Ethnicity in India: A History for the Present', *Economic and Political Weekly*, 30 December 1995, pp. 3373–80.

Chakravarti, Uma, and Nandita Haksar, *The Delhi Riots: Three Days in the Life of a Nation*, Delhi: Lancer International, 1987.

Chakravarti, Uma, 'Saffroning the Past: Of Myths, Histories and Right-Wing Agendas', *Economic and Political Weekly*, 31 January 1998, pp. 225–32.

Chandavarkar, Rajnarayan, *The Origins of Industrial Capitalism in India: Business Strategies and the Working Classes in Bombay, 1900–1940*, Cambridge: Cambridge University Press, 1994.

Chandra, Bipan, *Communalism in Modern India*, New Delhi: Vikas, 1984.

Chatterjee, Partha, *The Nation and its Fragments*, Princeton, NJ: Princeton University Press, 1993.

Choudhary, Kameshwar, 'Reservation for OBCs: Hardly an Abrupt Decision', *Economic and Political Weekly*, 1–8 September 1990, pp. 1929–35.

Chowdhury, Supriya Roy, 'Industrial Restructuring Unions and the State, Textile Mill Workers in Ahmedabad', *Economic and Political Weekly*, 24 February 1996, pp. L-7-L-13.

Datta, Pradip Kumar, *Carving Blocs: Communal Ideology in Early Twentieth-Century Bengal*, Delhi: Oxford University Press, 1999.

Davis, Natalie Zemon, 'The Rites of Violence', in *Society and Culture in Early Modern France*, Cambridge: Polity Press, 1987, pp. 152–87.

Desai, Anjana, *Indian Cities a Conglomeration of Culture: A Study in Behavioural Geography*, Jaipur: Illustrated Book Publishers, 1997.

Desai, Mihir, 'A Justification of Reservation and Affirmative Action for Backward Castes in India', *South Asia Bulletin*, vol. 11, no. 1–2, 1991, pp. 110–30.

Desai, Morarji, *The Story of My Life*, Vol. II, Oxford: Pergamon Press, 1979.

Dharmadhikari, Avinash, *Diary of a Decade of Agony*, Bombay: Orient Longman, 1995.

D'Souza, Paul, 'Dalit Identity in Gujarat', in Fernando Franco (ed.), *Pain and Awakening: The Dynamics of Dalit Identity in Bihar, Gujarat and Uttar Pradesh*, New Delhi: Indian Social Institute, 2002, pp. 156–267.

Engineer, Asghar Ali, 'Communal Fire Engulfs Ahmedabad Once Again', *Economic and Political Weekly*, 6 July 1985, pp. 1116–20.

Engineer, Asghar Ali, Shama Dalwani and Sundhya Mhatre, *Sowing Hate and Reaping Violence. The Case of Gujarat Communal Carnage*, Mumbai: Centre for Study of Society and Secularism, 2002.

Frankel, Francine R., 'Decline of Social Order', in Francine R. Frankel and M. S. A. Rao (eds.), *Dominance and State Power in Modern India*, Vol. II, Delhi: Oxford University Press, 1990, pp. 482–517.

Galanter, Marc, 'Changing Legal Conception of Caste', in Milton Singer and S. Bernard Cohn (eds.), *Structure and Change in Indian Society*, Chicago: Aldine Publishing Company, 1968, pp. 299–336.

Graham, Bruce, *Hindu Nationalism and Indian Politics*, Cambridge: Cambridge University Press, 1993.

Guha, Ashok, 'The Mandal Mythology', *Seminar*, vol. 375, November 1990.

Hasan, Zoya, 'Party Politics and Communal Mobilization in Uttar Pradesh', *South Asia Bulletin*, vol. 14, no. 1, 1994, pp. 42–52.

Hasan, Zoya, 'Representation and Redistribution: The New Lower Caste Politics of North India', in Francine Frankel *et al.* (eds.), *Transforming India: Social and Political Dynamics of Democracy*, New Delhi: Oxford University Press, 2000, pp. 146–75.

Hawthorn, Geoffrey, 'Caste and Politics in India since 1947', in Dennis B. McGilvray (ed.), *Caste Ideology and Interaction*, Cambridge: Cambridge University Press, 1982, pp. 204–20.

Henderson, Michael, *Experiment with Untruth: India under Emergency*, Delhi: Macmillan, 1977.

Hobsbawm, Eric, 'Cities and Insurrections', in *Revolutionaries*, London: Abacus, 1973, pp. 261–78.

Holmstrom, Mark, *Industry and Inequality: The Social Anthropology of Indian Labour*, Cambridge: Cambridge University Press, 1984.

Inden, Ronald, 'Orientalist Constructions of India', *Modern Asian Studies*, vol. 20, no. 3, 1986, pp. 401–46.

Iyengar, Sudarshan, and Sujata Patel, 'Violence with a Difference', *Economic and Political Weekly*, 13 July 1985, pp. 1174–5.

Jaffrelot, Christophe, 'BJP and the Challenge of Factionalism in Madhya Pradesh', in Thomas B. Hansen and Christophe Jaffrelot (eds.), *The BJP and the Compulsions of Politics in India*, Delhi: Oxford University Press, 1998, pp. 267–90.

Jenkins, Rob, 'Rajput Hindutva, Caste Politics, Regional Identity and the Hindu Nationalism in Contemporary Rajasthan', in Thomas B. Hansen and Christophe Jaffrelot (eds.), *The BJP and the Compulsions of Politics in India*, Delhi: Oxford University Press, 1998, pp. 101–20.

Kaviraj, Sudipta, 'The Imaginary Institution of India', in Partha Chatterjee and Gyanendra Pandey (eds.), *Subaltern Studies VII: Writing on South Asian History and Society*, Delhi: Oxford University Press, 1992, pp. 1–39.

Kaviraj, Sudipta, 'Crisis of the Nation-State in India', *Political Studies*, vol. 23, 1994, pp. 115–29.

Kaviraj, Sudipta, 'The General Elections in India', *Government and Opposition*, vol. 32, no. 1, 1997, pp. 3–24.

Kaviraj, Sudipta, 'Religion and Identity in India, *Ethnic and Racial Studies*, vol. 20, no. 2, 1997, pp. 325–44.

Kohli, Atul, 'Can Democracies Accommodate Ethnic Nationalism?', *Journal of Asian Studies*, vol. 56, no. 2, May 1997, pp. 325–44.

Kothari, Rajni (ed.), *Caste in Indian Politics*, London: Gordon and Breach, Science Publishers, 1970.

Kothari, Rajni, *Communalism in Indian Politics*, Ahmedabad: Rainbow Publishers, 1998.

Lal, Deepak, 'The Economic Impact of Hindu Revivalism', in Martin Marty and R. Scott Appleby (eds.), *Fundamentalism and the State: Remaking*

Politics, Economies and Militance, Chicago: University of Chicago Press, 1993, pp. 410–26.

Malik, Kenan, *The Meaning of Race*, London: Macmillan, 1996.

Marx, Karl, 'On the Jewish Question', in Joseph O'Malley (ed.), *Marx: Early Political Writings*, Cambridge: Cambridge University Press, 1994, pp. 28–56.

Mehta, Kapilrai and Kanto A. Shah, *Ahmedabad: 1958*, Ahmedabad: Gujarat Publishers, 1959.

Mehta, Meera, Dinesh Mehta and H. M. Shivanand Swamy, 'Metropolitan Housing Analysis: A Case of Ahmedabad', *Nagarlok*, vol. 20, no. 1, January–March, 1988, pp. 69–86.

Mehta, Meera and Dinesh Mehta, *Metropolitan Housing Market: A Study of Ahmedabad*, Delhi: Sage Publications, 1989.

Namboodiripad, E. M. S., 'Caste and Class', *Economic and Social Weekly*, 28 March 1981, p. 547.

Natraj, V. K., 'Reservations: New Perspectives', *Economic and Political Weekly*, 21–28 August, 1999.

Omvedt, Gail, *Dalits and the Democratic Revolution*, Delhi: Sage, 1994.

Omvedt, Gail, 'The Anti-Caste Movement and the Discourse of Power', in T. V. Sathyamurthy (ed.), *Region, Religion, Caste, Gender and Culture in Contemporary India*, Oxford and New Delhi: Oxford University Press, 1996, pp. 334–54.

Osborne, Evan, 'Culture, Development and Government: Reservations in India', *Economic Development and Cultural Change*, vol. 49, no. 3, April 2001, 659–85.

Panikkar, K. N., *Communal Threat, Secular Challenge*, Madras: Earthworm Books, 1997.

Peabody, Norbert, 'Collective Violence in Our Time', *American Ethnologist*, vol. 27, no. 1, 2000, pp. 169–79.

Peled, Yoav, 'Ethnic Exclusionism in the Periphery: The Case of Oriental Jews in Israel's Development Towns', *Ethnic and Racial Studies*, vol. 13, no. 3, 1990, pp. 345–67.

Perlin, Frank, 'The Material and the Cultural: An Attempt to Transcend the Present Impasse', *Modern Asian Studies*, vol. 22, no. 2, 1988, pp. 383–416.

Pollock, Sheldon, 'Ramayana and Political Imagination in India', *Journal of Asian Studies*, vol. 52, no. 2, May 1993, pp. 261–93.

Puri, Balraj, 'Can Caste, Region and Ideology Stem the Hindu Wave?', *Economic and Political Weekly*, 6 January 1990, pp. 15–16.

Rajgopal, P. R., *Communal Violence in India*, New Delhi: Uppal Publishing House, 1987.

Rao, M. S. A., *Economic and Political Weekly*, no. 3, 1968, pp. 779–82.

Rasam, V. P., *Swatantra Party: A Political Biography*, Nagpur: Dattsons, 1997.

Robinson, Francis, 'Islam and Muslim Separatism', in David Taylor and Malcolm Yapp (eds.), *Political Identity in South Asia*, London: Curzon Press, 1979, pp. 78–112.

Robinson, Francis, 'Nation Formation: The Brass Thesis and Muslim Separatism', *Journal of Commonwealth and Comparative Politics*, vol. 15, no. 3, 1977, pp. 215–30.

Roy, Ajit, 'Caste and Class: An Interlinked View', *Economic and Political Weekly*, Annual Number, February 1979, pp. 297–301.

Roy, Ashimk, 'Anti-Reservation Movement: A Political Assessment', *Economic and Political Weekly*, 10 August 1985, pp. 1343–4.

Rudolph, Loyd I. *et al.*, *In Pursuit of Lakshmi*, London: University of Chicago Press, 1987.

Sarkar, Tanika, and Urvashi Butalia (eds.), *Women and the Hindu Right*, Delhi: Kali for Women, 1995.

Shachar, Ayelet, *Multicultural Jurisdictions: Cultural Differences and Women's Rights*, Cambridge: Cambridge University Press, 2001.

Shah, Ghanshyam, 'Caste, Class and Reservation', *Economic and Political Weekly*, 19 January 1985, pp.132–6.

Shah, Ghanshyam, 'Social Backwardness and the Politics of Reservation', *Economic and Political Weekly*, vol. 26, no. 11–12, Annual Number, March 1991, pp. 601–10.

Shah, Ghanshyam, 'The BJP and Backward Castes in Gujarat', *South Asia Bulletin*, vol. 14, no. 1, 1994, pp. 57–65.

Shah, Ghanshyam, 'BJP's Rise to Power, *Economic and Political Weekly*, January 1996, pp. 20–30.

Sheth, D., L., 'Changing Terms of Elite Discourse: The Case of Reservation for "Other Backward Castes"', in T. V. Sathyamurthy (ed.), *Region, Religion, Caste, Gender and Culture in Contemporary India*, Oxford and New Delhi: Oxford University Press, 1996, pp. 314–33.

Srinivas, M. N., *Caste: Its Twentieth Century Avatar*, Delhi: Viking, 1996.

Thakur, Ramesh, 'Ayodhya and the Politics of India's Secularism: A Double-Standard Discourse', *Asian Survey*, vol. 33, no. 7, 1993, pp. 645–63.

Thompson, E. P., 'The Moral Economy of the English Crowd in the Eighteenth Century', *Past and Present*, vol. 50, February 1971, pp. 76–126.

Upadhyaya, K. K., 'The Political Economy of Reservations in Public Jobs in India. Implications for Efficiency in Public Administration and Equity in Society', *International Journal of Social Economics*, vol. 25, no. 6/7/8, 1998, pp. 1049–63.

Van den Berghe, Pierre, 'Race and Ethnicity: A Sociobiological Perspective', *Ethnic and Racial Studies*, vol. 1, no. 4, 1978.

Van der Veer, Peter, '"God Must be Liberated!" A Hindu Liberation Movement in Ayodhya', *Modern Asian Studies*, vol. 21, no. 2, 1987, pp. 283–301.

Valentine, Daniel E., *Charred Lullabies: Chapters in an Anthropology of Violence*, Princeton, NJ: Princeton University Press, 1996.

Vanaik, Achin, 'Reflections on Communalism and Nationalism in India', *New Left Review*, vol. 196, November/December 1992, pp. 43–63.

Wright, Eric O., *Class Counts: Comparative Studies in Class Analysis*, Cambridge: Cambridge University Press, 1997.

Xaxa, Virginius, 'Ethnography of Reservation in Delhi University', *Economic and Political Weekly*, 12 July 2002.

Yang, Anand A., 'Sacred Symbol and Sacred Space in Ritual India: Community Mobilization in the "Anti-Cow Killing" Riots of 1893', *Comparative Studies in Society and History*, vol. 22, no. 4, 1980, pp. 576–595.

Index